Colourful cabins in the fishing village of Bayahibe.
- *Michel Gagné*

One of the elegant residences lining Santo Domingo's Parque Colón.
- *Tibor Bognar*

The public markets of the Dominican Republic bustle with activity.
- *Claude Hervé-Bazin*

DOMINICAN REPUBLIC

5th Edition

Pascale Couture
Benoit Prieur

ULYSSES
TRAVEL PUBLICATIONS
Travel better... enjoy more

Authors Pascale Couture Benoit Prieur	*Page Layout* Jenny Jasper Clayton Anderson	*Photography*
		Cover Page Al Rubin Studio Superstock
Editors Daniel Desjardins	*Cartographers* Patrick Thivierge Yanik Landreville	
Project Director André Duchesne	*Computer Graphics* Stephanie Routhier	*Inside Pages* Claude Hervé-Bazin Tibor Bognar Michel Gagné
English Editing Jenny Jasper Tara Salman Jacqueline Grekin	*Artistic Director* Patrick Farei (Atoll)	Lorette Pierson Mégapress B. Pérousse Dugast
Translation Janet Logan Stéphanie Lemire	*Illustrations* Myriam Gagne Lorette Pierson Marie-Annik Viatour	T. Philiptchenko

Distributors

AUSTRALIA: Little Hills Press, 11/37-43 Alexander St., Crows Nest NSW 2065, ☎ (612) 437-6995, Fax: (612) 438-5762

BELGIUM AND LUXEMBOURG: Vander, Vrijwilligerlaan 321, B-1150 Brussel, ☎ (02) 762 98 04, Fax: (02) 762 06 62

CANADA: Ulysses Books & Maps, 4176 Saint-Denis, Montréal, Québec, H2W 2M5, ☎ (514) 843-9882, ext.2232, 800-748-9171, Fax: 514-843-9448, www.ulysses.ca

GERMANY and **AUSTRIA**: Brettschneider, Fernreisebedarf, Feldfirchner Strasse 2, D-85551 Heimstetten, München, ☎ 89-99 02 03 30, Fax: 89-99 02 03 31, Brettschneider_Fernreisebedarf@t-online-de

GREAT BRITAIN and **IRELAND**: World Leisure Marketing, Unit 11, Newmarket Court, Newmartket Drive, Derby DE24 8NW, ☎ 1 332 57 37 37, Fax: 1 332 57 33 99, office@wlmsales.co.uk

ITALY: Centro Cartografico del Riccio, Via di Soffiano 164/A, 50143 Firenze, ☎ (055) 71 33 33, Fax: (055) 71 63 50

NETHERLANDS: Nilsson & Lamm, Pampuslaan 212-214, 1380 AD Weesp (NL), ☎ 0294-494949, Fax: 0294-494455, E-mail: nilam@euronet.nl

PORTUGAL: Dinapress, Lg. Dr. Antonio de Sousa de Macedo, 2, Lisboa 1200, ☎ (1) 395 52 70, Fax: (1) 395 03 90

SCANDINAVIA: Scanvik, Esplanaden 8B, 1263 Copenhagen K, DK, ☎ (45) 33.12.77.66, Fax: (45) 33.91.28.82

SPAIN: Altaïr, Balmes 69, E-08007 Barcelona, ☎ 454 29 66, Fax: 451 25 59, altair@globalcom.es

SWITZERLAND: OLF, P.O. Box 1061, CH-1701 Fribourg, ☎ (026) 467.51.11, Fax: (026) 467.54.66

U.S.A.: The Globe Pequot Press, 6 Business Park Road, P.O. Box 833, Old Saybrook, CT 06475, ☎ 1-800-243-0495, Fax: 800-820-2329, sales@globe-pequot.com

OTHER COUNTRIES, contact Ulysses Books & Maps (Montréal), Fax: (514) 843-9448

Canadian Cataloguing in Publication Data
© October 1999, Ulysses Travel Publications.
All rights reserved
Printed in Canada

"...En verdad.
Con tres milliones
suma de la vida
una entre tanto
cuatro cordilleras cardinales
y une inmensa bahía y otra inmensa bahía,
tres penínsulas con islas adyacentes
y un asombro de ríos verticales
y tierra bajo los árboles y tierra
bajo los ríos y en la falda del monte
y al pie de la colina y detría del horizonte
y tierra desde el canto de los gallos
y tierra bajo al galope de los caballos
y tierra sobre el día, bajo el mapa, alrededor
y debajo de todas las huellas y en medio del amor.
Entonces
es lo que he declarado.
Hay un país en el mundo
Sencillamente agreste y depoblado..."

– Pedro Mir
Hay un país en el Mundo, 1913

"...In truth.
With three million
lives in total
to which can be added
four cardinal mountain ranges
and one large bay and another large bay,
three peninsulas with orbiting islands
and a surprising number of vertical rivers
and land under the trees and land
under the rivers and on the mountain slopes
and at the foothills and beyond the horizon
and land from the calling of the roosters
and land under horses' gallop
and land over the day, and under the map, all around
and under every footstep and even in the heart of love.
So
didn't I tell you.
There is
one country in this world
Quite simply rural and unpopulated...

– Pedro Mir
There is one country in this World, 1913
(Our translation)

Table of Contents

List of Maps

Map Symbols

✈ Airport	$ Bank	◓ Beach
🚌 Bus Station	(Telephone	◔ Park
🛥 Ferry	✉ Post Office	▲ Mountain
≍ Bridge	🏌 Golf	∴ Ruins

Symbols

🛶	Ulysses' Favourite
☎	Telephone Number
⊨	Fax Number
≡	Air Conditioning
⊗	Fan
≈	Pool
ℜ	Restaurant
⊕	Whirlpool
ℝ	Refrigerator
K	Kitchenette
△	Sauna
⊘	Exercise Room
tv	Colour Television
pb	Private Bathroom
sb	Shared Bathroom
fb	Full Board (Lodging + 3 Meals)
½ b	Half Board (Lodging + 2 Meals)
bkfst	Breakfast
♣	Casino

ATTRACTION CLASSIFICATION

★	Interesting
★★	Worth a visit
★★★	Not to be missed

The prices listed in this guide are for the admission of one adult.

HOTEL CLASSIFICATION

The prices in the guide are for one room, double occupancy in high season.

RESTAURANT CLASSIFICATION

$	$10 or less
$$	$10 to $20 US
$$$	$20 to $30 US
$$$$	$30 and more

The prices in the guide are for a meal for one person, not including drinks and tip.

All prices in this guide are in American dollars.

Write to us

Thanks to: Mayeline de Lara (Dominican Republic Tourist Office Montréal), Bolívar Troncoso, Ramón Cedano and luis Martínez (Dominican Republic Ministry of Tourism), Bárbara Polanco and Constance Hayward (Signature Vacations), Jean-Maurice and isabel Lemaire, Lorette Pierson, Carlos R. Batista and Précilio (our very devoted driver).

"We acknowledge the financial support of the Government of Canada through the Book Publishing Industry Development Program (BPIDP) for our publishing activities".

We would also like to thank SODEC (Québec) for their financial support.

Canadian Cataloguing in Publication Data

Couture, Pascale, 1966-

Dominican Republic

5th ed.
(Ulysses Travel Guide)
Translation of: République Dominicaine
Includes index.

ISBN 2-89464-209-1

1. Dominican Republic - Guidebooks.

I. Prieur, Benoit, 1965-   II. Title.   III. Series

F1934.5C6813 1999   917.29304'54   C99-940939-5

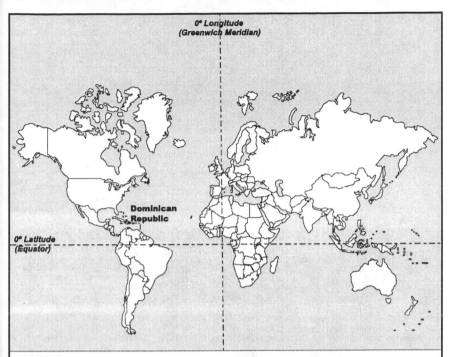

0° Longitude
(Greenwich Meridian)

Dominican
Republic

0° Latitude
(Equator)

 Where is the Dominican Republic?

18°N Santo
Domingo
69°O

Dominican Republic

Capital: Santo Domingo
Language: Spanish
Population: 8,000,000 inhab.
Currency: Dominican peso
Area: 48,442 km²

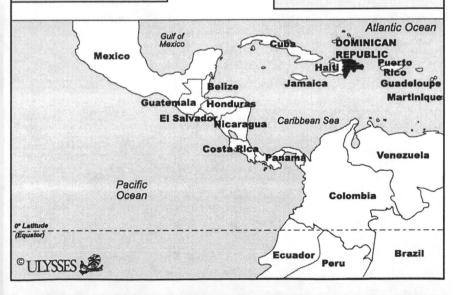

Atlantic Ocean

Gulf of
Mexico

Cuba

DOMINICAN
REPUBLIC

Mexico

Haiti

Puerto
Rico

Belize

Jamaica

Guadeloupe

Guatemala   Honduras

Martinique

El Salvador

Nicaragua

Caribbean Sea

Costa Rica

Panama

Venezuela

Pacific
Ocean

Colombia

0° Latitude
(Equator)

© ULYSSES

Ecuador   Peru

Brazil

Portrait

The Dominican Republic

shares with Haiti the island of Hispaniola, the second largest island in the Caribbean after Cuba.

Once the adopted land of the Tainos (Arawaks) and the Caribs, this island was "discovered" by Christopher Columbus and became home to the first European colony in the New World in 1492.

Known above all for the splendour of its white-sand beaches, the Dominican Republic is a country of tremendous diversity. The geography is a fascinating kaleidoscope, from the tropical rainforest to the desert-like expanses of the Southwest, from farming fields as far as the eye can see to the highest summit of the Caribbean, Pico Duarte, from the endless fields of sugar cane to verdant banana groves. The variety and spectacular beauty of its countryside is certainly one of its greatest riches.

But it is not the only one, for people also visit the Dominican Republic for the many remnants of its colonial past, of which the old area of Santo Domingo is one of the most shining examples, for its friendly hospitality and for the dynamic Caribbean culture and people.

Geography

With an area of 48,442 square kilometres, the Dominican Republic occupies the eastern two thirds of the island of Hispaniola. When crossing the country, it is hard not to be seduced by the astonishing diversity of the countryside.

Mountains

Five mountainous massifs rise from the Dominican territory. The most impressive is the Cordillera Centrale at the heart of which stands Pico Duarte, which with an altitude of 3,175 metres is the highest summit in the Caribbean. Southwest of and extending from this range are two small mountain chains, called "Neiba" and Baoruco". To the north, the whole Atlantic coast is isolated from the rest of the country by the Cordillera Septentrionale, which runs from Monte Cristi to San Francisco de Macoris. Finally, spanning the Samaná Peninsula on the eastern part of the island, is the Cordillera de Samaná.

The Plains

In between these mountain ranges stretch vast plains ideal for agriculture and grazing. In effect, 40% of Dominican land serves as grazing ground for animals, while one third is dedicated to agriculture. Fields stretch as far as the eye can see, especially sugar-cane fields, which have shaped the Dominican economy and countryside for centuries. The largest of these plains is the Cibao valley, in the centre of the country. This fertile land, where corn, rice, beans and tobacco are grown, is the coun-

try's most important agricultural region.

Tropical Rainforest

The heavy precipitation and constant humidity and temperature (never under 20°C) at the foot of the Cordillera Centrale have engendered the growth of a tropical rain forest. Three levels of vegetation can be distinguished in this verdant world. The first level, called the underbrush, consists of woody plants (young unmatured trees and shrubs that can survive in the shade) and herbaceous plants. All of these plants thrive on the little light that

manages to penetrate the canopy above them.

The second level consists of epiphytes (plants that do not touch the earth, but rather grow on other plants), such as mosses, lichens, creepers and bromeliads. These plants have adapted to dark and dank surroundings while making optimum use of the space available. Finally, the last level, the canopy, consists of the tallest trees in the forest, whose leaves absorb almost all of the solar energy. This forest is also populated by an incredible variety of animals, mostly birds and insects.

The Beaches

Most of the Dominican Republic's coastline is lined with beach, in many cases of pristine sand. The prettiest beaches are located along the northern coast and are washed by the Atlantic Ocean, as well as in the Punta Cana region in the eastern extremity of the island. A very particular vegetation grows along these beaches, made up essentially of creepers, seagrape trees and coconut palms.

Coconut Palm Trees

Mangrove Swamp

This strange forest grows in the mud and salt water and consists essentially of a few varieties of mangrove, recognizable by their large aerated roots which plunge into the submerged earth. Farther inland, the river mangrove grows in less salty waters. Shrubs and plants also grow in these swamps. Amidst this impenetrable tangle of roots and vegetation live various species of birds, crustaceans and above all insects. The Gri-Gri Lagoon, in Río San Juan, is an excellent spot to view the astonishing ecosystem of the mangrove

Red Mangrove Tree

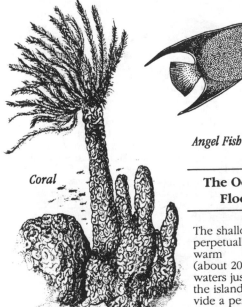

Coral

Angel Fish

The Ocean Floor

The shallow, perpetually warm (about 20°C) waters just off the island provide a perfect environment for the growth of coral. Formed by a colony of minuscule organisms called coelenterate polyps growing on a polypary (calcareous skeleton), coral takes many different forms. The abundant plankton around these formations attracts a wide variety of marine wildlife. Fish of all sizes also gravitate around the coral. These include tuna, kingfish and on rare occasions sharks, plus more colourful fish like parrot-fish, boxfish, mullet and angel-fish. The coral is also home to numerous other animals, like sponges and sea urchins.

Fauna

Very few mammals, apart from rodents (rats and mice) and cattle, inhabit Hispaniola. The island separated very early from the American continent, and therefore has few of the indigenous species that evolved later on the mainland. In fact, most of the mammals here were introduced during the colonial era. Wild pigs were among the species imported during the colonization of the island, and can still be seen in certain parts of the country.

Mongoose

The **mongoose** was introduced onto the island by colonists in an effort to eliminate the snakes and rats that lived in the fields and attacked workers. However, this little animal, which resembles a weasel, doesn't only hunt snakes (in fact, none of the island's snakes are really dangerous); it also goes after reptiles and ground-nesting birds, actually threatening the survival of some species. Mongooses can be spotted near fields, if you keep your eyes peeled.

Among the few species that inhabited the island before the arrival of colonists, the **agouti** is a small rodent from the shrew family, which is about the size of a hare. Their numbers are few, and they are spotted only rarely.

Iguana

Reptiles are more common. You are sure to see some little lizards sunning themselves here and there. Another, much larger reptile, the **iguana**, can be observed in the desert-like expanses of the southwest. This animal, which feeds on plants and insects, can grow to up to one

Turtle

metre long. Don't be afraid, though; the iguana is harmless. **Turtles** inhabit various areas, especially the islands of Siete Hermanos, north of Monte Cristi. Finally, **American crocodiles**, found only in Lago Enriquillo, are the largest animals on the

Humpback Whale

island.A few marine ammals populate the coastal waters, including the **manatee**, a bulky, gentle animal that resembles a large seal. Unfortunately, their numbers have diminished greatly in recent years, and they are spotted rarely. Another marine mammal, the **humpback whale**, which can grow to up to 16 metres, can be spotted near the coast of Bahía de Samaná. Arriving from the North Atlantic where they find an abundance of food during the summer, these whales head south to the warm waters of the Caribbean to reproduce (the gestation period lasts 12 months). Between January and March, whale-watching expeditions from Samaná allow visitors to become better acquainted with this fascinating mammal.

Manatee

Winged wildlife abounds all over the island, making a bird-watcher out of just about anyone who looks around. To help you identify these animals, we have included a description of the most common species below. With a bit of patience and a good pair of binoculars, you are sure to spot a few.

Brown Pelican

The **brown pelican** has greyish brown plumage and is identifiable by its long neck, enormous bill and long grey beak. It is usually seen alone or in small groups, flying in single file. These birds, which can grow to up to 140 centimetres, are commonly found near beaches.

The wingspan of the jet-black magnificent **frigate bird** can reach up to 2.5 metres. The colour of the throat is the distinguishing mark between the sexes; the male's is red, the female's white. These

birds can often be seen gliding effortlessly over the waves in search of food.

Herons are often found wading at the edge of ponds and mangrove swamps. Among the different types found in the Dominican Republic is the **great heron**, which can grow to up to 132 centimetres tall. It is identifiable by the large black feather extending from its white head and down its neck. Its body is covered with grey and white plumage.

Cattle Egret

The **cattle egret** is another bird in the same family commonly seen on the island, usually in the fields among cattle.

Frigate Bird

This bird is about 60 centimetres tall, with white plumage and an orange tuft of feathers on its head.

Great Heron

It arrived in the Caribbean during the 1950s; before that it was found only in Africa. It has adapted well and is found in large numbers throughout the Caribbean. Finally, you might hear the distinctive call of

the **small green heron**, which stands about 45 centimetres tall and has greenish-grey feathers on its back and wings.

The **pink flamingo**, another wader, is found along the shores of Lago Enriquillo. It feeds by turning its head upside down and dragging its beak through the mud while its tongue creates suction to trap small crustaceans and other organisms.

Coticas

Small green and red parrots called **coticas** can be seen in the gardens of several hotels. These domesticated birds are very popular with Dominicans, as they make friendly companions and can even learn to say a few words. The cotica, also known in Creole as the *verde cotorra*, is unfortunately being hunted into extinction.

The minuscule **hummingbird**, with its dark blue and green iridescent plumage, rarely grows more than 12 centimetres long, and some types weigh no more than 2 grams. It feeds on insects and nectar, and can be seen humming about near flowering bushes and   trees.

Hummingbird

The male **carib grackle** is completely black, while the female is paler. It is identifiable by its distinct yellow eyes. Its elongated claws allow it to run through fields in search of insects.

There are several types of **turtledoves** on the island, all about the size of a pigeon. The most widespread is the zenaida dove, with a brown back and a pinkish-beige breast, neck and head. It also has a blue spot on either side of its head. The common turtledove has greyish-brown plumage, with a black and white speckled neck.

Bananaquit

The **bananaquit**, also known as a yellow-breasted sunbird, is a small bird, about 10 centimetres tall, found throughout the Caribbean. It is easily identifiable by its dark grey or black upper-parts and its yellow throat and breast. It feeds on nectar and juice from various fruits including bananas and papaya. This greedy little bird often sits down on a patio table for a bit of sugar.

History

Well before the arrival of Christopher Columbus and the first Spanish conquistadors, large native populations inhabited the fertile island of Hispaniola. Like all native Americans, their ancestors were nomads from northern Asia who crossed the Bering

A BRIEF SUMMARY OF DOMINICAN HISTORY

Near the end of the ice age, nomads from northern Asia cross the Bering Strait and in successive waves of migration inhabit most of the American continent. Later, some migrate to the islands in the Caribbean.

1492: On his first voyage to the Americas, Christopher Columbus visits several islands, among them Hispaniola, where 39 soldiers stay behind while he returns to Spain.

1493: La Isabela is founded as the first European city in America.

1496: Bartholoméo Columbus, Christopher's brother, founds the city of Santo Domingo.

1535: Less than half a century after the arrival of the conquistadors, the native population on the island has been practically wiped out.

1603-1604: To combat trading between colonists and pirates, Spain forces the colonists to abandon the western regions of the island and resettle in the vicinity of Santo Domingo.

1697: France acquires the western part of the island under the Ryswick Treaty.

1795: French troops take possession of Santo Domingo and occupy it for more than a decade.

1809: Santo Domingo becomes a Spanish colony once again.

1822: The new Republic of Haiti takes over Santo Domingo and occupies it until 1844.

1844: After many years of guerilla fighting, the colonists of Santo Domingo oust the Haitian army. The newly independent nation adopts the name Dominican Republic.

1861: After a long period of political instability, the Dominican Republic reverts to being a Spanish colony until 1865.

1916: Already extensively involved in Dominican internal affairs, the United States invades the Dominican Republic, occupying it until 1924.

1930: General Trujillo seizes power by military force and imposes an excessively repressive dictatorship. He remains head of state for more than 30 years, until he is assassinated in May 1961.

1965: The United States sends in troops to prevent Juan Bosch, the legally elected president, from regaining the power he lost earlier at the hands of the military.

1966: Joaquín Balaguer becomes president of the country, and stays in power until 1978. During his 12 years in office, Balaguer often relies on repression as a political tool.

1978: Antonio Guzman, of the Dominican Revolutionary Party (PRD), is elected president. He is replaced in 1982 by Salvador Jorge Blanco, another member of the PRD.

1986: Frustrated by the corruption in Blanco's government, the people re-elect Joaquín Balaguer. The former autocrat is once again re-elected by a very small majority in 1990.

1994: Balaguer is elected once more, amid accusations by the opposition that he has fixed the election results. Under American pressure, Balaguer's term is cut to two years.

1996: Leonel Fernández is brought to power. Dominicans invest much hope in this new government.

Strait near the end of the ice age, and eventually inhabited almost all the Americancontinent through successive waves of migration.

Between 5500 and 3500 BC, the Ciboneys came from South America and settled on the island of Trinidad. From there they slowly migrated to the other islands in the West Indies, arriving in Hispaniola around 2500 BC. Little is known about this paleolithic society except that it came into contact with other Arawak peoples around the time of Christ: first the Guapoïdes (300 AD) and then the Salsdoïdes (between 300 and 800 AD). Then around 850 AD, a new wave of immigrants, the Caribs, drove the Arawak people from the Lesser Antilles to the Greater Antilles. There the Arawaks mixed with the people already on the islands, particularly on the island of Hispaniola, creating a new ethnic group called the Taïnos.

The island of Hispaniola, except the eastern extremity, which was populated with Caribs, became the adopted homeland of the Tainos. At the time of Columbus' arrival most of the territory was divided into five distinct kingdoms (Marien, Magua, Jaragua, Maguana and Higüey).

Each kingdom was governed by a grand chief, the cacique, and included several villages. The rest of the population was divided into three social strata: a group of nobles were in charge of all secular and spiritual ceremonies, while the common people worked the land with the help of slaves. The Tainos depended largely on agriculture for their survival, developing sophisticated irrigation and drainage techniques.

Columbus' first human contacts on the island of Hispaniola were with the Tainos, "Indians" that he judged to be fairly peaceable.

Scholars still do not agree on how large the native population of Hispaniola was at the time of the first Spanish explorations. Current estimations put the numbers at around 2 to 3 million individuals. Whatever the numbers, less than fifty years later, in 1535, only a few dozen native families remained on the island. A great many natives died because their immune systems were unable to combat the illnesses brought over by the Europeans. Many also perished in the colonial wars waged by Columbus and his successors. The survivors were then wiped out when the conquistadors imposed forced labour on them.

The Logbook of Christopher Columbus
(December 16, 1492)

"May Your Highness believe that these lands are so greatly good and fertile, and especially those of this island of Hispaniola, that there is no one who can tell it; and no one could believe it had he not seen it. And may you believe that this island and all the others are as much yours as Castille; for nothing is lacking except settlement and ordering the Indians to do whatever Your Highness may wish. Because I with the people that I bring with me, who are not many, go about in all these islands without danger; for I have already seen three of these sailors go ashore where there was a crowd of these Indians, and all would flee without the Spaniards wanting to do harm. They do not have arms and they are all naked, and of no skills in arms, and so very cowardly that a thousand would not stand against three. And so they are fit to be ordered about and made to work, plant, and do everything else that may be needed, and build towns and be taught our customs, and to go about clothed."

Christopher Columbus

August 3, 1492, the Genoese navigator Christopher Columbus set sail from the Spanish port of Palos, on an expedition financed by the Catholic kings of Castille and Aragon. Setting out to find a new route to Asia, he sailed westward across the Atlantic Ocean, heading a flotilla of three caravels: *The Santa Maria, The Pinta* and *The Niña.*

More than two months later, the expedition landed on an island in the Bahamian archipelago then known by its Taino name, Guanahani. That day, October 12, 1492 marked the official "discovery" of America; Columbus and his men believed they were just off the shores of Southeast Asia.

For several weeks, Columbus explored Guanahani and the neighbouring islands, encountering the natives for the first time. He then headed towards Cuba. After following its shores, the three caravels headed towards another island, known by some natives as Tohio. On the morning of December 6,

1492, this island was "discovered" by Columbus and christened *Isla Española* (or Hispaniola). Columbus was charmed by the beauty of this large island and wrote about it enthusiastically in his logbook. He sailed slowly along the northern coast, from west to east, making contact with natives and finding them peaceful and welcoming.

Caravel

The island seemed to Columbus an ideal place to establish the first Spanish colony on the American continent, especially after gold deposits were discovered in some of the rivers.

It was actually the foundering of the *Santa Maria* that precipitated the settling of this first colony. A fort was built with material salvaged

from the wreck. Completed on Christmas Day, 1492, it was christened *Fuerte de la Navidad* (Nativity Fort). A few weeks later, Columbus left 39 soldiers on the island under the command of Diego de Arana and returned to Spain, where news of his discoveries was received favourably by the Spanish monarchs.

This first Spanish colony on the American continent was soon wiped out. The details of what transpired after Columbus' departure are not known; perhaps the Spanish sailors left on Hispaniola wore out their welcome. One thing is certain: conflict erupted between the two groups, and the natives easily won out.

When Columbus returned ten months later with 1,500 men, he found no trace of the fort or the 39 soldiers. The explorer then launched the first retaliatory expeditions, which continued for many years and lead to the death of thousands of natives. Columbus later imposed forced labour on the island's inhabitants, and many were even sent to Spain to be sold as slaves. It was thus Christopher Columbus himself who initiated a process that led to the complete extinction of Hispaniola's native population in the decades to come.

The goal of Christopher Columbus' second voyage to America was to found a real Spanish city on Hispaniola. Columbus and his 1,500 men, with supplies, seeds and farm animals, chose a spot not far from the present city of Puerto Plata and founded La Isabela, the first Spanish city in the Americas, in 1493. The city remained the centre of the colony for some time, until it was abandoned due to famines and epidemics.

Gradually, several forts were built closer to the centre of the country to oversee the exploitation of the island's gold deposits. Then, in 1496, Columbus' younger brother Bartoloméo, founded Santo Domingo, which became the young colony's nerve centre.

In 1500, Christopher Columbus was relieved of his duties as Viceroy of the Indies after Francisco de Bodadilla, appointed by Queen Isabela of Spain to investigate colonial management, accused him of poorly administering the colony, needlessly killing natives and encouraging the slave trade.

Gold and Sugar

During the first quarter century of Spanish colonization, gold

mining fuelled Hispaniola's economy. Despite the *encomiendas* system, designed to protect natives from abuse, the island's inhabitants were used as slaves in the gold mines. Living conditions were deplorable, and natives died in such great numbers that the conquistadors eventually had to import slaves from other islands and from Central America.

By 1515, the gold deposits were becoming exhausted and the Spanish began to abandon Hispaniola in favour of other islands and regions in the Americas. Those who remained after the massive exodus of the Spanish population took up farming and stock breeding. On his second voyage to America, Columbus had provided the island with herds of cattle, which quickly grew in number, and crops such as sugar cane, which took well to the local climate. Sugar cane thus became Hispaniola's leading export and the driving force of its economy.

The sugar industry required an abundant workforce, which the island simply did not possess. The Spanish therefore came to depend largely on African slaves, so much so that by the middle of the 16th century, the African population on the island had grown to

more than 30,000 individuals

The sugar boom did not last long, however. During the final decades of the 16th century, the European demand for Dominican sugar cane products began to decline, due in large part to increased exports from Brazil. As a result, the island experienced a second exodus of Spanish colonists.

Sugar cane and cattle nevertheless remained the staples of the economy, but Hispaniola was relegated to a position of marginal importance in the Spanish Empire.

Pirates and Buccaneers

As the Spanish crown lost interest in the island and paid lower and lower prices for Dominican exports, the inhabitants of Hispaniola turned to smugglers to dispose of their merchandise. This angered the Spanish authorities, who decided to regain control of Hispaniola by forcing the Spanish colonists to move to the eastern part of the island, around Santo Domingo, and abandon the rest of the island. This harsh measure was enforced by the Spanish army in 1603 and 1604.
The western part of the island was thus completely deserted until several years later,

when French bucca-
neers were drawn to
the area. Many settled
here permanently and
tended the wild cattle
that had been left be-
hind. A very profitable
business was set up
between buccaneers,
who slaughtered the
animals for leather, and
pirates, who trans-
ported the leather to
Europe.

Although they tried
several times, the Span-
ish authorities never
succeeded in putting a
stop to the trade. Tak-
ing advantage of the
buccaneers' presence,
France gradually took
over this part of the
island, which became
an official French pos-
session in 1697, with
the signing of the
Ryswick Treaty.

The eastern part of the
island, still under Span-
ish control, experi-
enced many decades of
great economic hard-
ship before finally at-
taining a certain level
of prosperity towards
the middle of the 18th
century.

The division of Hispan-
iola between France
and Spain led to the
birth of the two coun-
tries that now share the
island: the Dominican
Republic and the Re-
public of Haiti.

Toward
Independence

The French Revolution
of 1789 had important
repercussions even for

Hispaniola. In 1791,
inspired by the winds
of change and the dis-
integration of France's
control, a slave upris-
ing led by Toussaint
L'Ouverture broke out
in the French colony in
the western part of the
island.

From the start, the
Spanish settlers of
Santo Domingo sup-
ported the insurgency.
However, things
changed drastically in
1794, when France
abolished slavery in the
colony. All of a sud-
den, Toussaint
L'Ouverture's men did
an about-face and
joined forces with the
French to overthrow
the Spanish colony on
the eastern part of the
island. Completely
overwhelmed, the
Spanish surrendered
Santo Domingo to
France (1795), which
ruled over the whole of
Hispaniola for a few
years.

In the years that fol-
lowed, France, under
the rule of Napoleon
Bonaparte, decided to
combat the rising au-
tonomy of Toussaint
L'Ouverture's govern-
ment. A military expe-
dition was sent to His-
paniola in 1802, and
L'Ouverture was taken
prisoner and brought to
France. However, the
western part of the
island continued to
strive for independence
from France. In fact, it
only became stronger,
this time under the
leadership of Jean
Jacques Desalines. The

French forces were
soon driven out by the
rebels, and on January
1, 1804, the Republic of
Haiti was declared.

The French maintained
control of the eastern
side of the island, but
not for long; in 1809,
Spanish colonists re-
captured Santo
Domingo for Spain
with the help of British
troops at war with Na-
poleon's France. How-
ever, Spanish authori-
ties showed very little
interest in the develop-
ment of this far-off
colony, leaving Santo
Domingo's settlers little
choice but to proclaim
their independence in
1821. This independ-
ence also proved short-
lived, for the Haitian
army invaded Santo
Domingo the following
year. Then, for a period
of more than 20 years,
until 1844, the Haitians
controlled the entire
island of Hispaniola.

Haitian domination
began to weaken near
the end of the 1830s,
when an underground
Dominican organiza-
tion began launching
attacks on the Haitian
army. This organiza-
tion, known as *La
Trinitaria*, was lead by
three men: Juan Pablo
Duarte, Ramón Mella
and Francisco del
Rosario Sanchez. After
a few years of fighting,
the Haitian army finally
retreated, and the east-
ern half of the island
declared itself officially
independent. On Feb-
ruary 27, 1844, this
new nation adopted

the name "Dominican Republic".

Years of Uncertainty (1844-1916)

Following the war of independence, *La Trinitaria* rebels faced opposition from several armed groups within their own country, who wished to take control for themselves. The members of *La Trinitaria* were quickly defeated at this game, and in September 1844 were completely ousted from power.

Thus began the battle for control, pitting the followers of General Pedro Santana against those of General Buenaventura Baez. For nearly a quarter century, the two military leaders wrestled for power through bloody civil wars. In 1861, General Santana even relinquished control of the Dominican Republic to Spain for a few years.

The Dominicans' string of misfortunes continued when General Ulysses Heureaux became president of the Republic in 1882. He headed a violent dictatorial regime, remaining in power until he was assassinated in 1899. During this time, his poor handling of internal affairs led the country into a series of economic crises.

Upon his death, a succession of governments took power for short periods, creating a period of instability and political chaos that exacerbated the country's economic problems.

It was this situation that precipitated the first of many incursions by the United States into the Dominican political arena. Worried that a European power might take advantage of the economic instability to gain a new foothold in the country, the United States, the new imperialist power that saw Latin America and the Caribbean as its private stomping ground, assumed control of the country's borders and economic affairs.

The American Occupation (1916-1924)

Attempts by the United States to increase their economic control in the Dominican Republic lead to an impasse in November of 1915, when Dominican authorities made it clear that they had no intention of giving in to American pressure. The U.S. reply was prompt: in May of 1916, the United States government ordered the invasion of the Dominican Republic; U.S. *marines* quickly took control of Santo Domingo and other major cities. Washington then or-

dered the dismantling of the Dominican army and the disarmament of the general population.

Under the eight-year American occupation, the Dominican economy was largely remodelled to suit the needs of the United States. For example, as the First World War had made the Americans fear a sugar shortage, the Dominican Republic increased its production of sugar, while the production of other goods needed locally was put aside.

The United States also used this period to eliminate import barriers for American products in the Dominican Republic. The resulting American penetration into the Dominican market forced many small local enterprises out of business. The occupation did have some positive results, however, including an expansion of road and railway networks and an improvement of the educational system.

The American occupation of Dominican territory ended in 1924. In return, the Americans left a semblance of political legitimacy and a powerful National Guard.

The Trujillo Dictatorship

In 1924, Horacio Vasquez won the first free election held in the Dominican Republic. However, this period of democratic rule was short, as *General Rafael Leonidas Trujillo (1891-1961)*, leader of the National Guard, took over the country by military force in 1930 and became the mastermind of one of the darkest periods in Dominican history.

During his "reign", Trujillo, backed by the National Guard and a solid network of spies, imposed an absolute dictatorship with a heinous combination of violence, intimidation, torture, political assassinations and deportations. Under Trujillo, elections were vulgar shams, held only to cover up the excesses of a regime that was nothing less than one of the most terrible dictatorships in the history of the continent.

Trujillo ran things as if they were his personal business. He exercised almost complete control over the development of the Dominican economy by maintaining, either directly or indirectly, a controlling interest in most of the country's industries. Rarely in history has a ruler been as extreme a megalomaniac as Trujillo. Portraits and statues honouring the Generalissimo, who declared himself the nation's "Benefactor", were put up everywhere in the country. In 1936, he even went

so far as to change the name of the capital, Santo Domingo, to Ciudad-Trujillo (Trujillo City).

Relations between the Dominican Republic and Haiti were poor during Trujillo's reign. The dictator's rejection of Haiti and its "black" culture were central to Dominican nationalism. Trujillo actually believed that Dominicans had a "civilizing" mission on the island. Relations between the two countries deteriorated even further when, in 1937, under orders from Trujillo, the National Guard massacred between 10,000 and 20,000 Haitians living in the Dominican Republic.

In contrast to the situation between the Dominican Republic and Haiti, Trujillo established excellent relations with the U.S. by offering extremely favourable conditions to American investors and by taking a stand against communism. By the end of the 1950s, maintaining ties with Trujillo became burdensome for the U.S. In Washington, the fear was that the extreme brutality of Trujillo's regime only served to fire up communist revolutionaries in other parts of the continent. Trujillo finally succeeded in completely alienating the Americans in 1960, following the aborted attempt to assassinate Venezuelan

president Romulo Bétancourt. From that point on, Trujillo's days were numbered.

This terrible dictatorship, which lasted more than 30 years, ended abruptly on May 30, 1961, when Trujillo was assassinated. At the time of his death, Trujillo was considered one of the 10 richest men in the world, with about 600,000 hectares of productive farmland to his name and a personal fortune valued at $500 million US. The three-decade-long Trujillo regime is estimated to have cost the lives of some 100,000 Dominicans.

The Second American Invasion

After Trujillo's death, the vice-president of the country, Joaquín Balaguer, took over. He soon had to relinquish control to a state council, which organized a presidential election on December 20, 1962. The people elected Juan Bosch of the Dominican Revolutionary Party (PRD). His term did not last long, however; believing that Bosch was determined to re-establish civil liberties, the army ousted him in a coup in September, 1963.

After two years of disastrous economic policies, the increasingly dissatisfied Dominican working classes rose up and, with the help of a dissident army faction, re-established constitutional order on April 24, 1965. Under the pretext that the uprising had been infiltrated by communists, the nervous American government reacted by sending in the marines to assist the Dominican military in putting down the "revolution". Fighting began, causing heavy casualties, and soon the rebels were forced to give in.

A provisional government led by Hector Garcia Godoy was established. Then in a rigged election, one of Trujillo's former comrades-in-arms, Joaquín Balaguer, was elected president in June 1966.

The Contemporary Period

Balaguer led the country for 12 years, winning rigged elections in 1970 and 1974, for which the opposition refused even to put up candidates. During this entire period, Balaguer ruled as an authoritarian, using violence and intimidation to maintain power.

Things took a new turn during the 1978 election, when the Dominican Revolutionary Party (PRD) supported Antonio Guzman in a bid for the presidency.

Dominicans were ready for change, yet Balaguer had no intention of relinquishing his control. On election day, when poll results were leaning in favour of Guzman, Balaguer tried to put an end to the vote counting. He almost succeeded, but was forced to give in to outside pressure, mainly from the United States, and admit defeat.

Antonio Guzman remained in power until 1982, but his presidency ended on a tragic note, when he committed suicide upon learning that some of his closest allies had embezzled public funds. After an interim period of a few months, Salvador Jorge Blanco, the new head of the PRD, was elected president and remained so until 1986.

During the presidencies of Guzman and Blanco, many civil liberties were reinstated, which contributed greatly to the popularity of the two men. Unfortunately, with the collapse of sugar markets and the rise in oil prices, the Dominican Republic endured severe economic hardships during this period, leading to deep dissatisfaction among the population. The axe fell on the PRD, when its president, who was also the president of the country, Salvador Jorge Blanco,

was personally found guilty of corruption.

In 1986, a disillusioned Dominican electorate facing an unprecedented political void opted to support the former dictator, octogenarian Joaquín Balaguer, in a national election. Balaguer was re-elected in 1990, defeating a disorganized and divided opposition.

Once again, in 1994, he remained in power, not without difficulty, however, and despite accusations that he had fixed the election results in his favour. In a bid to silence critics who questioned the election results and under pressure from the Americans, Balaguer agreed to cut his term to two years and hold another election in 1996. During these last terms, Balaguer governed with a much softer hand than he had previously.

The 1996 election should have belonged to José Francisco Pena Gómez, of the Dominican Revolutionary Party (PRD). Everything indicated he would win, but it was not to be. On the second ballot, a coalition was formed between the Social-Christian Reform Party and the Dominican Liberation Party

The First Inhabitants of the West Indies

When the first European explorers arrived, the majority of the West Indies were occupied by two native peoples, the Tainos and the Caribs. These peoples were descended from several tribes that migrated to the Caribbean from the South American continent.

The first people that lived in the West Indies were the Ciboneys. Originally from South America, they established themselves first on the island of Trinidad between the years 5500 and 3500 BC. Being excellent navigators, the Ciboneys then migrated to other islands in the West Indies. In the Dominican Republic, the remains of Ciboney sites dating from 2500 BC have been found at Pedernales and Barrera Mordan (near Azua). The Ciboneys were a seminomadic people who lived essentially from hunting, fishing and gathering fruit.

From the time of Christ, successive waves of migrants settled in the Lesser Antilles: the Guapoids from South America (from the 1st to the 4th century), followed by the Saladoids from Central America (from the 4th to the 9th century). These peoples, both Arawak-speakers, lived off the earth: they had advanced tool-making and irrigation techniques, and they produced beautiful pottery which they decorated with drawings. The Gaupoids and the Saladoids soon came in contact with the Ciboneys from the West Indies.

The last people to come to the West Indies from the South American continent were Caribs from Guyana at the beginning of the 9th century. Expelling the then-resident Arawak-speakers to the Greater Antilles, the Caribs settled mainly in the Lesser Antilles and soon mixed with the already-present Ciboneys creating a new ethnic group called the Tainos. When the Europeans discovered Hispaniola in the 15th century, it was mainly populated by the Tainos.

The Tainos developed a well structured society and an efficient trading system with the other peoples of the Antilles. They generally lived next to the ocean in villages that consisted of about 50 family huts (*bohios*) with 1,000 inhabitants; but the largest villages could have up to 5,000 inhabitants. These villages were part of an empire that was lead by a single ruler called the *cacique*. Beneath the ruler were three social groups: the nobles who took care of religious functions, the common people and the slaves, who were essential to the economic survival of the empire.

Because they had several food sources, the Tainos were self-sufficient when the Europeans arrived. They grew corn and peppers which they had brought from Mexico, and cassava, also known as manioc, from which they made a bread that served as a staple in their diet. They ate fish, mollusks and wild game, as well as parrots and tiny, voiceless dogs without fur, which were raised by the Tainos strictly for consumption. The Tainos also developed cotton-weaving techniques and created beautiful fabrics. They also made hammocks

which became popular with Spanish sailors shortly after the Conquest.

Contrary to popular belief, these island people were not isolated from other peoples in the Americas. The Tainos were great navigators and were familiar with wind and water currents, which allowed them to travel from one island to another. Of all the peoples on the American continent, they seem to have traded the most with native communities in Mexico. The Tainos travelled in canoes that were up to 10 m long and could hold 50 sailors. In these ships they sailed as far as Mexico and Venezuela, where they sold cottonfabric.

The Tainos are often considered pacifists, while the Caribs are seen as war-like people, an image that seems to have been based on some distorted ob-

servations made by their Spanish conquerors. The Caribs were certainly fierce warriors who conquered Taino villages and violently opposed European settlement on their lands. Moreover, it seems that the Caribs engaged in cannibalistic rituals after defeating their enemies. The Spanish had the impression that the Taino, by comparison, were a peaceful people, when in fact, they too were valiant warriors. This image of the Taino has persisted: during the European conquest the Taino had a difficult time fending off the Caribs and were ultimately unable to resist the better armed Europeans. The Taino left no descendants; the only remaining native peoples of the West Indies are the Caribs on the island of Dominica.

allowing the latter's candidate, Leonel Fernández, to narrowly defeat Pena Gómez. The results of the election were nevertheless greeted with enthusiasm by the Dominican people, as Fernández offers a real alternative to the Balaguer regime. Quite young (he is in his early-forties) and educated in the United States, Leonel Fernández intends to modernize the country by combatting corruption and investing in health and education.

Politics, Economy and Society

The 500 years that have passed since Columbus' first voyage to America in 1492 have seen an independent Dominican nation emerge. Like most populations in Latin America, Dominicans continue to struggle for real political, economic and social freedom. They must continuously deal with numerous uncertainties that linger over the future of their country. Whatever choices are made in the years to come, the country must first learn to invest in its extraordinarily young population.

Politics

Like the U.S. system, on which it is based, the Dominican legislative system is made up of two chambers, the Senate and the Chamber of Deputies. The Senate has 30 representatives, one for each province in the country and one for the national district; the Chamber of Deputies has 120 members. The president of the country has considerable power; he is elected by universal suffrage to a four-year term.

Though there are about 20 political parties, only three play a significant role in the political power play of the country. Up until 1996, the Social-Christian Reform Party (PRSC) (previously called the Reform Party or PR) dominated political life. As leader of the PR and then the PRSC, Joaquín Balaguer was elected president in 1966, 1970 and 1974, then in 1986, 1990 and 1994. The PRSC is the result of the coming-together of the Reform party and the Social-Christian Revolutionary Party.

Founded in Havana (Cuba) by Juan Bosch, in 1939, the Dominican Revolutionary Party (PRD) was headed by José Francisco Pena Gómez until recently. In 1973, in-party fighting forced Juan Bosch and his supporters to leave the PRD to found the Dominican Liberation Party. It was as head of the PRD that Juan Bosch was elected president in 1962 before being overthrown by a coup d'état the

following year. The PRD was re-elected in 1978 and 1982 with Antonio Guzmán as their leader and then Salvador Jorge Blanco. The most recent election, held in 1996, was won by Leonel Fernández of the Dominican Liberation Party.

In the last few years, Dominican politics have been marked mainly by the growing impatience of the country's working classes, exasperated by the widespread corruption that has reached even the highest levels of government, and by a forced economic austerity plan that has greatly reduced consumer buying power.

Only a few months after his election, Leonel Fernández had to deal with general strikes, which broke out in certain regions of the country. These social ills, which shake things up politically from time to time in the Dominican Republic, are the result of a profound malaise that is particular to many Latin American societies and is linked to the constant growth of the immense gap separating the rich and the poor.

Presently, in the Dominican Republic, while large segments of the society often cannot afford basic foodstuffs and live in humble shacks without running water or electricity, a small minority enjoys fabulous riches and material wealth. This marginalization of a large part of the population is a major stumbling block on the road to true democratization.

As well, until very recently the government of the Dominican Republic stood accused by the international community of participating in the exploitation of Haitian braceros (sugar cane cutters). Often surrounded by armed guards, thousands of Haitians had long worked in the fields for a pittance, barely making enough to survive. The Dominican government promised many times to rectify the problem; then, in June 1991, it deported all the illegal workers back to Haiti.

Many Haitians have nevertheless remained in the country, usually working at menial, low-paying jobs in the construction or agricultural sectors. Working conditions remain unbearable on sugar plantations, and, generally, the situation of Haitians living in the Dominican Republic is still a problem. The country's new president, Leonel Fernández, seems to show much more goodwill than his predecessor. A meeting with his Haitian counterpart at the end of 1996 lead to an agreement concerning the wages paid to cane-cutters.

The Economy

The Dominican economy has become somewhat more modern and diverse in recent decades, but farming and raising livestock are still central activities. More than 40% of the country's total surface area serves as pasture for cattle, and approximately one third is used for growing food for human consumption. Contrary to the situation in many Caribbean countries, most of the dietary staples consumed on the island are produced locally.

Sugar cane, which was introduced to the island by Columbus, is still the largest crop in the country. Its cultivation requires a large work force, and refined cane sugar is the country's primary agricultural export.

Among the other commodities exported by the Dominican Republic, the most important are tobacco, cocoa, coffee, rice and various tropical fruits. Dairy production and the breeding of cattle, pigs and poultry serve mainly to satisfy local demand.

The Dominican Republic is rich in mineral resources, though many are still largely untapped. The only large-scale mining operations focus on silver, gold, nickel and iron.

In recent years, nickel has come to occupy an important place on the foreign markets. In terms of value, it is presently the most important export. The Dominican Republic also produces large quantities of salt, which is extracted primarily from deposits along the shores of Lago Enriquillo. In addition, hydroelectric facilities produce about 20% of the country's energy requirements. As with most Caribbean countries, the Dominican Republic is still largely dependent on foreign imports for energy.

Despite recent efforts to diversify industrial production, sugar cane refinement is still the biggest Dominican industry. Sugar cane is used mainly to produce raw sugar, and secondarily for rum and molasses.

Labour-intensive light industries, such as the production of textiles, shoes, clothing and food products, have grown steadily in the last few decades. The Dominican Republic's heavy industries are mostly in the plastic, metallurgy and oil refining sectors.

The Dominican government continues to favour the development of industrial zones near several large cities for the use of foreign businesses. As a consequence, many companies, mostly American,

Canadian and Asian ones, now assemble their products in the Dominican Republic, thus taking advantage of a cheap labour force.

Tourism is also one of the mainstays of the economy; it is now the major source of foreign currency in the country. Though largely dominated by companies not owned by Dominican interests, tourism directly employs close to 200,000 people Realizing the economic importance of tourism with respect to the development of the country, the new government has increased its support for this sector. The tourism industry is nonetheless a key sector of the Dominican economy and contributes about 70% to the gross national product.

Tourism began to develop in the 1980s, and since then the Dominican Republic has marketed itself as an inexpensive sun destination. Thanks to local production of most of the necessary foodstuffs, many hotel complexes are able to offer "all-inclusive" packages (room, meals and drinks) at very competitive rates compared to what is offered in other islands in the region.

Finally, the country's continued dependence on sugar markets constitutes a recurring problem for the structure of the national economy. The economic crisis that has plagued the Dominican Republic for over ten years is tied to a reduction in American sugar imports and the resulting sharp drop in the price of sugar. The Dominican Republic also has a considerable foreign debt, which seems out of control, further hindering the country's economic development. The employment situation is just as dismal, with more than a quarter of the potential workforce left idle.

Population

Covering two thirds of the island of Hispaniola, which it shares with Haiti, the Dominican Republic has a population of 7,900,000, according to the most recent census. A majority of Dominicans live in either Santo Domingo or the Cibao valley. The population density in the country has reached 150 inhabitants per square kilometre, and the birth rate is among the highest in the Caribbean. Presently, 48% of Dominicans are under 14 years old. The poor economic conditions in recent years have pushed the number of Dominicans emigrating to Puerto Rico to as many as 500 per week.

Although it is difficult to present a precise picture of the Dominican Republic's racial composition, there are three main population groups in the country: mulattos make up about 75% of the population, while whites and blacks represent 15% and 10%, respectively. A marked economic disparity exists between whites and blacks, generally favouring whites.

The origins of the Dominican population are diverse, but most have Spanish or African backgrounds. A smaller percentage, typically working at lower-paying jobs, are of Haitian descent. Generally speaking, citizens of Haitian origin are poorly accepted; the conflicts that have marked relations between the two countries are not soon forgotten.

In addition, the country's large urban centres often have small Asian communities, while a number of the residents of Sosúa are descendants of Eastern European Jews who escaped Nazi Germany in the 1930s. There are no descendants of the indigenous peoples that once inhabited the island of Hispaniola; this group was completely wiped out at the beginning of colonization.

More than 95% of Dominicans consider themselves Catholic, while a small number of people, most of whom live in mountainous areas, practise voodoo.

The official language of the Dominican Republic, and the mother tongue of 95% of the population, is Spanish. Along the Haitian border a few people speak Creole. Throughout the country, even in tourist areas, visitors will be addressed in Spanish, though many people speak English and French as well.

Culture, Traditions and Lifestyle

The Dominican Republic was a Spanish colony for many years during which time it absorbed thousands of African immigrants. The artistic activity on the island has been shaped by these two cultures. During the early years of colonization, the arts flourished, especially in the 16th century. It was not until the 19th century, when the country gained independence and a certain stability, that artistic expression began to develop. From the end of the 19th century to the present, the arts have thrived continually. Unfortunately, censorship has often thrived as well.

Literature

The first writer to document the charms of Hispaniola was none other than Christopher Columbus; his log books provide the first descriptions of the region. Very early in the country's colonial history, Dominican writers emerged with a style of their own. The **Santo Tomas de Aquino University**, founded in 1538, was central to the development of this literature. The earliest Dominican works consist essentially of essays, journals and chronicles written by the first explorers and missionaries, and aim mainly to describe the territory and spread knowledge of its existence. Among the first texts of note are *The Historia Natural y General de Indias* by Gonzalo Fernandez de Oviedo, *Doctrina Cristina* by Brother Pedro de Cordoba, and *Historia de las Indias* by Brother Bartoloméo de las Casas.

The French invasion and the difficulties with Spain in the 17th and 18th centuries slowed the literary development of the country. Dominican literature did not enjoy a resurgence until the 19th century. Several influential writers emerged during that period, most notably Felix Maria del Monte, known for his patriotic poetry. The texts of

Salomé Ureña, advocating an improvement in conditions for women on the island, are also significant. *Enriquillo*, a historical text written by Manuel de Jesus Galvan in the late 19th and early 20th centuries, also ranks among the most important works of the time.

The period immediately following the country's independence (1880), though marred by the American invasion (1916), saw the development of a literature that emphasized an awareness of social realities, as well as more patriotic writings. It was in this context that Federico Bermúdez wrote *Los Humildes*, denouncing the suffering of the Dominican people.

Federico Garcia Godoy recounts the advent of independence in three powerful short stories: *Rufinito*, *Alma Dominicana*, and *Guanuma*. Though fairly conservative in his choice of subjects, Gaston Fernando Deligne is a master of the Spanish language and one of the country's most important poets. Another writer by the name of Domingo Moreno Jimines headed a group that sang the praises of the good and simple values of peasant life.

Later, during the dictatorship of President Trujillo, literary activity slowed down. In a climate of brutal repression, Dominican authors had much less freedom of expression. Writers such as Manuel Rueda and Lupo Fernandez Rueda used symbols and metaphors to covertly protest certain aspects of the political regime. Others were forced into exile. It was in such a context, while in Cuba, that Pedro Mir wrote his beautiful poem "Hay un país en el Mundo".

During the 1940s, a greater openness toward foreign literary movements led to the emergence of the "*surprise*" poetry movement. Among the so-called "*independent*" poets, Tomas Hernandez Franco became known for his modern works, which protested the existing regime. Works with wider appeal were also created during this period.

Antonio Fernandez Spencer published collections of poetry that gained international recognition. One of the most important authors of the 20th century, Juan Bosch, did most of his writing during the Trujillo dictatorship. His engaging, beautifully written essays describe the daily life of Dominican peasants. After the fall of the Trujillo regime, Bosch led the Dominican Republic for a few months, and remained an important political

figure for many years. However, during the 30 years of Trujillo, many authors opted for silence or exile, publishing their texts only after Trujillo's death in 1961. Despite these difficult years, Dominican literary movements remained dynamic and innovative.

Literary expression has since been granted more and more freedom and several authors, often influenced by foreign literary trends, stand out for the quality of their work. The most important are Ivan Garcia Guerra, Miguel Alfonseca, Jeannette Miller, Alexis Gómez and Soledad Alvárez and the former president of the country, Joaquín Balaguer.

Painting

The Dominican Republic has been and is home to numerous talented painters who have gained renown in Dominican and international artistic circles. Usually vibrantly coloured and buoyant, local painting is quite emblematic of the artistic intensity of the island. Among the distinguished artists of the country are Guillo Pérez, Elsa Núñez, Fernando Ureña Rib, Candido Bibo and Manuel Severino. Two celebrated painters in particular, Giorgi Morel and Jaime Colsón,

stand out among the country's masters.

Music and Dance

Music and dance occupy a very important place in the cultural landscape of the Dominican Republic. Much more than an occasional pastime, music accompanies every part of a Dominican day, whether it be on a crowded bus, in the most humble of market stalls, at work, at home, or late at night in the nightclubs of Santo Domingo and other cities.

Among the current musical trends, a Dominican favourite is the *merengue*, that rousing, furiously rhythmic music that has its origins on the island. Though originally identified with the rural classes, the popularity of the merengue cuts through the various social divisions of the country. It was in the Dominican countryside that this accordion, tambourine, saxophone and drum music, with its son rhythm, was conceived.

The merengue became fashionable throughout the country in the 1930s, under the regime of General Trujillo, who was a true fan of this music. The talented artist Francisco Uloa made a name for himself during this period. At the end of the 1950s, the major groups had their turn at fame, most notably Johnny Ventura. Since then, while conserving its original rhythms, the merengue has been developed: leaving more space for the saxophone ; replacing the accordion with an electric guitar and the piano with a synthesizer. Contemporary Merengue has also been influenced by various other styles, such as salsa, rock, zook and reggae.

Among the other Dominican merengue stars we should mention Tonio Rosario and Fernandito Villalona.

Although the Dominicans adore merengue, they also appreciate *batchata*, their other national music. The batchata is becoming more popular among most of the social classes of the Dominican Republic. This music, with rhythms slower than merengue, has traditionally been associated with Dominican workers and peasants. Love remains the essential theme that colours the songs of batchata singers. Currently, the popular artists of the country are Antony Santos, Raúl Rodríguez and Luis Vargas.

For a while now, the appeal of the merengue has extended beyond the borders of the Dominican Republic. Some of the country's great-

est talents have become international stars, as well known the world over as they are throughout the Caribbean and in other Spanish-speaking countries. In the 1980s, the group 4:40 and its leader *Juan Luís Guerra* were a huge success on the international scene.

Though Dominicans adore merengue, which they consider their national music, they are also very fond of other types of music. Spanish and Latin-American singers are common and very well-liked with locals. North American "top-40" music, as well as Afro-American and Caribbean movements, such as reggae, are also prevalent in the country. Classical music enjoys a following here as well. Santo Domingo even has its own reputed symphony orchestra.

Baseball

Baseball is at least as popular in the Dominican Republic as it is in the United States, where it originated. Young Dominicans practise this sport more than any other; there are baseball fields in every neighbourhood in the capital and every village of the country. And with equipment requirements limited to a glove, a ball and a bat, it is very economical to play, a definite plus in a country

where money is an issue for the majority of the population.

Baseball is the national sport of Dominicans, and is also a very popular pastime. The exploits of the big Dominican stars of professional baseball are followed passionately and reported upon at length in the local media.

Professional baseball has existed in the Dominican Republic for more than 100 years. The professional league currently numbers five teams, two in Santo Domingo and the others in San Pedro de Macorís, Santiago de los Caballeros and La Romana. Each team plays about 60 games between the months of October and February, and the season ends with a championship series between the best teams in the Caribbean.

Discussions are currently underway to grant Puerto Plata its very own professional team. There is talk of completely renovating the old stadium at the entrance to the city (near The Brugal Rum Distillery), in order to accommodate a Puerto Plata team that could prove to be very popular with tourists.

The reputation of Dominican baseball grew in the fifties following the successes of the first Dominicans to play in the majors. In 1956, Ozzie Virgil became

the first player to make a name for himself in the United States. But it was thanks to the remarkable talent of right-handed pitcher Juan Marichal, signed by the San Francisco Giants and of the Alou brothers (Felipe, Mateo and Jesús) that the quality of Dominican players became known.

Since Virgil, Marichal and the Alou brothers, more than 200 young Dominicans have stepped up to the plate in the major leagues. Some of the more noteworthy players include Rico Carty, Manny Mota, César Cedeno, Pedro Guerrero, Frank Taveras, Pepe Fria, Alfredo Griffín, Rafael Landestoy, Joaquín Andujar, Tony Pena, George Bell, Damaso García, Pasqual Pérez, Mario Soto, Raul Mondesi, Julio Franco, Vladimir Guerrero, Moises Alou, Mel Rojas, Carlos Pérez and Sammy Sosa. After the United States, the Dominican Republic that has produced the most major league players. The city of San Pedro Macoris actually claims to have spawned more players *per capita* thanany other city in the world.

Felipe Alou: a star player and manager *par excellence* !

Born in 1935 in Haina, Felipe Alou has had a remarkable career in major-league baseball, which started in 1958 with the San Francisco Giants. Over the course of his 2,082 games Felipe maintained a batting average of .286, and hit a total of 206 home runs. In 1966, *Sporting News* magazine named him first-baseman of the year in the National League. When his career as a player ended in 1979, he joined the Montreal Expos organization and was named manager in 1992 (Felipe Alou thus became the first "Latino" to occupy this position in the major leagues). His success led to his being named National League manager of the year in 1994. Felipe Alou is very popular with Montreal fans, as well as fans back in the Dominican Republic, where he is seen as a pioneer for having had a major-league career that has spanned decades. Other family members have also known success as professional baseball players: his brothers Mateo and Jesús played in the major leagues, and his son Moises enjoys quite a reputation among the professionals today.

Cockfighting

Introduced by the Spanish, cockfights are held all over the Dominican Republic. Men gather around the "*pits*" (packed-dirt arenas) to watch and cheer on a battle between two cocks.

Beforehand, there is a ceremony, during which the cocks are weighed and fitted with spurs, and their owners are introduced. Then, once the judges have decided that the birds qualify, the fight begins. Victory goes to the cock left breathing at the end.

Practical Information

Whether alone or with a group, it is easy to travel anywhere in the Dominican Republic.

In order to make the most of your stay, it is important to be well prepared. In addition to providing information on local customs, this chapter is intended to help you plan your trip.

Entrance Formalities

Make sure you bring all the necessary papers to enter and exit the country. Though requirements are not very strict, you will need certain documents to travel in the Dominican Republic. You should therefore keep your important papers safe at all times.

Passport

To enter the Dominican Republic, citizens of Canada, the United States and the European Union are advised to bring their passport, making sure it is valid for the length of their stay. It is also possible to enter the country with an official birth certificate or a citizenship card accompanied by an identificatin card and a photograph. Be reminded though, that in case of problems with the authorities, the most official proof of your identity is your passport.

It is a good idea to keep a photocopy of the key pages of your passport, and to write down your passport number and its expiry date. This way, in case the document is lost or stolen, it will be much easier to replace (do the same with your birth certificate or citizenship card). If this should occur, contact your country's consulate or embassy to have a new one issued.

Tourist Card

To enter the country, all visitors are required to have a tourist card (tarjeta del tourista) which is valid for 60 days. In most cases the card is issued by the travel agent, at the airport, or on the airplane with the plane ticket. The price of your airline ticket or package will usually include the cost of the card, which is about $10 US. Keep it in a safe place during your stay, as it must be returned to authorities upon departure.

Visas

A visa is not required for visitors from Canada, the United States, and the European community. Citizens of other countries must contact the closest embassy or consulate of the Dominican Republic to obtain a visa.

Departure Tax

Each person leaving the Dominican Republic must pay a departure tax of $10 US. The tax is collected at the airport when you check in for your return flight. Remember to keep this amount in cash, as credit cards are not accepted.

Customs

Visitors may enter the country with up to one litre of alcohol, 200 cigarettes and up to $100 US worth of goods (not counting personal belongings). Bringing in illegal drugs and firearms is, of course, prohibited.

Embassies and Consulates

Embassies and consulates can be an invaluable source of help to visitors who find themselves in trouble. For example, consulates can provide names of doctors or lawyers in the case of death or serious injury. However, only urgent cases are handled. The cost of these services is not absorbed by the consulates.

Belgium Agencias
Navieras Báez
504 av. Abraham Lincoln
☎ *(809) 562-1661*
⇌ *(809) 562-3383*

Canada
30 Avenida Máximo Gomez
☎ *(809) 685-1136*
⇌ *(809) 682-2691*

United States
At the corner of Calle Cesar Nicolas Pension and Calle Leopold Navarro
☎ *(809) 541-2171*

Germany
37 Calle Lic. Juan Tomás Mejía y Cotes
Apartado Postal 1235
☎ *(809) 565-8811*
☎ *(809) 565-8812*

Great Britain
Saint George School 552 Av. Abraham Lincoln,
☎ *(809) 562-5015*
or
Apartado Postal 30341
Av. Romulo Betancourt # 1302 apt. 202
☎ *(809) 532-4216*

Switzerland
26, av. José Gabria García
☎ *(809) 685-0126.*

Dominican Embassies and Consulates Abroad

Belgium
160-A av. Louise
1050 Bruxelles
☎ *648-0840*
⇌ *640-9561*

Canada
1650 de Maisonneuve West, Suite 302
Montreal, Quebec
☎ *(514) 933-9008*
☎ *1-800-563-1611*

United States
1715 22nd St. N.W., Washington, D.C. 20008, U.S.A.
☎ *(202) 332-6280*
or
1501 Broadway, 4th floor,· New York, N.Y. 10036, U.S.A.
☎ *(212) 768-2480*
or
1038 Brickell Ave., Miami, FLA 33131, U.S.A.
☎ *(305) 358-3221*
or
870 Market St., Suite 915, San Francisco, Calif. 94102, U.S.A.,
☎ *(415) 783-7530*

Germany
Burgstrasse # 87
5300 Bonn, 2nd floor, Germany
☎ *00228-36-4956*

Switzerland
16 rue Genus, Genève
☎ *738-0018*

Tourist Offices

These offices exist to help travellers plan their trips to the Dominican Republic. Their personnel can answer questions and provide you with brochures.

Canada
2080 Crescent,
Montreal, Quebec
H3G 2V8
☎ *(514) 499-1918*
⇌ *(514) 499-1393*
or

74 Front St. E., Unit 53,
Market Square,
Toronto, Ontario ,
M5E 1B8
☎ *(416) 361-2126*
or *1-888-494-5050*
₰ *(416) 361-2130*

Italy
Iazza Castello 25,
20121 Milano, Italia
☎ *(392) 805-7781*
₰ *(392) 865-8611*

Great Britain
1 Hay Hill, Berkely Square,
London W1X 7LF
England
☎ *(171) 495-4322,*
₰ *(171) 491-8689*

United States
136 East 57th Street, Suite 803,
New York, N.Y., 10022
☎ *(212) 588-1012/13/14*
₰ *(212) 588-1015*
or
2355 Salzedo St., Suite 307,
Coral Gables
Miami, Fla., 33134
☎ *(305) 444-4592*
₰ *(305) 444-4845*
or
561 West Diversey Bldg, Suite 214,
Chicago, IL
60614-1643
☎ *(773) 529-1336*
☎ 1-888-303-1336
₰ *(773) 529-1338*

Tourist Information in the Dominican Republic

Santo Domingo
Secretaria de Estado de Turismo
Oficinas Gubernamentales
Block D, Mexico Ave.
at the corner of Calle 30 de Marzo
Suite 497
Santo Domingo

☎ *(809) 221-4660*
₰ *(809) 682-3806*

Boca Chica
Tourist Information
Calle Juan Rafael
Plaza Comercial
☎ *523-5106*

Higuey
Tourist Information
Calle Agustín de Guerrero
Edificio de la Gobernacíon
☎ *554-2672*

Puerto Plata
Tourist Information
1, Avenida Hermanas Mirabel
Parque Costeroé
☎ *586-3676*

Las Terrenas
Tourist Information
147, Calle Principal
☎ *240-6363*

On the Net

www.dominican.com.do

Entering the Country

Several tour operators offer packages including accommodation, meals and airfare on a charter flight. Theses "all-inclusive" deals generally bring visitors to tourist villages like Playa Dorada, Sosua, Punta Cana or Juan Dolio. Check with your travel agent to find out which packages are available.

It is also easy to head off with just an airline ticket and to find accommodation on location, due to the abundance of hotels situated in all regions of the island. The advantage of this type of travel is that you will see much more of the island and can choose where to stay each day. Except during peak travel times (Christmas vacation and the week leading up to Easter week), you should not have any trouble finding accommodation without reservations, either in out-of-the-way Dominican villages (if you don't require the utmost in comfort) or in the popular resorts.

Most flights from Canada are aboard charter flights, so check with a travel agent. At press time, American Airlines and Air France were among the major carriers offering flights to Santo Domingo.

By Plane

The Dominican Republic has seven international airports which are located in Santo Domingo (Las Américas and Herreras), Puerto Plata, Punta Cana, La Romana (Cajuiles) and Barahona. The most important airports are in Santo Domingo and Puerto Plata.

The Airports

Both The Las Américas Airport in Santo Domingo and The Puerto Plata International Airport are expansive, full-service facilities. Several boutiques sell

Practical Information

local products here, though at prices slightly higher than in the city.

Las Américas Airport
Located 20 km east of Santo Domingo
☎ 549-0651

Puerto Plata International Airport
Located 18 km east of Puerto Plata
☎ 586-0219

Punta Cana Airport
☎ 686-8790

At these airports there are taxis and public buses that can take travellers to the surrounding cities. Though taxi rates are always posted (and non-negotiable), it is best to use the services of drivers who are members of The AILA association in order to avoid any hassles. When it comes to rates for buses, always ask for the fare to the town where your hotel is located before getting on.

All of the car rental companies have branches at the airports, so you can rent a car as soon as you arrive. They are all right beside each other, making it easy to compare prices.

Domestic Flights

Air Santo Domingo (☎ 683-8020) offers flights to different cities in the country leaving from Santo Domingo. Flights depart from The Las Americas International

Airport or The Herreras Airport (situated on the west side of the city). There are four departures daily to Puerto Plata and Punta Cana and one departure daily to El Portillo (The Samana Peninsula) and to Port au Prince (Haiti).

Ferry

From Puerto Rico

There is now a ferry that does a return route between Puerto Rico (Mayaguez) and the Dominican Republic (Santo Domingo). The trip lasts about 10 hours and the ferry is equipped to carry both passengers and vehicles. Departures from Puerto Rico are Monday, Wednesday and Friday and from Santo Domingo Tuesday, Thursday and Sunday. A one-way fare is $70 per passenger and $90 per vehicle.

Ferries Del Caribe
Avenida El Puerto
Santo Domingo
☎ (809) 688-4400
⇌ (809) 688-4963

By Car

To Haiti

To drive to Haiti, take the highway that leads to the town of Jimaní in the Dominican Republic. Anyone wishing to visit Haiti must have a valid passport.

Depending on your country of origin, you may or may not need a visa (Canadian residents, for example, do not). Visas can be obtained through the Haitian Consulate in your country or in Santo Domingo at:

Haitian Consulate
33 Avenida Juan Sanchez Ramires
Santo Domingo
☎ 686-6094

Short excursions to Haiti are also offered from the major resort towns (notably Puerto Plata, Santo Domingo, Sosua and Cabarete).

Insurance

Health Insurance

Health insurance is the most important type of insurance for travellers and should be purchased before your departure. A comprehensive health insurance policy that provides a level of coverage sufficient to pay for hospitalization, nursing care and doctor's fees is recommended. Keep in mind that health care costs are rising quickly everywhere. The policy should also have a repatriation clause in case the required care is not available in the Dominican Republic. As patients are sometimes asked to pay for medical services up front, find out what provisions your policy makes in this case.

Always carry your health insurance policy with you when travelling to avoid problems if you are in an accident, and get receipts for any expenses incurred.

Theft Insurance

Most residential insurance policies in North America protect some of your goods from theft, even if the theft occurs in a foreign country. To make a claim, you must fill out a police report. Usually the coverage for a theft abroad is 10% of your total coverage. If you plan to travel with valuable objects, check your policy or with an insurance agency to see if additional baggage insurance is necessary. European visitors should take out baggage insurance.

Cancellation Insurance

This type of insurance is usually offered by your travel agent when you purchase your air ticket or tour package. It covers any non-refundable payments to travel suppliers such as airlines, and must be purchased at the same time as initial payment is made for air tickets or tour packages. This insurance allows you to be reimbursed for the ticket or package deal if your trip must be

cancelled due to serious illness or death. This type of insurance can be useful, but weigh the likelihood of your using it against the price.

Health

The Dominican Republic is a wonderful country to explore; however, travellers should be aware of and protect themselves from a number of health risks associated with the region, such as malaria, typhoid, diphtheria, tetanus, polio and hepatitis A. Travellers are advised to consult a doctor (or travellers' clinic) for advice on what precautions to take. Remember that it is much easier to prevent these illnesses than it is to cure them. It is thus worthwhile to take the recommended medications, vaccinations and precautions in order to avoid any health problems.

Illnesses

This section is intended to give a brief introduction to some of the more common illnesses and thus should be used for information purposes only.

Malaria

Malaria (or paludism) is caused by a parasite in the blood called Plasmodium sp. This

parasite is transmitted by anopheles mosquitoes, which bite from nightfall until dawn. In the Dominican Republic, the rural and urban zones of the whole country, especially along the Haitan border, can sometimes be hot-spots. The risk is minimal and anti-malaria drugs are not necessary for short stays in resort areas. It is nevertheless a good idea to take measures to prevent mosquito bites (see p 41).

The symptoms of malaria include high fever, chills, extreme fatigue and headaches as well as stomach and muscle aches. There are several forms of malaria, including one serious type caused by P. falciparum. The disease can take hold while you are still on holiday or up to 12 weeks following your return; in some cases the symptoms can appear months later.

Hepatitis A

This disease is generally transmitted by ingesting food or water that has been contaminated by faecal matter. The symptoms include fever, yellowing of the skin, loss of appetite and fatigue, and can appear between 15 and 50 days after infection. An effective vaccination by injection is available. Besides the recommended vaccine, good hygiene is important. Always wash your hands before every meal, and ensure that the food and preparation area are clean.

Hepatits B

Hepatitis B, like hepatitis A, affects the liver, but is transmitted through direct contact with body fluids. The symptoms are flu-like, and similar to those of hepatitis A. A vaccination exists but must be administered over an extended period of time, so be sure to check with your doctor several weeks in advance.

Dengue

Also called "breakbone fever", Dengue is transmitted by mosquitoes. In its most benign form it can cause flu-like symptoms such as headaches, chills and sweating, aching muscles and nausea. In its haemorrhagic form, the most serious and rarest form, it can be fatal. There is no vaccine for the virus, so take the usual precautions to avoid mosquito bites.

Typhoid Fever

This illness is caused by ingesting food that has come in contact (direct or indirect) with an infected person's stool. Common symptoms include high fever, loss of appetite, headaches, constipation and occasionally diarrhea, as well as the appearance of red spots on the skin. These symptoms will appear one to three weeks after infection. The type of vaccination you get (it exists in two forms, oral and by injection) will depend on your trip. Once again, it is always a good idea to visit a travellers' clinic a few weeks before your departure.

Diphtheria and Tetanus

These two illnesses, against which most people are vaccinated during their childhood, can have serious consequences. Before leaving, check that your vaccinations are valid; you may need a booster shot. Diphtheria is a bacterial infection that is transmitted by nose and throat secretions or by skin lesions on an infected person. Symptoms include sore throat, high fever, general aches and pains and occasionally skin infections. Tetanus is caused by a bacteria that enters your body through an open wound that comes in contact with contaminated dust or rusty metal.

Other Health Tips

Cases of illnesses like hepatitis B, AIDS and certain venereal diseases have been reported; it is therefore a good idea to be careful.

Near the villages of Hato Mayor, Higüey, Nisibon and El Seibo, fresh water is often contaminated by an organism that causes schistosomiasis. This infection, which is caused by a parasite entering the body and attacking the liver and nervous system, is difficult to treat. It is therefore best to avoid swimming in fresh water.

Remember that consuming too much alcohol, particularly during prolonged exposure to the sun, can cause severe dehydration and lead to health problems.

Due to a lack of financial resources, Dominican medical facilities may not be as up-to-date as those in your own country. Therefore, if you need medical services, expect them to be different from what you are used to. The clinics outside large urban centres might seem modest to you. In general, however, clinics are better equipped than hospitals, so head to a clinic first. In tourist areas, there are always doctors who can speak English. Before a blood transfusion, be sure (when possible) that quality control tests have been carried out on the blood.

Insufficiently treated water, which can contain disease-causing bacteria, is the cause of most of the health problems travellers are likely to encounter, such as stomach upset, diarrhea or fever. Throughout the country, it is a good idea to drink bottled water (when buying bottled water, make sure the bottle is properly sealed), or to purify your own with iodine or a water purifier. Most major hotels treat their water, but always ask before you drink.

Ice cubes should be avoided, as they may be made of contaminated water. In addition, fresh fruits and vegetables that have been washed but not peeled can also pose a health risk. Make sure that the vegetables you eat are well-cooked and peel your own fruit. Do not eat lettuce, unless it has been hydroponically grown (some vegetarian restaurants serve this type of lettuce; ask). Remember: cook it, peel it or forget it.

If you do get diarrhea, soothe your stomach by avoiding solids; instead, drink carbonated beverages, bottled water, or weak tea (avoid milk) until you recover. As dehydration can be dangerous, drinking sufficient quantities of liquid is crucial. Pharmacies sell various preparations for the treatment of diarrhea, with different effects. Pepto Bismol and Imodium will stop the diarrhea, which

slows the loss of fluids, but they should be avoided if you have a fever as they will prevent the necessary elimination of bacteria.

Oral rehydration products, such as Gastrolyte, will replace the minerals and electrolytes which your body has lost as a result of the diarrhea. In a pinch, you can make your own rehydration solution by mixing one litre of pure water with one teaspoon of sugar and two or three teaspoons of salt. After, eat easily digested foods like rice to give your stomach time to adjust. If symptoms become more serious (high fever, persistent diarrhea), see a doctor as antibiotics may be necessary.

Food and climate can also cause problems. Pay attention to food's freshness, and the cleanliness of the preparation area. Good hygiene (wash your hands often) will help avoid undesirable situations.

It is best not to walk around barefoot as parasites and insects can cause a variety of problems, the least of which is athlete's foot.

Mosquitoes

A nuisance common to many countries, mosquitoes are no strangers to the Dominican Republic. They are particularly numerous during the rainy season (May to October). Protect yourself with a good insect repellent. Repellents with DEET are the most effective. The concentration of DEET varies from one product to the next; the higher the concentration, the longer the protection.

In rare cases, the use of repellents with high concentrations (35% or more) of DEET has been associated with convulsions in young children; it is therefore important to apply these products sparingly, on exposed surfaces, and to wash it off once back inside. A concentration of 35% DEET will protect for four to six hours, while 95% will last from 10 to 12 hours. New formulas with DEET in lesser concentrations, but which last just as long, are available.

To further reduce the possibility of getting bitten, do not wear perfume or bright colours. Sundown is an especially active time for insects. When walking in wooded areas, cover your legs and ankles well. Insect coils can help provide a better night's sleep. Before bed, apply

Practical Information

insect repellent to your skin and to the head-board and baseboard of your bed. If possible, get an air-conditioned room, or bring a mosquito net.

Lastly, since it is impossible to completely avoid contact with mosquitoes, bring along a cream to soothe the bites you will invariably get.

The Sun

Its benefits are many, but so are its harms. Always wear sunscreen (SPF 15 for adults and SPF 30 for children) and apply it 20 to 30 minutes before exposure. Many creams on the market do not offer adequate protection; ask a pharmacist. Too much sun can cause sunstroke (dizziness, vomiting, fever, etc.). Be careful, especially the first few days, as it takes time to get used to the sun. Take sun in small doses and protect yourself with a hat and sunglasses.

First-Aid Kit

A small first-aid kit can prove very useful. Bring along sufficient amounts of any medications you take regularly as well as a valid prescription in case you lose your supply. It can be difficult to find certain medications in small towns in the Dominican Republic. Other medications such

as anti-malaria pills and Imodium (or an equivalent), can also be hard to find. Finally, do not forget self-adhesive bandages, disinfectant cream or ointment, analgesics (pain-killers), antihistamines (for allergies), an extra pair of sunglasses or contact lenses, contact lens solution, and medicine for upset stomach. Though these items are all available in the Dominican Republic, they might be difficult to find in remote villages.

Climate

There are two seasons in the Dominican Republic: the cool season (from November to April) and the rainy season (from May to October). The cool season is the most pleasant, as the heat is less stifling, the rain less frequent and the humidity lower. Temperatures hover around 29°C during the day and dip to about 19°C at night.

During the rainy season, the showers are heavy, but short, so it is still possible to travel. Rain is most frequent from May to mid-June. In the rainy season, the average temperature is 31°C during the day and 22°C at night. The number of hours of daylight remains fairly constant throughout the

year. Hurricanes, though rare, occur during the rainy season.

Packing

The type of clothing required does not vary much from season to season. In general, loose-fitting, comfortable cotton or linen clothes are best. When exploring urban areas, wear closed shoes that cover the entire foot rather than sandals, as they will protect against cuts that could become infected. Bring a sweater or long-sleeved shirt for cool evenings, and rubber sandals (thongs or flip-flops) to wear at the beach and in the shower.

During the rainy season, an umbrella is

useful for staying dry during brief tropical showers. To visit certain attractions you must wear a skirt that covers the knees or long pants. For evenings out, you might need more formal clothes, as a number of places have dress codes. Finally, if you expect to go hiking in the mountains, bring along some good hiking boots and a sweater.

Safety and Security

Although the Dominican Republic is not a dangerous country, it has its share of thieves, particularly in the resort towns and in Santo Domingo. Keep in mind that to the majority of people in the country, some of your possessions (things like cameras, leather suitcases, video cameras, and jewellery) represent a great deal of money, especially when you consider that the minimum monthly salary is 3,800 pesos ($250 US).

A degree of caution can help avoid problems. For example, do not wear too much jewellery, keep your electronic equipment in a nondescript shoulder bag slung across your chest, and avoid revealing the contents of your wallet when paying for something. Be doubly careful at night, and stay away from dark streets, especially if there are strangers lurking about. Finally, some neighbourhoods of Santo Domingo — around the Puente Duarte and behind Calle Mella, for example — should be avoided, particularly at night. To be safe, do not wander into an area you know nothing about.

A money belt can be used to conceal cash under your clothes, traveller's cheques and your passport. If your bags should happen to be stolen, you will at least have the money and documents necessary to get by. Remember that the less attention you draw to yourself, the less chance you have of being robbed.

If you bring valuables to the beach, you are strongly recommended to keep a constant eye on them. It is best to keep your valuables in the small safes available at most hotels.

In a case of a theft you also have the option of dialing 911.

Getting Around

Distances can be long in the Dominican Republic, especially since the roads, though generally in good condition, often pass through small villages where drivers must slow down. Furthermore, very few roads have passing lanes, and the condition of some of the smaller roads make it difficult to drive faster than 40 kph. Thus, it is important to plan your itinerary carefully.

By Car

Renting a car in the Dominican Republic is easy, as most of the large companies have offices in the country. It will cost an average of $50 US a day (unlimited mileage) for a compact car, not including insurance and taxes. The minimum age for renting a car is 25 and you must possess a credit card. Choose a vehicle that is in good condition, preferably a new one. A few local companies offer low prices, but their cars are often in poor condition, and they do not offer much assistance in case of breakdown. Therefore, before heading off on a long journey, choose your car carefully.

It is strongly recommended that you take out sufficient automobile insurance to cover all costs in case of an accident. A $700 US deductible is fairly standard. Before signing any rental contract, make sure the methods of payment are clearly indicated. Finally, remember that your credit card must cover both the rental fees and the deductible in case of an accident. While some credit cards insure you automatically, you should check if the coverage is complete.

A valid driver's license from your country is

Practical Information

accepted in the Dominican Republic.

Driving and the Highway Code

In general, the main roads and highways in the Dominican Republic are in good condition, but the odd pothole does crop up here and there. Furthermore, even though there are no shoulders, traffic still moves pretty fast.

Driving on the secondary roads is a whole other story. They are often gravel-covered, narrow and littered with potholes of all different sizes. As well, animals tend to wander across the roads (dogs and chickens in particular), forcing drivers to brake unexpectedly. Drivers must be particularly careful when passing through villages where there are many pedestrians. Cautious driving is imperative at all times.

Speed bumps have been placed on some village roads to slow down traffic, but unfortunately they are poorly marked. They are usually located on the way into villages and near military barracks.

Road signs, such as speed limit indications, stop signs or no-entry signs are few and far between. The rules of the road are still to be respected, however. Slow down at intersec-

tions and do not go over the speed limit of 80 kph. Dominicans drive very fast, often with little regard for these rules, meaning travellers must be particularly vigilant. Many locals do not check their blind spot, and cars equipped with turn signals are rare. Motorcyclists are numerous and quite reckless. Finally, the most hair-raising experiences are almost always associated with passing. There are no passing lanes, except the lane for oncoming traffic. Some drivers weave in and out of traffic, passing at every chance, no matter how slim.

Although significant improvements have been made in recent years, road signs are still insufficient in many places. If you get lost, therefore, the only way of finding your way might be to ask local villagers, who are usually more than happy to help out.

Heavy traffic is rare on roads in the Dominican Republic, except in Santo Domingo, where driving can get tricky, especially at peak hours.

Due to the lack of signs and street lights on Dominican roads, driving at night is strongly discouraged. If your car breaks down you will be stranded. If you do have to drive at night, keep in mind that you are at greater risk of

being robbed, so do not pick up hitchhikers or stop at the side of the road, and keep your doors locked.

The speed limit is 80 kph on the highways, 60 kph near cities and 40 kph within city limits.

Accidents

In the event of a road accident, the police will be called to the scene to assess the situation. If there are injuries or damages, witnesses will be asked to testify in court; the information they provide is central to the outcome of the case. Occasionally, the principal witnesses to an accident will be held in jail until the authorities can interview them. The wait can take up to 48 hours. This rarely happens, but should you find yourself in such a situation, stay calm and be patient.

Animals that roam freely along the roads near small villages can be hard to avoid, even for the most careful drivers (chickens seem to be particularly attracted to moving cars). If you do hit one, the local inhabitants might react aggressively, so it is best to drive to the nearest police station and deal with the situation through official channels.

Table of distances (km)
Via the shortest route

	Barahona	Higüey	Jarabocoa	La Romana	Monte Cristi	Puerto Plata	Río San Juan	Samaná	San Francisco de Macorís	Santiago de los Caballeros
Higüey	366									
Jarabocoa	248	326								
La Romana	298	154	244							
Monte Cristi	343	443	270	366						
Puerto Plata	421	387	114	309	135					
Río San Juan	470	435	147	358	232	83				
Samaná	452	416	212	337	320	226	142			
San Francisco de Macorís	339	304	65	230	175	118	119	145		
Santiago de los Caballeros	360	323	50	249	120	60	110	203	55	
Santo Domingo	204	168	157	89	276	219	270	248	136	157

Example: The distance between Santo Domingo and Puerto Plata is 219 km.

Car Watchers

Throughout the Dominican Republic, youths will offer to wash or keep an eye on your car — for a small fee, of course. Sometimes they will even perform these services without asking, and still expect to get paid. Windshield washers are common at traffic lights. Usually a simple refusal is enough, though sometimes they will wash it anyway. You have every right to refuse to pay; just make sure your windows are up, or you may get a bucket of water in your lap. When it comes to car watchers, it is often best to pay a small sum (to avoid some mysterious scratches appearing on the car). Expect to pay between 10 and 15 pesos for an evening of car surveillance and about 15 pesos for a car wash. Of course, you will have to pay up front.

The Police

Police officers are posted all along Dominican highways. In addition to stopping drivers who break traffic laws, they are authorized to pull over any car they wish and ask to see the identification papers of the driver. The police have been told not to harass tourists, but occasionally some still ask for a few pesos. If you are sure you have not broken any laws, there is no reason to pay anything. Do not be alarmed if the police pull you over to check your papers. In general, they are approachable and ready to help if you have problems on the road.

Gasoline (Petrol)

There are gas stations all over the country. Gas is reasonably priced, generally at par with North American prices. Most stations are open until 10pm, and many stay open 24 hours. More stations are now accepting credit cards.

By Motorcycle or Scooter

In most resort areas it is possible to rent a motorcycle for $30 to $40 US a day. You will need to leave a deposit, such as your passport (or another valid piece of identification) or sometimes even your plane ticket. Drive carefully. Even though motorcycles are common in the Dominican Republic, car drivers are not always cautious around them. Always determine the price and payment conditions before leaving with your rental.

By Taxi

Taxi services are offered in every resort area and moderate-sized city. The cars are often very old, but they will get you where you want to go. The rates are fairly high, and are usually posted at the taxi stand. They vary little from one city to another. Make sure to agree on the fare with the driver before starting out, and do not pay until you arrive at your destination.

By Motorcyle-Taxi

Motorcyclists offer rides to pedestrians in most cities, providing a quick and inexpensive way to cover short distances. You will have to sacrifice some comfort and security, so avoid long distances and highways. Set a price before getting on; a few kilometres should cost about 10 pesos.

By Collective Taxi

In a collective taxi, the cost of the trip is shared between all the passengers, even if their destinations vary. These taxis operate within cities or travel between them. The vehicles are often in terrible shape (especially in Santo Domingo), but are still more comfortable than the bus. They are identifiable by their license plate reading *público*.

By Public Bus (Guagua)

Public buses, called *guaguas* by the Dominicans, (pronounced "oua-oua") travel along every type of road in the Dominican Republic and are an efficient way of getting around the island. To catch one, simply go to the local bus station (often near the central park) or wait by the side of a main road and flag one down. These buses stop frequently, and are often jam-packed and very uncomfortable. On the positive side, this is the cheapest way to get around the island.

By Coach

Coach service is offered by two bus companies, Metro Bus and Caribe Tours. While the vehicles in question are fairly old, they are air conditioned and reasonably comfortable. Coaches make fewer stops than guaguas and thus cover longer distances quite quickly. The fares are higher than those for guaguas, but quicker for long trips.

Hitchhiking

It is fairly easy to get around the country by hitchhiking. Dominicans are friendly and like chatting with visitors. However, a reasonable amount of caution is advised, especially for women travelling alone.

Plane

Air Santo Domingo (☎683-8020) guarantees connections between the main cities of the country. Daily flights from Santo Domingo link this city to Puerto Plata, Punta Cana and El Portillo (Samana). From Punta Cana, there are daily flights going to Santo Domingo, Punta Cana, El Portillo (Samana) and La Romana. Daily departures from El Portillo (Samana) allow passage to Santo Domingo, Puerto Plata and Punta Cana.

From La Romana you can reach Puerto Plata and Punta Cana.

Money and Banking

Currency

The country's currency is the peso. Bills are available in 100, 50, 20, 10, and 5 peso denominations; coins come in 50, 25 and 5 centavo pieces (100 centavos = 1 peso).

Banks

Banks are open Monday to Friday, from 8:30am to 3pm. They can be found in all large and medium-sized cities. Most can exchange US dollars, while fewer deal in other foreign currencies. In certain small villages and on holidays, it is impossible to change money. It is best to carry some cash with you at all times.

Cash advances from your credit card are easy to obtain. Most large banks offer this service. You can also withdraw money using your credit card from automatic teller machines, which are found mostly in Santo Domingo and in a few larger towns. However, it is difficult.

US Dollars

It is best to travel with cash or traveller's cheques in US dollars since they are easier to exchange and generally fetch a better rate.

Exchanging Money

It is illegal to exchange money in the street. However, in some cities you may be approached by people offering to buy your dollars. It is safer to go to an official currency exchange bureau, especially since

Practical Information

the rates are usually about the same.

Traveller's Cheques

It is always best to keep most of your money in traveller's cheques, which are accepted in some restaurants, hotels and shops (if they are in American dollars or pesos). They are also easy to cash in at banks and exchange offices. Always keep a copy of the serial numbers of your cheques in a separate place; that way, if the cheques are lost, the company can replace them quickly and easily. Do not rely solely on travellers' cheques. Always carry some cash.

Credit Cards

Most credit cards, especially Visa and MasterCard, are accepted in many businesses. However, many of the smaller places only take cash. Once again, remember that even if you have a credit card and traveller's cheques, you should always have some cash on hand.

When paying with your credit card, always check your receipt carefully to make sure that the abbreviation for the peso — "RDS" — appears, rather than the letters "US". If there is an error, make sure

to have it corrected before signing.

Taxes and Service Charges

An 8% tax and a 10% service charge are automatically added to restaurant bills. For hotels the tax is 5%, and the service charge 6%.

Telecommunications

Mail

There are post offices in every city, and some hotels offer mailing services and sell stamps. Regardless of where you mail your correspondence from, do not expect it to reach its destination quickly; the postal service in the Dominican Republic is not known for its efficiency. If you have something important to send, you are better off using a fax machine at a Codetel. Stamps are sold in post offices and in some shops.

Telephone and Fax

International telephone calls can be made from the larger hotels or from Codetel centres, which are found in all cities. Calling abroad from a Codetel is very easy. The simplest way

is to dial direct, but collect calls can also be made. The length of a call is measured on a computer, and customers pay at a counter when leaving, eliminating the need for handfuls of change. Credit cards are accepted. Codetel centres also offer facsimile (fax) services.

The area code for the entire country is 809. When calling the Dominican Republic from the United States or Canada, dial 1-809 and the number you wish to reach. The personnel at the Codetel centres can provide instructions (usually in Spanish, but occasionally in broken English) on how to dial long distance.

Using Foreign Operators

It is possible to use the operator in the country you are calling.

Canada Direct
☎ *1-800-333-0111*

AT&T USA
☎ *1-800-872-2881*

Sprint USA
☎ *1-800-751-7877*
(from pay phone) or 1166 (wait for tone) 77 (from private phone)

MCI USA
☎ *1-800-999-9000*

British Telecom Direct
☎ *1-800-751-2701*

Bus Schedule - Santo Domingo

Jarabacoa
7h   10h   13h30   16h30

Barahona
6h30   9h45   13h30   17h

Monte Cristi
6h30   8h   9h30   14h   15h30

Río San Juan
7h   8h   9h   13h45   15h

Samaná
7h30   9h   10h   13h30   15h45

Sosúa
6h   7h   8h   9h   10h
12h   13h   14h

Santiago
6h   6h30   6h45   7h   7h15
12h   12h30   13h   13h30

Puerto Plata
6h   7h   8h   9h   10h
12h   13h   14h   15h

La Vega
6h   6h30   6h45   7h15   7h30
12h   13h   13h30   14h   14h30

San Francisco de Macorís
7h   7h30   8h   9h   10h
12h30   13h30   14h   15h   15h45

Guaguas Rates

Santo Domingo	-	La Romana	:	18 pesos
Santo Domingo	-	Barahona	:	30 pesos
Santo Domingo	-	Santiago	:	25 pesos
Santo Domingo	-	Puerto Plata	:	50 pesos
Santiago	-	Constanza	:	20 pesos
Santiago	-	Puerto Plata	:	20 pesos
Puerto Plata	-	Samaná	:	60 pesos
Puerto Plata	-	Monte Cristi	:	60 pesos

Exchange Rates

10 peso	=	$0.06 US	$1 US	=	16 pesos
$1 CAN	=	$0.68 US	$1 US	=	$1.47 CAN
$1 AUS	=	$0.66 US	$1 US	=	$1.50 AUS
1 EURO	=	$1.07 US	$1 US	=	$0.93 EURO
1 £	=	$1.65 US	$1 US	=	0.60 £
1 DM	=	$0.54 US	$1 US	=	1.82 DM
1 guilder	=	$0.52 US	$1 US	=	2.05 guilders
1 SF	=	$0.67 US	$1 US	=	1.48 SF
10 BF	=	$0.03 US	$1 US	=	37.56 BF
1000 lire	=	$0.55 US	$1 US	=	18.03 lire
100 SPA	=	$0.65 US	$1 US	=	154.94 SPA

Tolll-free 1-800 and 1-888 numbers included in this guide can only be reached from North America.

Direct Dialing

Calls dialed directly go through a Dominican operator and are charged accordingly.

To call North America, dial 1, the area code and the telephone number. For other countries dial 011 then the international country code (see below), the area code and the telephone number.

United Kingdom 44

Australia 61

New Zealand 64

Belgium 32

Italy 39

Germany 49

Netherlands 31

Switzerland 41

Accommodations

When it comes to accommodations in the Dominican Republic, the choices are endless, especially in the tourist areas (Sosúa, Cabarete, Boca Chica) and in Santo Domingo. The rate varies enormously depending what type of establishment you choose, from the smallest hotel to the resort complex. Every room is subject to the 5% tax and the 6% service charge, however. It is customary to leave an extra 10 to 15 pesos per day for the room cleaning services; this can be left at the end of your stay. Most large hotels accept credit cards, while smaller hotels usually do not.

Hotels

There are three categories of hotels. The low-budget places near the downtown areas offer only the basics in comfort. The rooms generally have a small bathroom and an overhead fan.

Medium-budget hotels typically offer simple air-conditioned rooms that are reasonably comfortable. These can usually be found in resort towns and larger cities.

Finally, there are the luxury hotels, found in resort towns and on large, secluded properties in Santo Domingo. They all try to surpass each other in comfort and luxury. Several hotels in this last category belong to international hotel chains like Occidental Hoteles, LTI, Caribbean Village, Riv, Barcelo, Alegro, Marriott, Jack Tar Village and Sheraton.

Except for budget hotels, most places have their own generator, as power cuts are frequent in the Dominican Republic. Security guards keep watch over medium- and high-priced hotels.

Some hotels offer all-inclusive packages, which usually include two or three meals a day, all locally produced drinks (such as rum and beer), taxes and the service charge. When a package deal is available, it will be indicated next to the room rate in the hotel listings.

Apart-hotels

Apart-hotels offer all the services of a hotel, but each room has an equipped kitchenette. This is the most economical option for longer stays in the Dominican Republic.

Cabañas

This type of accommodation is only slightly different than a hotel. *Cabañas* offer rooms in separate little buildings. They are usually inexpensive, and some are equipped with kitchenettes.

Bed and Breakfasts

Some people have adapted their homes to receive guests. However, the level of comfort varies greatly from one place to another.

A few of our favourites...

For its colonial charm
L'Embajador (Santo Domingo) . . . . p 88
Le Palacio (Santo Domingo) . . . . p 86

For its lively ambiance
Méson de Isabel (Boca Chica) . . . . p 112
El 28 (Boca de Yuma) . . . . p 116
Waterfront (Sosúa) . . . . p 203
Caribe Surf (Cabarete) . . . . p 206
Bahía Blanca (Río San Juan) . . . . p 207
Tropic Banana (Las Terrenas) . . . . p 228

For its superb view of the ocean
Marco Polo Club (Sosúa) . . . . p 204
Bahía Blanca (Río San Juan) . . . . p 207
Gran Bahía (Samaná) . . . . p 231

For its pleasant location
La Catalina (Cabrera) . . . . p 209
Villa Serena (Las Galeras) . . . . p 231
Coyamar (Las Terrenas) . . . . p 227

For children
Club Med Punta Cana . . . . p 131

For its landscaping
Casa de Campo (La Romana) . . . . p 115
Bahía Principe (Río San Juan) . . . . p 209
Melia Bavaro (Punta Cana) . . . . p 129
La Hacienda (Playa Cofresi) . . . . p 200
Paradise Beach Club (Playa Dorada) . . . . p 201

For its beautiful beach
Club Med (Punta Cana) . . . . p 131
Punta Cana Beach Resort . . . . p 131
Melia Bavaro (Punta Cana) . . . . p 129
Iberostar (Punta Cana) . . . . p 131
Ríu (Punta Cana) . . . . p 129
Caribbean Village Playa Grande . . . . p 209
Playa Naco (Playa Dorada) . . . . p 201
Jack Tar (Playa Dorada) . . . . p 201

For it unique design
Natura Park . . . . p 130

Generally, guests do not have a private bathroom.

Youth Hostels

There are no youth hostels in the Dominican Republic, but many of the country's small hotels offer very good rates.

Camping

The only designated camping grounds in the Dominican Republic are in **Armando Bermudez National Park**, in the middle of the country. Campers sometimes stop here on their way to Pico Duarte. Though Dominicans are generally not big on camping, there is no law against pitching your tent wherever you want such as on one of the country's many deserted beaches. Obviously, some discretion is advised, and don't camp on private property without obtaining permission first.

Restaurants

There is something for every taste in the Dominican Republic, from little cafeterias serving local inexpensive dishes to gourmet restaurants offering refined fare. The choice is particularly varied in Santo Domingo and near the resort areas. Elsewhere, however,

often the choice is limited to local specialties. Service is usually friendly and attentive in both small and large restaurants. An 8% tax and 10% service charge are added to every bill.

Dominican Cuisine

Only slightly spiced, Dominican cuisine above all simple and nourishing, being prepared from local ingredients. Dishes are usually of meat, fish, chicken or seafood accompanied by rice, beans or plantain. By visiting a few local restaurants you will certainly have the chance to enjoy some local specialties like *mondongo, asopao* or *sancocho*.

Drinks

There are a few local Dominican beers, including *Quisqueya*, the new *Soverana* and *El Presidente*. All three are of export quality, though the most popular is El Presidente. Most hotels and restaurants also serve imported beers.

Wine is not very popular in the Dominican Republic, and little is produced locally. The imported wines served in restaurants are often quite expensive — particularly the French ones. We would advise you to try one of the Chilean wines which

deliver good quality for the price.

Rum, whether golden, white, dark or aged, whether served as an aperitif or digestif, is definitely the most sought after alcohol. Sold everywhere (it is sometimes easier to find than bottled water), rum has been close to the hearts of all Dominicans since sugar cane has been grown here, and grown well, we might add. Do not miss the chance to savour some *Brugal Extra Viejo* or *Ron Bermúdez*.

Shopping

Opening Hours

Most stores are open from 9am to 5pm. Stores rarely close at lunchtime, especially in resort areas.

Alcohol

Alcohol, most often rum and beer, is sold in all convenience stores (*mercados*).

What to Bring Back

The boutiques in Santo Domingo and the resort areas are full of all sorts of merchandise like summer outfits and t-shirts. On the street and in the few craft shops in the tourist areas you might find

Here is a short food glossary to help you understand Dominican menus:

Agua . . . . water
Ajo . . . . garlic
Almuerzo . . . . lunch
Asopao . . . . a tomato-, rice-, seafood- or fish-based dish
Arroz . . . . corn
Batida . . . . a fruit juice made with ice and milk
Camarones . . . . shrimps
Carne . . . . meat
Carne de res . . . . beef
Cena . . . . supper
Cerveza . . . . beer
Chicharón . . . . cooked marinated chicken or beef
Chivo . . . . kid
Chuleta . . . . cutlet
Conejo . . . . rabbit
Desayuno . . . . breakfast
Empanadas . . . . small pastries filled with meat or vegetables
Filete . . . . steak filet
Granadilla . . . . grenadine
Habichuela . . . . plate of beans
Habichuela con dulce . . . . sweet red beans
(during the week of Easter only)
Huevo . . . . egg
Jalao . . . . coconuts and molasses
Jamón . . . . ham
Jugo . . . . juice
Lambi . . . . small mollusks (also called Lambis in English)
Langosta . . . . lobster
Leche . . . . milk
Limón . . . . lemon
Mangu . . . . green bananas and meat
Mariscos . . . . seafood
Masitas . . . . coconut powder and brown sugar
Mermelada . . . . preserve
Mofongo . . . . ripe bananas with grilled sesame
Mondongo . . . . tripes
Naranja . . . . orange
Pan . . . . bread
Papas fritas . . . . fried potatoes
Postulad . . . . wheat pancake filled with
seafood, meat or vegetables
Pescado . . . . fish
Pica pollo . . . . fried chicken
Piña . . . . pineapple
Plátanos fritos . . . . fried bananas
Pollo . . . . chicken
Postre . . . . dessert
Queso . . . . cheese
Sancocho . . . . meat dish boiled with vegetables
Sopa . . . . soup
Tamarindo . . . . tamarin
Tortilla . . . . omelette
Tostada . . . . toast
Vino . . . . wine
Zanahoria . . . . carrot

something interesting amongst the wood sculptures, mahogany boxes, straw hats and naive (Haitian) art for sale. Jewellery made with amber (the price of which has increased since the release of the film Jurassic Park), larimar and shells are also sold throughout the country. Finally, rum is a must; it is both good and inexpensive.

Miscellaneous

Tour Guides

You will likely be approached in tourist areas by Dominicans speaking broken English or French, offering their services as tour guides. Some of them are quite capable and trustworthy, but many have little valuable information to share. Be careful. If you want to hire a guide, ask for proof of his or her qualifications. Instead of vending their knowledge at a bargain-basement price, qualified guides will usually charge a substantial fee. Before starting off on a guided tour, establish precisely what services you will be getting and at what price - and then - pay only when the tour is over.

Duty-Free Shops

There are duty-free shops in the airports and in Santo Domingo. Most of the products sold are foreign. All purchases must be paid for in American dollars.

Mercados

You can buy all kinds of things in these little grocery stores, including food, beauty products, alcohol and cigarettes.

Holidays

All banks and many businesses close on official holidays. Plan ahead by cashing traveller's cheques and doing last-minute souvenir shopping the day before. Things generally slow down during holidays.

January 1
New Year's Day
January 6
Epiphany
January 21
Nuestra Señora de la Altagracia Festival
January 26
Birthday of J.P. Duarte
Variable
Mardi gras
February 27
Independence Day
Variable
Good Friday
May 1
Labour Day
Variable
Corpus Christi
August 16
Restoration of the Republic Day
September 24
Nuestra Señora de las Mercedes Festival
December 25
Christmas Day

The Semana Santa

During the days leading up to Easter, called the *Semana Santa* or Holy Week, various festivities are organized by the Catholics to celebrate this auspicious holiday. On Thursday, the pious visit churches throughout the country to pray. On Good Friday the festivities reach their peak as countless processions take to the streets of the country's towns and villages. Many Dominicans take advantage of this holiday to travel within the country, and hotels are often full.

Taxes

The Dominican government charges a tax on hotel rooms (see p 48) and another on restaurant bills. The tax should be clearly indicated on the bill.

Tips

To show gratitude for good service it is customary to give a tip. In staurants there is a 10% service charge already added to the total on the bill. In addition to this sum, a tip of 10 to 15% should be left - according to the quality of service, of course.

Electricity

Like in North America, wall sockets take plugs with two flat pins and work on an alternating current of 110 volts (60 cycles). European visitors with electric appliances will therefore need both an adaptor and a converter. There are frequent power cuts in the Dominican Republic. The more expensive hotels compensate with generators.

Women Traveling Alone

Women travelling alone should not encounter any problems. For the most part, people are friendly and not aggressive. Generally, men are respectful toward women, and harassment is uncommon, although Dominican males do have a tendency to flirt. Of course, a certain level of caution should be exercised; avoid making eye contact, ignore any advances or com-

ments and do not walk around alone in poorly-lit areas at night.

Smokers

There are no restrictions with respect to smokers. Cigarettes are not expensive, and smoking is allowed in all public places.

Gay Life

The situation of gays and lesbians in the Dominican Republic is similar to that found in other Latin American countries. Gays still suffer from a certain form of repression, which stems from old family and chauvinistic values and politics. *Machismo*, the notion of male superiority, is alive and well and its insistance oupon maintaining rigid, stereotypical gender roles contribute more than anything else to the oppression of homosexuals, while at the same time keeping women in traditional roles.

Prostitution

Veritable scourge of the Dominican Republic, prostitution became rampant in the 1980s following the arrival of masses of tourists. Whether it is male or female prostitution, it exists in the every town that is the least bit touristy. In certain areas, notably Boca

Chica and Sosúa, it became such a problem that merchants began to complain. In an effort to restore order, Dominican authorities closed many bars in Sosúa toward the end of 1996.

Time Change

The Dominican Republic is one hour ahead of Eastern Standard Time, and four hours behind Greenwich Mean Time. In the winter it is one hour ahead of New York and Montreal and four hours behind London. There is no daylight savings time, therefore in the summer it is on the same time as New York and Montreal and five hours behind London.

Weights and Measures

Officially, the Dominican Republic uses the metric system. However, businesses often use the imperial system. The following conversions may be helpful.

Weights
1 pound (lb) =
454 grams (g)

Linear Measure
1 foot (ft) =
30 centimetres (cm)

1 mile =
1.6 kilometres (km)

Outdoors

The Dominican Republic

has a wide range of exceptionally beautiful natural attractions, including the highest summit in the Caribbean, Pico Duarte, at 3,175 metres.

There are mountain ranges, blanketed with forests at times lush and other times sparse, and protected by national parks. The country also boasts idyllic beaches, stretches of golden sand that make it a veritable paradise for those who like to bask in the sun and enjoy the crystal-clear waters of the Caribbean Sea and the Atlantic Ocean. The coral reefs that have developed in the waters off these beaches attract a vibrant variety of plant and animal life that can be observed by scuba divers and snorkellers alike. Finally, visitors can seek out the fascinating wildlife that inhabits the island, particularly in the winter, when humpback whales can be spotted in waters off Samaná.

The resources in the Dominican Republic make it easy for outdoor enthusiasts to enjoy both a slew of activities and sports and the natural beauty of the setting.

This chapter contains tips and advice on various sports and activities to help you get the most out of them in a safe and environmentally conscious manner.

National Parks

Much of the Dominican Republic's natural beauty is preserved by the island's national parks and its wildlife and science reserves. These wilderness retreats are found in every corner of the country, each protecting a distinct natural environment. There is an increased effort to create infrastructures that would open these areas to visitors, but not all parks are easily accessible. Some, like Parque Los Haïtises near

Samaná, and Parque Armando Bermudes around Pico Duarte, are starting to welcome more travellers, and companies have begun organizing excursions there. Others still remain isolated from the resort areas, however, and have virtually no facilities or services to offer. Because some parks are very demanding to explore - containing few, if any, marked trails - the wayfarers who venture in these wild parts should be very careful. Theoretically, to enter a national park, you must have a permit issued by the:

National Parks Service
Santo Domingo
☎ *221-5340*

Permits are also available on site, but often things are poorly organized, and it can be difficult to find the person in charge. The parks, however, are not

exploring the parks of the Dominican Republic, here is a short description of them. A more detailed description is found in each chapter.

There are two national parks in the southeastern part of the country:
Located 22 km west of Santo Domingo, **Parque Nacional La Caleta** is a marine park that was created to protect the coral reefs and the enormous amount of fish that visit them. In 1984, a boat was deliberately sunk here to make an artificial reef.

A fascinating park in the southeastern tip of the country, **Parque Nacional del Este** encompasses the small peninsula between Bayahibe and Boca de Yuma, as well as magnificent Isla Saona. Bordered by sandy beaches and seldom visited, this park has a rich variety of flora and fauna: more than a hundred species of birds, reptiles and marine animals such as the manatee have been sighted here.

There are four national parks in the southwestern part of the country:

Parque Nacional Jaragua is the largest park in the country. It stretches from Perndales to Oviedo on the tip of the Barahona peninsula. Although the park is difficult to reach, it is definitely worth the visit for its beautiful fine-sand beaches that shelter numerous birds and reptiles.

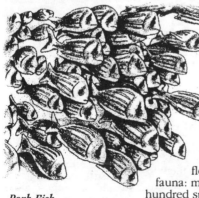

Pork Fish

well supervised. If you are interested in

The small islands of Beata and Alto Velo are also part of the park.

North of the Parque Nacional Jaragua, the **Parque Nacional Sierra de Bahoruco** protects part of the Bahoruco mountain range and is not easily accessible to visitors. The vegetation on the mountain slopes changes with altitude as does the level of precipitation.

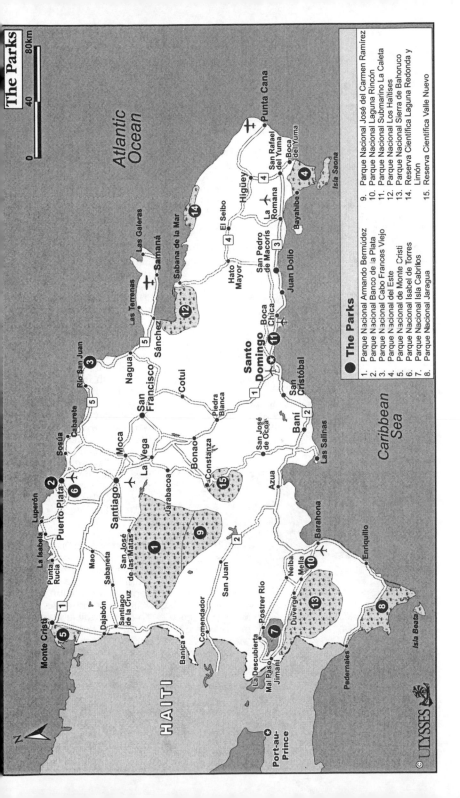

The Parks

0 40 80km

Atlantic Ocean

Caribbean Sea

HAITI

Port-au-Prince

Monte Cristi La Isabela Punta Rucia Luperón **Puerto Plata** Sosúa Cabarete Río San Juan Nagua Las Galeras Las Terrenas **Samaná** Las Terrenas

Dajabón Mao Sabaneta **Santiago** Moca **La Vega** San Francisco Cotuí Piedra Blanca Sabana de la Mar

Banica Santiago de la Cruz San José de las Matas Jarabacoa Bonao Constanza San José de Ocoa Hato Mayor El Seibo

Comendador San Juan Azua **Baní** Las Salinas Juan Dollio **San Pedro de Macorís** Higüey San Rafael del Yuma Boca del Yuma Punta Cana

Postrer Río La Descubierta Mal Paso Jimaní Duvergé Neiba Mella Barahona Enriquillo Pedernales

Santo Domingo Boca Chica San Cristóbal

Isla Saona Isla Beata

● The Parks

1. Parque Nacional Armando Bermúdez
2. Parque Nacional Banco de a Plata
3. Parque Nacional Cabo Frances Viejo
4. Parque Nacional del Este
5. Parque Nacional de Monte Cristi
6. Parque Nacional Isabel de Torres
7. Parque Nacional Isla Cabritos
8. Parque Nacional Jaragua
9. Parque Nacional José del Carmen Ramírez
10. Parque Nacional Laguna Rincón
11. Parque Nacional Submarino La Caleta
12. Parque Nacional Los Haitíses
13. Parque Nacional Sierra de Bahoruco
14. Reserva Científica Laguna Redonda y Limón
15. Reserva Científica Valle Nuevo

© ULYSSES

The park is known for its **orchids**, of which no less than 166 species have been counted.

Orchids

Parque Nacional Isla Cabritos is perhaps one of the most fascinating parks in the Dominican Republic. It is located in the middle of Lago Enriquillo, the largest saltwater lake in the Caribbean. This lake attracts unusual fauna, including reptiles and birds such as the pink flamingo. American crocodiles nest on the shores of Isla Cabritos.

The smallest of the parks, **Parque Nacional Laguna Rincón** protects the country's largest fresh-water lagoon.

In the country's mountainous centre, two national parks and a scientific reserve have been created:

The **Parque Nacional Armando Bermudez** encompasses the northern part of the Cordillera Centrale (766 km²) and boasts the Caribbean's highest peak, Pico Duarte, at 3,090 m. Tourist facilities are gradually being set up to make the beautiful hike up the mountain less arduous.

Bordering Parque Nacional Armando Bermudez, the **Parque Nacional José del Carmen Ramirez** covers 764 km² of the southern Cordillera Central. Like its neighbour, this park has no roads and can only be visited on foot.

The **Reserva Cientifica Valle Nuevo** protects a microclimate with a very special vegetation composed of numerous kinds of trees

(mostly conifers) that are generally found in more northerly countries. The temperature can even drop below the freezing mark at certain times of the year.

There are four national parks on the country's northern coast:

Located south of the Samaná Peninsula, the **Parque Nacional Los Haïtises** is relatively easy to explore because there are many organised excursions to it. You can discover amazing mangrove swamp with a diversified wildlife, as well as caves with pre-Colombian drawings.

The **Parque Nacional Isabel de Torres** protects the Pico Isabel de Torres, which is near Puerto Plata. In the past, the summit of this mountain was easily accessible by a cablecar that is now out of service.

The **Bancó de la Plata** is a large coral reef north of Puerto Plata. Each year, humpback whales come to these calm waters to reproduce. To protect these marine mammals, the **Parque Nacional Banco de la Plata** was created. The park is difficult to access because of the coral reefs.

A Fragile Ecosystem

Coral reefs are formed by minuscule organisms called coelenterate polyps, which are very sensitive to water pollution. The high level of nitrates in polluted water accelerates the growth of seaweed, which in turn takes over the coral, stops it from growing and literally smothers it. Sea urchins (whose long spikes can cause severe injuries) live on the coral and play a major role in controlling the amount of seaweed that grows on the coral by eating what the fish cannot. An epidemic threatened the survival of many reefs in 1983, when the waters became so polluted that sea urchins were affected and seaweed flourished in the Caribbean waters. Scientific studies have since proved the importance of urchins to the ecological balance, and the species has thus been restored on certain reefs. These little urchins, however, cannot solve the problem on their own. Pollution control is essential if the coral reefs, upon which 400,000 organisms depend, are to survive.

Parque Nacional de Monte Cristi covers a large portion of land from Monte Cristi to the Haitian border, including seven small islands, the Cayes Siete Hermanos. The park is frequented by sea turtles, but fewer come each year because overhunting threatens the animal with extinction.

Swimming

Along every coast of the Dominican Republic, there are beaches that are perfect for swimming or just lounging about. The currents can be strong, though, so be careful. You are better off staying close to shore when the waves get high. Also, never swim alone if you don't know how strong the currents are.

Greater efforts have been made to sensitize people about the importance of keeping the beaches clean, especially on the northern coast. Please respect these natural areas.

A completely deserted beach is a rarity in the Dominican Republic. The good beaches are usually overrun with visitors, and to satisfy their every need, vendors roam about selling juice, fruit, beach-wear and souvenirs of all sorts. Generally a "*no, gracias*" will suffice if you are not interested. Of course, if you look at the merchandise of one vendor, the others will assume you are a potential customer and will come along one by one to hawk their wares. Set a price first if you decide to buy.

Beach chairs and parasols can be rented at almost all beaches near resort towns; the cost is around 20 pesos per day per item.

Beaches are not private in the Dominican Republic. Hotels are nevertheless often built right on the ocean. Anyone is allowed to use the beach in front of a hotel, but not necessarily the facilities. These beaches have the advantage of being free of vendors, and

Outdoors

are also better maintained.

Scuba Diving

Several diving centres offer visitors the opportunity to explore the underwater world. Reefs are numerous, and there are diving centres on the northern coast (notably along the Playa Sosua and De Las Terrenas) and the southern coast (close to Isla Saona).

Certified divers can explore the secrets of the Dominican coastline to their heart's content. Others can still experience breathing underwater, but must be accompanied by a qualified guide, who will supervise their descent (to a depth of 5 m). Although there is little danger, be sure that the supervision is adequate. Before diving for the first time, it is very important to at least take an introductory course in order to learn basic safety skills: how to clear the water from your mask, how to equalize the pressure in your ears and sinuses, how to breathe underwater (don't hold your breath), to become comfortable with the change in pressure underwater, and to familiarize yourself with the equipment. Many hotels offer a resort course of about

one hour before taking first-timers under water. Equipment can easily be rented from the different centres along the coasts.

Scuba diving makes it possible to discover fascinating sights like coral reefs, schools of multi-coloured fish and amazing underwater plants. Don't forget that this ecosystem is fragile and deserves special attention. All divers must respect a few basic **safety guidelines** in order to protect

these natural sites: do not touch anything (especially not urchins, as their long spikes can cause injury); do not take pieces of coral (it is much prettier in the water than out, where it becomes discoloured); do not disturb any living creatures; do not hunt; do not feed the fish; be careful not to disturb anything with your flippers and, of course, do not litter. If you want a souvenir of your underwater experience, disposable underwater cameras are available.

Snorkelling

It doesn't take much to snorkel: a mask, a snorkel and some flippers. Anyone can enjoy this activity, which is a great way to develop an appreciation for the richness of the underwater world. Not far from several beaches, you can go snorkelling around coral reefs inhabited by various underwater species. Some companies organize snorkelling trips. Remember that the basic rules for protecting the underwater environment (see scuba diving section) must also be respected when snorkelling.

Surfing and Windsurfing

Some beaches in the Dominican Republic, especially near Cabarete, are known for their great waves. Others, like those in Boca Chica bay, where the waters are usually calm, are better suited to novice surfers. If you would like to try these sports, you can rent equipment on the beach (particularly at Cabarete, Boca Chica

Typhoons, Cyclones and Hurricanes

Whether its called a typhoon in Asia, a cyclone in the Indian Ocean or a hurricane in the Caribbean Sea, they all have one thing in common: they always start with a tropical disturbance. Hurricanes occur when a tropical disturbance develops into a tropical low pressure area with winds up to 34 (noeuds) mph, it is upgraded to a tropical storm when the winds reach 64 mph, and finally, becomes a hurricane with even stronger winds. Hurricanes usually occur in September.

Hurricanes form in warm ocean water. In order for one to develop, the water must be over 26EC and 30 to 40 metres deep. Winds from the ocean surface must also rise more than 9,000m in the atmosphere and blow in the same direction and at the same speed as this water mass. When the water evaporates, water molecules rise up and come into contact with air molecules, creating an energy transfer. The faster the air molecules move, the more water evaporates, and this is the beginning of a hurricane. This process speeds up then the water molecules cause the air to cool and condense into vapour. When the vapour becomes liquid, the energy is transformed into air molecules. The air then heats up, becomes lighter and rises.The whole process repeats itself until it gets so strong that it becomes a tropical storm and finally a hurricane. Hurricanes move from east to west until they hit land where they begin to die off, but not before causing vast amounts of damage.

Hurricanes have been scientifically recorded in the Caribbean since 1950. The Dominican Republic and Haiti have been ravaged several times by devastating hurricanes: Hazel in 1954, Katie in 1955, Edith and Flora in 1963, Cleo in 1964, Inez in 1966, Beulah in 1967, David in 1979, Allen in 1980, Emily in 1987 and more recently George in 1998 with record-breaking winds over 195£km/h.

Hurricanes are named by the World Meteorological Association. This association draws up six lists of names which are reused every six years. Hurricanes are given the first names of boys and girls in French, English and Spanish and are listed in alphabetical order. When a hurricane is particularly devastating its name is sometimes "retired" much like the number of an exceptional sports star.

Here are several Internet sites where you can watch the progression of a hurricane:
www.usatoday.com/weather
www.storm.com

Outdoors

and Playa Grande as well as Punta Cana). Some places offer courses as well.

If you have never tried these sports, a few safety pointers should be followed before hitting the waves: choose a beach where the surf is not too rough; keep well clear of swimmers; don't head too far out (don't hesitate to make a distress signal by waving your arms in the air if you need to) and wear shoes to avoid cutting your feet on the rocks.

Sailing

Excursions aboard sailboats and yachts offer another enchanting way to freely explore the sea's sparkling waves. Some centres organize trips, while others rent sailboats to experienced sailors. You'll find a few addresses throughout the guide.

Deep-Sea Fishing

Deep-sea fishing enthusiasts will be pleased to note that several places offer fishing excursions, particularly out of Boca Chica, Playa Dorada and Rio San Juan. Whether you are

interested in big fish (like marlin, for example) or smaller ones will determine how far from the island you go. These trips usually last about 3 hours. Equipment and advice are provided. Even if you come back empty-handed, this is still a great way to spend the day.

Hiking

Hiking and walking are undoubtedly the most accessible activities in the Dominican Republic. Parks with well-marked trails, however, are hard to find, so anyone heading off to explore must be well prepared. A few trails near the resort towns are worth a quick visit; just be sure to bring along everything you

might need during your outing.

There are a few things to keep in mind when hiking. Before heading off on any trail try to find out its length and level of difficulty. Remember that there are no maps available at the parks, and that if you should get lost, there are no rescue teams.

You will have to be well prepared and bring along anything you might need during your hike. The longer the hike, the better prepared you must be. First of all, bring a lot of water (you won't find any along the way) and sufficient food. Remember that the sun sets between 6pm and 7pm, and you can't do much hiking afterwards, so plan to be back before dark. Ideally, you should start out early in the morning in order to avoid hiking when the sun is at its hottest, and get back before the day is done.

Sunstroke

Some trails include long sections in the open, with no shade. The risk of sunstroke, which threatens anyone hiking in the tropics, is thus even higher. Cramps, goose bumps, nausea, and loss of balance are the first signs of sunstroke. If these symptoms arise, the affected person needs immediate shade, water and ventilation.

To avoid this problem, always wear a hat and a good sunscreen. By getting an early start, you'll have time to hike in cooler temperatures.

Clothing

Appropriate clothing is one of the best ways to avoid the little inconveniences of the outdoors. It is thus important to remember the following: Wear lightweight and light-coloured clothing; long pants to protect your legs from underbrush, thorny bushes and bug bites; and thick-soled hiking boots with good traction that are lightweight but solid. Bring water resistant clothing, as downpours are frequent, especially in the rainforest, and don't forget your bathing suit if you plan on cooling off in one of the many waterfalls in the mountains.

What to Bring

To be prepared for the unexpected, it is a good idea to bring along a few necessities, including a water bottle, a pocketknife, antiseptic, bandages (both adhesive and non-adhesive), scissors, aspirin, sunscreen, insect repellent, food and above all enough water for the trip.

Bicycling

The road system in the Dominican Republic is mostly made up of one-lane highways with no shoulders and secondary roads strewn with potholes - not exactly a cyclist's dream. In addition, it gets very hot during the day, and the roads are not always shady. Caution is advised as people drive fast. This said, cycling can still be a very pleasant way to see the countryside outside the large cities. Bicycles can be rented in most of the tourist centres for a few dollars. If you plan on travelling long distances, bring along a few tools, since bike repair shops are few and far between on the island.

Motorcycling

Motorcycles are the most common mode of transportation in the Dominican Republic, and can be rented in any tourist area for about $35 US per day. You may be asked to leave your passport or return plane ticket as a deposit. A motorcycle makes it easy to explore smaller roads, some of which lead to untouched beaches away from the touristy

areas. Motorcycles are a convenient means of getting around, but once again, caution is strongly advised.

Horseback Riding

A very popular activity among Dominicans, horseback riding is another interesting way to see the country. In some parts of the island, especially on the Eastern Point, the inhabitants use horses as their main form of transportation on the often narrow dirt roads of the region. Many of the large hotels, including Casa de Campo and Punta Cana organize excursions on horseback. Small riding stables can also be found in some cities, including Bayahibe, Río San Juan and Las Terreras.

Golf

To meet the demands of golf enthusiasts, anumber of golf courses have been developed around the country. Among the most renowned is the one at the Casa de Campo hotel complex; laid out along a stretch of the Caribbean coast, it is simply magnificent. One can also find fantastic greens on the

Outdoors

North Coast close to most of the tourist villages. Among the most beautiful are those of Playa Dorada and Playa Grande.

In Punta Cana, on the grounds of The Barcelo Bavaro Resorts, you will find not just one, but four well-groomed courses.

Finally, a charming 9-hole course can now be found close to Boca Chica.

Santo Domingo

The first city

founded in the Americas, Santo Domingo has some 500 years of history under its belt.

In 1496, after a fruit-less effort to colonize the north shore of the island, Bartolomé, son of the great Genoese admiral Christopher Columbus, decided to build a city on the shores of the Caribbean Sea, at the mouth of the Río Ozama. Founded on the east bank of the river, this city was christened Nueva Isabel. A hurricane destroyed its first buildings, however, and in 1502, Nicolás de Ovando, the colonial governor at the time, decided to reconstruct the town on the west bank of the Ozama, a location he deemed more strategic.

The seat of the government of Spain's colonies in the New World, Santo Domingo thrived right from the start, and the numerous buildings dating from that period serve as evidence of this. Spain began losing interest in Santo Domingo in 1515, when the island's gold mines were finally exhausted and fabulous riches were discovered elsewhere, most notably in Peru and Mexico, prompting the authorities to relocate the colonial government. Despite its decline in relation to the other Spanish colonies, Santo Domingo remained a nerve centre and continued to play a major role in the development of the country.

It was not long before Europe's other great powers began to show interest in the New World colonies, and, envying the riches Spain had found there, tried to conquer them. Wars, invasions and destruction thus became the lot of the colonists. Santo Domingo was no exception, and many of its buildings were destroyed in an attack by English pirate Sir Francis Drake in 1586. An English offensive in 1655 and French domination from 1795 to 1809 disrupted life in the capital, whose inhabitants managed, often through bitter combat, to resist and drive back the invaders. In the mid-19th century, Haitian troops invaded the country and took control of it in 1822.

The 19th century brought a desire for independence, which changed the course of Dominican history. Juan Pablo Duarte, a fervent defender of these aspirations, succeeded in gaining the country's independence from Haiti in 1844. Santo Domingo was named capital of the Dominican Republic. The young republic was not safe from invaders, however, and was repeatedly attacked by Haitian troops, which the Dominicans, with considerable difficulty, succeeded in driving back. Less than 20 years later, in 1861, Spain annexed the country once again, putting an end to its independence and stripping Santo Domingo of its status as capital. This annexation only lasted a short time, however, and in 1865, the country was declared independent once and for

all. Santo Domingo has been the capital ever since. Only its name has changed; during the Trujillo (1930-1961) dictatorship, the generalissimo renamed it Ciudad Trujillo (1936). Immediately following the president's death, the city became Santo Domingo again.

Trujillo's death also had harsh consequences for the capital, however, as it sparked major social unrest. The climate was so unstable that the Americans deemed it necessary to intervene to put some order back into the country's internal affairs.

In 1965, American troops entered Santo Domingo and shelled parts of the old city, damaging a number of old buildings.

Today, with over 2,000,000 inhabitants, Santo Domingo is the largest and most populated city in the Dominican Republic. It is the country's financial, industrial and commercial centre. Its petrochemical, metallurgical, textile and plastic industries are thriving. It also has the busiest port in the country. Despite the frantic pace of life here, Santo Domingo is a pleasant city, especially in the colonial zone. Nicolás Ovando drew up the plans for the city in 1502. With the aim of reducing the existing traffic problems, he used a grid pattern for the streets. Elsewhere, however, the city has not always developed in such an organised manner.

Coboba

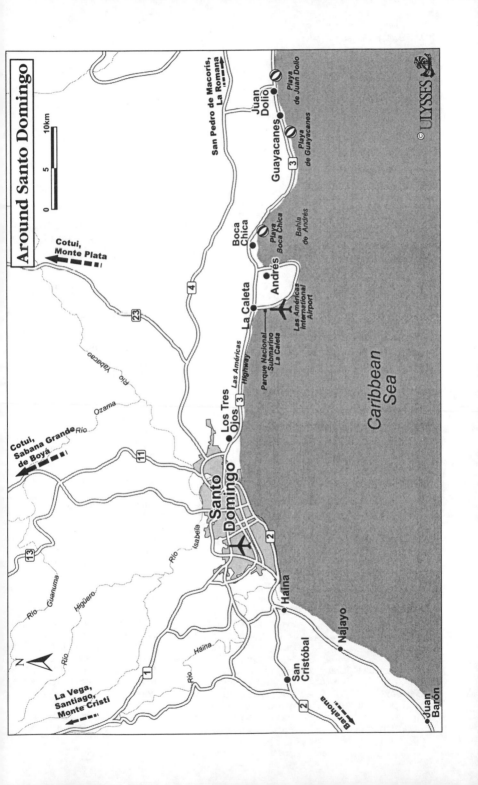

Around Santo Domingo

0 5 10km

Cotui,
Monte Plata

San Pedro de Macorís,
La Romana

Juan
Dolio

Playa
de Juan Dolio

Guayacanes

3

Playa
de Guayacanes

Boca
Chica

Playa
Boca Chica

Bahía
de Andrés

Andrés

Caribbean
Sea

Las Américas
International
Airport

La Caleta

Parque Nacional
Submarino
La Caleta

Las Américas
Highway

3

Los Tres
Ojos

4

23

Río Yabacao

Ozama

Río

Cotui,
Sabana Grande
de Boyá

11

Santo
Domingo

Isabela

Río

13

Río Guanuma

Higüero

Río

Haina

Río

N

2

Haina

San
Cristóbal

Najayo

2

Barahona

Juan
Barón

1

La Vega,
Santiago,
Monte Cristi

© ULYSSES

Finding Your Way Around

The road system in Santo Domingo is relatively modern. At rush hour, however, the streets swarm with an overwhelming number of *guaguas*, buses, motorcycles and cars heading in every direction at once, their drivers intent on weaving their way through traffic to get ahead. It is a truly "unforgettable" experience. Traveling by car between 8am and 9:30am and 4pm and 6pm is best avoided.

Although a road bypassing the downtown area is in the works, the project could take several years to complete. Until then, it is the main highway that cuts through the city, adding to the congestion of downtown traffic. It takes at least an hour to cross the city on this highway.

Santo Domingo International Airport

Las Américas Airport
Located 20 km east of Santo Domingo
☎ 549-0651
This airport, the largest in the country, has all the conveniences one would expect: ticket counters for major airlines, exchange offices, an assortment of boutiques and several restaurants.

Rental Cars

Several major car rental agencies also have counters at the airport, including the following:

Avis
☎ 549-0468

Budget
☎ 549-0351

Hertz
☎ 549-0454

Nelly Rent-A-Car
☎ 549-0505

When arriving at the airport by car, you will likely be approached by employees offering to carry your bags to the check-in counters. A tip is expected in return. If you do not need help, make this clear right away.

Taxis and Public Buses

It is easy to reach Santo Domingo and the surrounding cities from the airport. Taxis are available for the trip, but if you are on a tight budget, the public buses (*guaguas*) will get you to your destination. Comfort is not the first priority, but the trip will only cost you about ten pesos. If you decide to take a bus,

make sure to agree on the price before leaving the airport. Drivers will sometimes take advantage of new arrivals, charging far more than the usual rate. It should not cost much more than ten pesos to get to Boca Chica or Santo Domingo from the airport.

Getting In and Out of the City

If you take the highway from the airport or from the eastern part of the country, you will cross the **Río Ozama** on the **Puente Duarte**. On the other side of this bridge, take a left on one of the main perpendicular roads and you will soon be downtown.

By taking the road that follows the river south of the Zona Colonial to get out of Santo Domingo and head east, you will avoid a few headaches, not to mention many intersections and traffic lights. At the end, turn left (follow the signs) to reach Puente Duarte.

The highway from San Cristóbal and the western part of the country becomes Avenida George Washington once it enters Santo Domingo; it then follows the shore all the way downtown.

If you are coming from Santiago or the north

Santo Domingo

N

2km
0   1   2km

San Vicente de Paul

Sánchez Bridge

Castellanos

José Fabrea

Av. Duarte

Juan P. Duarte Bridge

Mella Bridge

Malecón

Av. Las Américas

Av. del Puerto

Pedro Livio Cedeno

Gómez

Av. San Martin

Av. John F. Kennedy

See map of Downtown

Av. 30 de Marzo

27 de Febrero

Máximo

Parque Independencia

Av. Bolívar

Paseo Billini

Av. Tiradentes

Independencia

Río Ozama

Caribbean Sea

Av. Lope de Vega

Av. Abraham Lincoln

Av. Jiménez Moya

Av.

See map of the modern city

Av. de los Próceres

Av. John F. Kennedy

Av. Winston Churchill

Hatuey

Av. 27 de Febrero

Av. Prolongación Bolívar

Av. Anacaona

Av. Sarasota

Av. Mirador del SUR

Av. George Washington

Av. Núñez de Cáceres

Av. Faro a Colón

Parque Mirador del Este

Av. Mirador del Este

Av. Estados Unidos

Cuarta

Av. España

Airport Boca Chica

6

5

4

3

2

1

© ULYSSES

ern part of the country, you will cross several main arteries, such as Winston Churchill, Abraham Lincoln and Máximo Gomez. Take one of these to the right, then turn left on Avenida Independencia or Avenida George Washington. The downtown area lies straight ahead.

Remember that there are toll booths at the western and eastern entrances to the city; the toll is five pesos.

In the City

The city's large arteries make it easy to get around. Running along the Caribbean Sea, Paseo Billini (which becomes Avenida George Washington) is a two-way street. Avenida Independencia, which is one-way, goes from west to east, while Avenida Bolivar, also one-way, runs in the other direction.

The main streets running north-south are Avenidas Churchill, Lincoln, Tiradentes and Gomez. The Zona Colonial is bordered by the Río Ozama on one side and Parque Independencia on the other. Countless, inexpensive taxis, guaguas, and collective taxis crisscross the city. Always make sure you indicate your destination clearly. If you have any trouble finding your way around the city, do not hesitate to ask directions from a local. The following are a few tips for those getting around by car.

By Car

Once in the city, be aware that in Santo Domingo there are many one-way streets, heavy traffic and pedestrians who seem to pop up everywhere. It can get quite confusing, especially because the road signs are sometimes inadequate. Decide where you are headed before you set out, keep your map in hand and do not hesitate to ask questions. This last solution may take a few tries, since many Dominicans do not know the street names, and their directions are often sketchy.

At intersections you may also be solicited by vendors trying to sell you peanuts, fruit and just about anything else. They can be fairly insistent, but be patient and make your refusal clear if you are not interested. The "windshield washers" are the most troublesome; they see you coming, wash your windshield without asking and then expect a few pesos.

Parking can also be a problem. If you stop next to Parque Colón or the Zona Colonial it is recommended that you ask someone to keep an eye on your car in order to prevent having it scratched. In return for the favour, you should offer about 10 pesos. To avoid these inconveniences, we would advise you to park a few streets away from the park. If you do not have to go downtown, avoid driving in the city by picking up your rental at the airport.

Car Rental Agencies

These major car rental agencies have offices in Santo Domingo:

Avis
Avenida Abraham Lincoln
☎ 533-3530

Budget
J.F. Kennedy Lope de Vega
☎ 567-0175
≈ 567-0177

Honda
J.F. Kennedy Pepillo Saloedo
☎ 567-1015
≈ 541-0039

Hertz
454 Avenida Independencia
☎ 221-5333
≈ 221-8927

National
1056 Avenida Abraham Lincoln
☎ 562-1444
≈ 544-3030

Nelly
139 Jose Conteras
☎ 535-1233
≈ 685-4933

Thrifty
Jose María Heredia
☎ 686-0133
≈ 685-4933

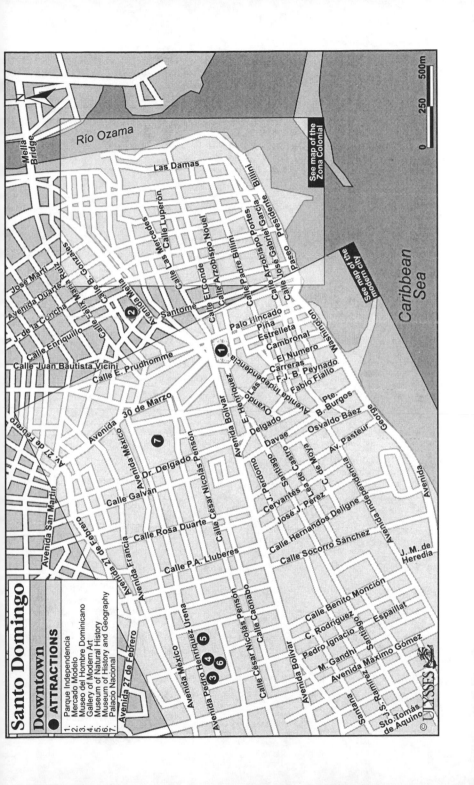

Santo Domingo

Downtown

● ATTRACTIONS

1. Parque Independencia
2. Mercado Modelo
3. Museo del Hombre Dominicano
4. Gallery of Modern Art
5. Museum of Natural History
6. Museum of History and Geography
7. Palacio Nacional

Río Ozama

Mella Bridge

Las Damas

See map of the Zona Colonial

See map of the modern city

Caribbean Sea

0   250   500m

José Martí

Avenida Duarte Ruiz

J. de la Concha

Calle Enriquillo

Calle Félix María González

Calle Gabriel Ruiz

Avenida Mella

Santomé

Calle Juan Bautista Vicini

Calle E. Prudhomme

Calle Las Mercedes

Calle Luperón

Calle Arzobispo Nouel

Calle El Conde

Calle Arzobispo Portes

Calle Padre Billini

Calle José Gabriel García

Calle presidente

Billini

Palo Hincado

Piña

Estrelleta

Cambronal

El Numero

Carreras

F. J. B. Peynado

Fabio Fiallo

Pte. B. Burgos

Osvaldo Báez

Av. Pasteur

George

Mesarruón

Avenida Independencia

Las Ovando

E. Henríquez

Avenida Bolívar

Delgado

Davae

J. Perdomo

Santiago

Cervantés

José J. Pérez

C.

Calle Hernandos Deligne

Calle Socorro Sánchez

J. M. de Heredia

Avenida Independencia

30 de Marzo

Avenida México

Dr. Delgado

Calle Galván

Calle Rosa Duarte

Calle P.A. Lluberes

Calle César Nicolás Pensón

Cervantés de la Moya

Avenida San Martín

Avenida 27 de Febrero

AV. 27 de Febrero

Avenida Francia

Avenida Pedro Henríquez Ureña

Avenida México

Calle César Nicolás Pensón

Calle Corabo

Calle Benito Monción

C. Rodríguez

Pedro Ignacio

M. Gandhi

Santiago

Espaillat

Avenida Bolívar

Avenida Máximo Gómez

Santana

S. S. Ramírez

Sto. Tomás de Aquino

⬤ 1
⬤ 2
⬤ 3
⬤ 4
⬤ 5
⬤ 6
⬤ 7

© ULYSSES

Taxis

Taking a taxi is definitely the fastest and most convenient way to get around town. Rather than waiting to be flagged down, taxi drivers will often approach tourists to offer their services. Taxis can often be found near the major hotels and main tourist attractions. A ride within the limits of Santo Domingo rarely costs more than $5 US, but always negotiate the price beforehand. The vehicles are generally in good condition. In the capital, there are two main taxi companies that should be mentioned:

Taxi Agua
☎ 596-6060

Apolo Taxi
☎ 537-0000

Buses

Several bus companies link Santo Domingo to other towns in the country. The following are the main ones:

Caribe Tours
27 de Fevrero corner of Leopoldo Navarro
☎ 221-4422

Emely Tours
58 San Francisco de Macorís
☎ 687-7114
⇄ 686-0775

Metro
Winston Churchill corner of Fco Pratts
☎ 566-7126

Omni Tours
204 Roberto Pastoriza
☎ 565-6591
⇄ 567-4710

Terra Bus
27 de Febrero
Plaza Criolla
☎ 472-1080

Caribe Tours and Metro serve most regions.

Collective Taxis and Public Buses

Collective taxis can be identified by the word **Público** on their license plates. They are often in poor condition and jam-packed, but work well and cost very little to ride. For most destinations, you will be charged about 5 pesos. The drivers of collective taxis and buses tend to be honest, so it is not necessary to negotiate a price in advance. However, if you suspect you are being overcharged, ask other passengers how much they paid. To take a collective taxi or a bus, wait by the side of a main road and flag one down, since stops are often poorly marked. Buses and collective taxis heading east out of the city can be caught at the corner of Duarte and 27 de Febrero.

Motorcycles

Many Dominicans ride motorcycles, avoiding traffic jams by making their way between the backed-up cars. Some drivers take passengers for a few pesos, but al-

ways negotiate the price first. This mode of transport can be unsafe in the busier parts of the city and is best reserved for the quieter neighbourhoods.

Practical Information

The following section includes the addresses of several organizations that might be of help to you during your stay in the Dominican capital. Because the offices of some of these organizations are not always easy to find, it is often simpler to ask locals for directions.

Tourist Information Office

Tourist Information
Secretaria de Estado de Turismo Oficinas Gubernamentales
Block D, Mexico Ave.
corner of Calle 30 de Marzo
Suite 497
Santo Domingo
☎ 809-221-4660
⇄ 809-682-3806

The main tourist information office lies opposite the Palacio Nacional, on the second floor of a building at the corner of Avenidas 30 de Marzo and Mexico.

There is also a tourist information office in the Colonial Town:

Tourist Information
103 Isabel La Católica
☎ 686-3858

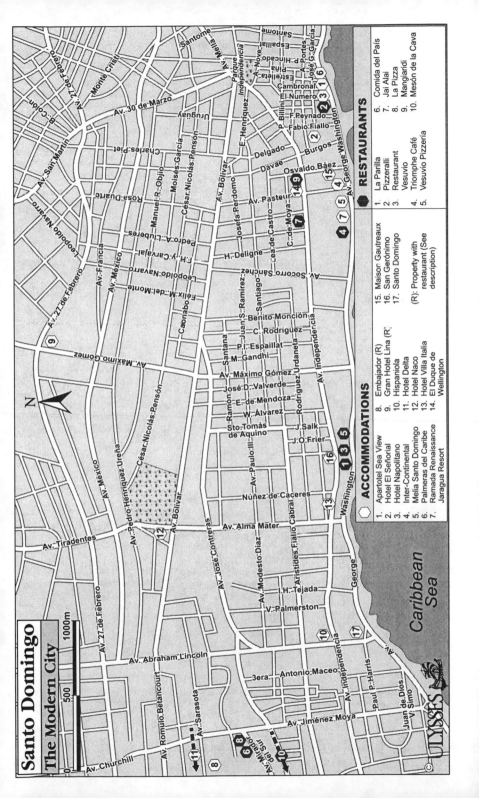

Santo Domingo
The Modern City

0   500   1000m

N

Caribbean Sea

© ULYSSES

National Parks Service

If you are planning to visit any of the parks in the Dominican Republic, be aware that permits are required. Most outfitters furnish these permits, so in theory it is only those travellers planning to visit parks without the benefit of a tour operator who must obtain permits at the national parks office (*Ave. Independencia, behind The Sheraton Hotel*, ☎ *221-5340*). Security at park entrances is generally relatively lax, and it is also possible to buy permits in villages on the outskirts of parks (if you succeed in finding the park's official!).

Post Office

The post office is located on Calle Isabela la Católica (in the Zona Colonial), at the corner of Calle Arzobispo Portes.

Codetel Centres

Santo Domingo has about 15 Codetel centres. In the Zona Colonial, the easiest one to find is at 20 Calle El Conde.

Safety

Despite its size, Santo Domingo is not a particularly dangerous city. While it is important to maintain a level of caution, you can walk about most parts of the city without worry. Tourists may run into trouble if they make a display of

material goods (camera, jewellery) in certain poorer sectors; other areas are to be avoided altogether, especially north of Calle Mella. Outside these areas, anyone walking about is generally treated well. Of course, if you decide to explore at night, avoid dark streets and be careful.

A number of children wander the streets of the city begging for small change from passersby; some have no family, while others just want to make some money. They offer their services, usually a shoe-shine, to tourists and locals alike for a few pesos. The younger ones usually just wait for a charitable soul to give them a few centavos or a bit of food. Though these children can be brusque, they are generally harmless.

Exploring

Of its rich history, Santo Domingo has preserved fabulous treasures, concentrated in **The Zona Colonial**. Whether you visit **Catedral Santa María la Menor**, built in 1521, **Las Casas Reales Museum**, **Alcázar de Colón**, or any other building in this sector of the city, you will be awestruck by these stone buildings that have dominated the city for centuries. While history has proffered these priceless gifts, the capital is also endowed with sites of natural beauty such as **Los Tres Ojos Park** and typical Dominican neighbourhoods that are both dis-

orienting. To help you become familiar with this vibrant capital, and allow you to appreciate its treasures, we first lead you to **the Zona Colonial**. We then take you through some of the more noteworthy tourist attractions.

The Zona Colonial

To visit the Zona Colonial is to climb streets that are imbued with memory and history, discovering buildings that may be as much as 500 years old, to marvel at the still palpable colonial past. For those interested in old stonework, this is doubtless the most rewarding visit in the country. A stroll through these streets is even more pleasant than it is effortless, the buildings being set in a relatively limited perimeter and the traffic being much lighter than in nearby downtown.

Once called "Mayor Place", **Parque Colón** (*at the corner of Calle Arzobispo Meriño an Calle El Conde*), at the center of which stands a bronze stature of the Genoese sailor, is the departure point for the tour. Many guided tours leave from this park and buses full of tourists stop here in great numbers, which explains the hordes of vendors and self-proclaimed private-tour guides who make the park less pleasant than one would hope.

The magnificent **Catedral Santa María de la Encarnación** ★★★ (*facing Parque Colón*), constructed during the 1540s on the order of Real Miguel de Pasamonte, dominates an entire side of the park. It is famous as the first cathedral constructed in the Americas and also constitutes the oldest building of the Plateresque-Gothic style (which allies the characteristics of Gothic and Spanish Renaissance architectural styles with baroque ornamentation).

From the outside, this squat building of grey stone can seem dull, but it conceals an extremely beautiful interior. First, there is its elegant door and then, once your eyes have adjusted to the dimly-lit interior, its graceful arches, its magnificent mahogany altar dating from 1684 and its 14 little chapels dispersed on either side of the cathedral. Until 1992 one of these chapel enclosed the tomb of Christopher Columbus, which is now located at the **Faro a Colón** (see p 85). After being left to deteriorate over many years, the cathedral has recently been restored. Visits to the cathedral are free. Proper dress (no shorts or miniskirts) is required.

The **Palacio de Borgella** (*on Isabel la Católica, facing Parque Colón*), dates from the 19th century, and was once the seat of executive power for the country. It now houses administrative offices.

After visiting the area around **Parque Colón**, *turn left on Calle Pellereno Algaz* (*the first little stone passage*).

The **Casa Diego Caballero** and **The Casa Sacramento** (*Calle Pellereno Algaz*) both face a small cobblestone lane, the first pedestrian street in Santo Domingo. The latter was home to many important colonial figures, including archbishop Alonso de Fuenmayor, who ordered the construction of the city walls. The Casa Diego Caballero was built around 1523. Its façade is distinguished by two square towers, while its interior features galleries formed by solid stone arches.

Keep walking until you reach Calle Las Damas.

★★★
Calle Las Damas

Calle Las Damas is like nothing else in Santo Domingo. This splendid little street, where some of the oldest and most beautiful buildings in the old city stand in succession, will doubtless be inscribed in your memory and constitute one of themost remarkable moments of your trip.

Fortaleza Santo Domingo ★ (*10 pesos; Mon to Sat 9am to 5pm, Sun 10am to 3pm; Calle Las Damas*), the oldest military building in the Americas, stands proudly at the edge of a cliff presiding over both the Caribbean and Río Ozama, a location originally chosen for its strategic value in the protection of the colony.

Fortaleza de Santo Domingo

The walls surrounding this vast military complex shelter an attractive garden, at the center of which stands a statue of Gonzales de Oviedo, which you will notice upon entering. The munitions building is located to the right of the entrance. At the end of the garden, there is a square structure known as the **Torre del Homenaje**, whose struction began in 1505 by order of Nicolás de Ovando.

The Casa de Bastidas (*Calle Las Damas*) was built at the beginning of the 16th century for Don Rodrigo de Bastidas, a comrade of Nicolás de Ovando, who arrived in Santo Domingo in 1502. The neoclassical portal was added in the 17th century. A charming inner garden enhances the beauty of the residence. Two small art galleries have been set up in the rooms adjoining the entrance.

The Casa de Hernán Cortes (*Calle Las Damas*) was constructed in the early 16th century to accommodate representatives of public institutions. It has been restored and now houses the offices of the Maison de la France (*French Tourist Board*). It was from here that Cortés planned and organized the conquest of Mexico.

Santo Domingo: Fortified City

Like European cities of the time, Santo Domingo, the first city in the New World, was built within fortifications. These fortifications, with their high stone walls punctuated by forts and doors, served to fend off attacks by the colony's enemies: the English, Portuguese, French and natives. Today, ruins of these fortifications can be seen along several streets in Santo Domingo; on Las Damas and Del Puerto, which run along the Caribbean Sea, as well as on Palo Hincado and Juan Isidro in the Zona Colonial.

The larger forts were built on Calle Las Damas, which was the most strategic point to defend the city because the street faced the Ozama River and was the entrance to the city. Going north on Calle Las Damas, the forts include the Fortaleza de Santo Domingo, built in 1503 (see p 77); the Fuerte de San Diego with its Puerta de San Diego, once the main entrance to the city; and right next to the Puerta, the Batería del Almirante, which was built to better defend the city and the port.

Two forts were built facing the Caribbean Sea: the Fuerte de San José (Paseo Billini, corner of 19 de Marzo) and the Fuerte de San Gil (Av. George Washington, corner of Palo Hincado). The latter fort is located at the western end of the Zona Colonial.

Calle Palo Hincado also has some interesting fortifications. At the corner of Arzobispo Portes, you will pass through the Puerta de la Misericordia, built in 1543 and a fine example of a medieval-style fortified door. Further north along Calle Palo Hincado are the ruins of Fuerte de Santiago and the Puerta del Conde (corner Calle Le Conde), another entrance to the city, and the Fuerte de la Concepción (corner Mercedes), built in 1678.

Finally, there are several forts in the north part of the Zona Colonial such as the Fuerte de la Caridad (Calle Isidro Pérez), the Fuerte de San Lazaro and the ruins of the Fuerte de San Miguel. All these forts were built during the 17th century. Last but not least is the Fuerte de San Antón, built near the Ozama River in 1672.

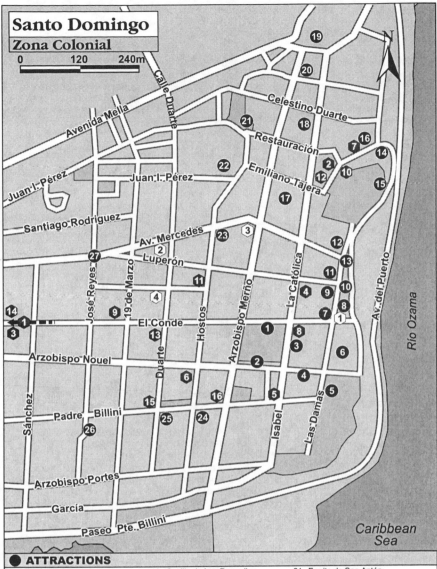

Santo Domingo
Zona Colonial

0   120   240m

Calle Duarte
Avenida Mella
Juan I. Pérez
Juan I. Pérez
Santiago Rodriguez
Celestino Duarte
Restauración
Emiliano Tajera
Av. Mercedes
Luperón
José Reyes
19 de Marzo
El Conde
Arzobispo Nouel
Sánchez
Padre Billini
Arzobispo Portes
García
Paseo Pte. Billini
Duarte
Hostos
Arzobispo Meriño
La Católica
Isabel
Las Damas
Av. del Puerto
Río Ozama
Caribbean Sea

● **ATTRACTIONS**

1. Parque Colón
2. Catedral Santa María de la Encarnación
3. Palacio de Borgellá
4. Casa de Diego Caballero and Casa Del Sacramento
5. Fortaleza de Santo Domingo
6. Casa de Batisdas
7. Casa de Hernán Cortés
8. Casa de Nicolás de Ovando
9. Panteón Nacional
10. Capilla de Los Remedios
11. Casa de los Jesuitas
12. Museo de Las Casas Reales
13. Reloz de Sol
14. Alcázar de Colón
15. Fuerte San Diego
16. Calle Atarazana
17. Casa del Cordón
18. Museo de Juan Pablo Duarte
19. Fuerte y Iglesia Santa Bárbara
20. Museo de Ambar
21. Ermita de San Antón
22. Monasterio de San Francisco
23. Hospital San Nicolás
24. Imperial Convento de Santo Domingo
25. Capilla de la Tercera Orden de Los Dominicos
26. Iglesia Regina Angelorum
27. Iglesia Conventual de las Mercedes

◻ **ACCOMMODATIONS**

1. Hostal Nicolás de Ovando
2. Hostal Nader
3. Hotel Frances
4. Hotel Palacio

◆ **RESTAURANTS**

1. Bariloche
2. Brasserie Pat'e Palo
3. Café de Las Flores
4. Café Galería
5. Coco's Restaurant
6. De Nosotros
7. Fonda Atarazana
8. L'Avocat
9. La Cafetería
10. La Crêperie
11. Meson D'Bari
12. Museo del Jamón
13. Panadería Sum
14. Petrus Cafetería
15. Retazos
16. Ristorante La Briciola

© ULYSSES

Now a hotel, **The Hostal Palacio Nicolás de Ovando** (*Calle Las Damas*) was the residence of the governor of the colony from 1502 to 1509. Nicolás de Ovando was an important figure in Santo Domingo's history, as he enhanced the city's development by instituting various construction standards. The house is certainly among the most beautiful and elegant residences of its era. Built of high quality cut stones, it has a Gothic-style portal, a very rare feature in the architecture of the New World.

Once a Jesuit church, **The Panteon Nacional ★** (*Every day 9am to 4:40pm; Calle Las Damas*) was built between 1714 and 1745. This imposing neoclassical church is made of large grey stones; a sculpted Dominican coat of arms adorns the façade. The interior consists of a single nave hung with magnificent wrought-iron chandeliers. In 1950, Trujillo ordered that the building be renovated and transformed into a pantheon in honour of the country's heroes. Although it is open to the public; you must, be appropriately dressed (no shorts or mini skirts) to visit.

In the 16th century, **The Capilla de Nuestra Señora de los Remedios** (*Calle Las Damas*) was a private church belonging to a wealthy family, the Davilas. The pretty little red brick chapel has a campanile with three arches. The building was restored at the end of the 19th century after being abandoned and partially destroyed.

The Casa de Los Jesuitas ★ (*Calle Las Damas*), made of brick and stone, is one of the oldest buildings in the city. Constructed by order of Nicolás de Ovando, it was given to the Society of Jesus in 1701. The Jesuits used the building for a college, which became a university in 1747. In 1767, when the Jesuits were expelled from the Dominican Republic, the house was taken over by the Spanish Crown.

The Museo de Las Casas Reales ★★ (*10 pesos; Tue to Sun 10am to 5pm; Calle Las Damas, at the corner of Calle Las Mercedes*) is located in two impressive palaces that originally housed the offices of royal institutions governing the territories, hence the name: museum of the "royal houses". The buildings were completed in the 1520s. Although they look fairly modest from the outside, their interior is richly decorated. Objects relating to the social, political, economic, religious and military history of the country are on display here. Among other things, there is a magnificent collection of weapons from different countries. The museum makes for an interesting visit, though not all rooms contain treasures.

Alcázar de Colón

At the end of Calle Las Damas stands the **Sundial** (*at the corner of Calle Las Mercedes*) built in 1753. This spot offers a splendid view of the port and the Río Ozama. An extensive park can be viewed from here, which is slightly uninviting because of the lack of shade. A statue of Nicólas de Ovando stands at the center of the park and at the very end lies **The Alcázar de Colón ★★★** (*20 pesos; Tue to Sun 9am to 5pm; Calle Las Damas at the far end of the park*). It dates from 1509-1510 and was built for Christopher Columbus' son, Diego Columbus, and his family. Diego Columbus succeeded Nicolás de Ovando as Viceroy of the colony in 1509. The beautiful façade, graced with 10 stone arches, looks out onto a large paved park where visitors will find a handful of benches and, in the center, a statue of Nicolás de Ovando. The Alcázar was abandoned for many years until architect Javier Borroso undertook reconstruction work in the 1950s. It has since been opened to the public. Each room is decorated with beautiful period furniture, making this a visit not to be missed.

Near the Alcázar de Colón is the **gate** to the **Fuerte San Diego** (*Calle Las Damas*). Constructed in 1571, it served as the main entrance to Santo Domingo in the late sixteenth century. Part of the wall of the fortress that protected the city in the early colonial days can be seen here. Designed to face the river, this fortress was the main base of defense for the city.

At the edge of Parque Colón, follow the first little street on the right to reach **Calle Atarazana** ★ where, in 1509, the first group of shops in the New World was built. Visitors will find a row of small white houses with brick foundations, whose architectural style is unique in the country. Besides their architectural significance, they form a harmonious ensemble, which still houses a few little shops to this day.

Double back to Calle Emilo Tejera and turn left on Isabel la Católica.

Calle Isabel la Católica

The architecture on Isabel la Católica is less harmonious than that on Calle Las Damas. There are, however, a few beautiful colonial buildings scattered among the much more recent additions.

The Casa del Cordón (*Calle Isabel la Católica, at the corner of Calle Tejera*), constructed in 1502, was one of the first stone residences in the New World. Upon arriving in 1509, Diego Colón lived here with his family before moving into the palace in 1510. The house is easy to spot, thanks to a large sculpted sash on the façade, the symbol of the Franciscan religious order.

The Museo de Juan Pablo Duarte ★ (*10 pesos; Mon to Fri 9am to noon and 2pm to 5pm, Sat and Sun 9am to noon; on Calle Isabel la Católica, at the corner of Calle Celestino Duarte*) is located in the house where Juan Pablo Duarte was born on January 26th, 1813. This national hero became famous as the leader of *La Trinitaria*, a secret organization that sought to liberate the Dominican Republic from Haitian domination. As a result of his efforts, the country declared independence on February 27th, 1844. Ousted from power,

Duarte took exile in Venezuela, where he stayed until 1864, when Spain annexed the Dominican Republic (1861-1865). He returned to the Dominican Republic to oppose the Spanish takeover, but his efforts were in vain. Forced to leave the country again, he was never able to return and died in Carácas, Venezuela on July 15th, 1876. The museum highlights the important moments in his life, and displays many of his belongings. The building itself is unremarkable, but the exhibit is quite good.

The Iglesia Santa Bárbara and its connected **fort** (*Calle Isabel la Católica, at the corner of Avenida Mella*) erected in 1562, form a unique construction featuring elements from various architectural styles, including Gothic and baroque. The façade is distinguished by two square towers of different sizes and three brick arches at the entrance. The fort was erected in the 18th century at a point where the soldiers could keep an eye on a part of the city and on the Río Ozama. The church, for its part, constructed at the end of the 16th century, was destroyed by a hurricane a few years later. The sanctuary was then reconstructed and up to eight chapels have been designed here over the years.

After leaving the fort, take Calle Arzobispo Meriño to get to the Ermita San Anton.

Calle Arzobispo Meriño

After visiting the monastery, continue to Calle Hostos. A portion of the road is lined with pretty, colourful little houses.

The privately funded **Museo del Ámbar ★** *(452 Arzobispo Meriño)* aims to increase public knowledge of amber, the hardened sap of an extinct species of pine. It takes no more than 30 minutes to tour the museum, where you can learn about how amber was created and how insects and leaves were trapped in it. A number of fine specimens are displayed. Visitors will also have a chance to see amber of all different colours—not just yellow, but red, green and blue as well. The exhibit is also intended to help consumers learn to distinguish between real and imitation amber, and some useful tips are provided.

The Ermita San Anton *(Calle Hostos, at the corner of Calle Restauración)* is located just a few steps from the Monasterio San Francisco. Nicólas de Ovando had already planned the construction in 1502, but the building was not finished until 1586. A few years later, when the city was sacked by Drake, it was damaged in a fire. In 1930, after being entirely destroyed by a hurricane, the hermitage was reconstructed.

Built on a small hill in the heart of the old city, **the Monasterio de San Francisco ★★** *(4 pesos; everyday except Sun, 10am to 5pm; Calle Hostos, at the corner of Calle Tejera)* is impressive, though only ruins remain. Construction began in 1505 and the monastery was nearly completed during the 16th century, but in 1673, an earthquake completely destroyed it. Originally, it consisted of three distinct but connected buildings: the convent, the church and the chapel. The thick wall that surrounded the monastery still stands. Among the ruins, the little chapel is the easiest building to identify, as its brick vault remains.

Soon after Santo Domingo was rebuilt on the right bank of the Río Ozama, Nicolás de Ovando ordered the construction of **The Hospital de San Nicolás** *(Calle Hostos, at the corner of Calle Mercedes; you will need to double back)* to provide care for the city's poor and needy. In ruins today, the building was shaped like a cross, a traditional Spanish design.

It was surely the first hospital in the New World.

Parque Duarte is a little island of tranquillity, the perfect place to relax. It is beautifully landscaped and well worth a stop.

Dominating an entire side of the park, **Imperial Convento de Santo Domingo ★** *(Calle Hostos, at Calle Padre Billini)* is a magnificent stone structure that was built in several stages: the monastery itself dates from 1510, and the church from 1517 (though the original building was destroyed by an earthquake in the 16th century), both constructed in Gothic style. It encloses five chapels including the rosary chapel (1649) which is done in a 16th Century Spanish ornate architecture. The monastery also had the privilege of housing the first university in the Americas, **Universidad Santo Tomás de Aquino**. The building is still in good condition, but is scheduled for renovations and is thus closed to the public for the time being.

A few steps away from the convent, the Capilla de la **Tercera Ordén de los Dominicos** *(Calle Padre Billini, corner of Duarte)* dates from 1729 and served as the *Imperial Convento de Santo Domingo* in bygone days. It is adorned with a baroque façade and houses only one little nave in addition to its three small chapels.

Calle José Reyes

To continue your tour of
the Zona Colonial, take
Calle Arzobispo Portes to
Calle José Reyes, where
you will find another
series of interesting buildings dating from the 16th
century. These are some-
what out-of-the-way,
however, so you will
have to walk a bit farther
to reach them.

With elements that hint at
Baroque influences, the
**Iglesia del Convento de Re-
gina Angelorum** (*Calle José
Reyes, at the corner of Paseo Padre Billini*) is one
of the city's major 18th
century constructions.
The cut-stone exterior
features a small campa-
nile with three arches.
The church, having been
seriously damaged by
seismic activity and hurricanes since the end of
the 16th century, required
a thorough restoration.
Though the interior is
very simple, with only
one nave, its ornamenta-
tion is striking. Take the
time to admire the mag-
nificent wood retable (an
ornamental screen sur-
rounding an altar) behind
the altar.

**The Iglesia y Convento de las
Mercedes** (*Calle José Reyes,
at the corner of Calle Las
Mercedes*) was built du-
ring the first half of the
16th century, in homage
to the Virgin Mary. The
cut-stone church has a
massive tower. The
richly-carved wooden
retable is one of the most
beautiful in the city. The
convent, even more
stark-looking than the
church, was heavily dam-
aged by earthquake in
1673 and 1684. The cloist-
er is the only existant
structure of its kind from
the era.

At the Edge of the Colonial Zone

Located at the end of
Calle El Conde, **The
Parque Independencia** is
surrounded by noisy,
traffic-ridden streets, making it seem like an oasis
of greenery and peace. A
monument containing the
tombs of three Domi-
nican heroes who fought
for the country's inde-
pendence, Mella, Sanchez
and Duarte, stands in the
center of the park.

Sundays on Calle Mella
once brought out droves
of Dominicans to sample
unique dishes prepared
according to African culinary traditions. The street
has changed considerably
and is no longer an Af-
rican neighbourhood, but
a large commercial artery
with countless shops selling all kinds of products.

The **Mercado Modelo** ★ is
also located here. Domin-
icans come to this enor-
mous indoor market to
sell foodstuffs, jewellery
made of shells, *larimar*
or amber, beachwear and
crafts. This place is picturesque, but be careful (the
aisles are narrow and
sometimes dark) and
always bargain before
buying.

Plaza de la Cultura

The Plaza de la Cultura
(*Calle Máximo Gomez,
between Calles Cesar
Nicola Penson and Pedro
Henriquez Urena*), or
cultural centre, includes
four museums and the
Teatro Nacional. The
museums can all be
visited on the same day.

**The Museo del Hombre
Dominicano** ★★ (*10 pesos;
Tue to Sun 10am to 5pm*)
is certainly the most
interesting museum in
Santo Domingo, if not the
whole Dominican Repub-
lic. A rich collection of
Taino art is displayed on
the main floor. This indigenous people had already
lived in the Dominican
Republic for over a thou-
sand years when Colum-
bus arrived, and large
numbers of them were
wiped out during coloni-
zation. The entire ground
floor of the museum is
devoted to an exhibit of
the art, religion and daily
life of this society, which
changed radically follow-
ing the arrival of the
Europeans. The few
information panels in the
museum are written only
in Spanish.

The exhibits on the sec-
ond floor retrace various
events that have marked
the colonization of the
country. Many subjects
are explored, and slavery
is given special attention.
The difficult living conditions faced by the thou-
sands of Africans forced
to come to the Domi-
nican Republic are de-
scribed. The last room
houses a magnificent

collection of carnival masks from different regions of the country.

The Gallery of Modern Art (*20 pesos; Tue to Sun 10am to 5pm*) houses a beautiful collection of modern art by Dominican and foreign artists, and offers visitors a chance to familiarize themselves with local trends in modern art. While the extensive permanent collection merits a visit on its own, the museum presents interesting temporary exhibitions as well.

The mandate of **The Museum of Natural History** (*10 pesos; Tue to Sun 10am to 5pm*) is to further the public's knowledge of various aspects of the country's natural history. Some rooms contain taxidermy exhibits that focus on animals found in the Dominican Republic, including some beautiful birds. Unfortunately, some of these specimens have been around for a long time and look more like the remains of dead birds than the work of a taxidermist. Other rooms deal with more general themes, such as astronomy. The information provided is a little brief (and only in Spanish), but covers a multitude of subjects relating to animal life, vegetation and minerals.

The Museum of History and Geography (*10 pesos; Tue to Sun 10am to 5pm*) houses a collection of objects from everyday and military life in the Dominican Republic. It is divided into three rooms, each with exhibits covering a specific period: 1822 to 1861, 1861 to 1916 and 1916 to 1961.

Although certain objects on display belonged to important figures in Dominican life, such as President Trujillo, this museum holds few objects of great interest and has limited appeal, unless you are a specialist or real fan of these types of exhibits.

Other Attractions

The Palacio Nacional ★ (*Calle Dr. Delgado*) was built in the 1940s to house President Trujillo's government offices. The long, imposing building is neoclassical in design and has an elegant dome, 34 metres high and 18 metres across. The building is still the seat of government. The main façade looks onto a quiet little street. An impressive staircase, flanked by two stone lions, leads to the main entrance. The building is surrounded by a pretty park, which is unfortunately closed to the public. To enter the palace, visitors must wear long pants or skirts that cover the knees.

Extending over several kilometres, The **Mirador del Sur** park ★ is a welcome green space perfect for a stroll far from the hustle and bustle of Santo Domingo.

The Jardín Botánico ★★ (*everyday; Avenida de Los Proceres*) is the largest park in the city, and without a doubt the most pleasant. The multitude of tropical plants and trees on display are well laid out and provide a good introduction to the plant life of the island. Another attraction is the pretty Japanese garden. We recommend taking the little train (*10 pesos*) that crisscrosses the garden, carrying passengers through a lush forest one moment and flowering gardens the next. This is an ideal way for those in a hurry to visit the entire garden. These gardens provide a welcome break from the frantic pace of the city.

The **Parque Zoológico Nacional** (*Paseo de Los Reyes Católicos*) is home to a good number of animal species, some of African origins (giraffes, lions, rhinoceros) and others from the Dominican Republic (pink flamingos). Special care has been taken to recreate the natural environments of these animals. A big section of the park has been laid out without any cages, thus allowing visitors to observe the animals roaming almost freely. There is also an aviary with a large variety of tropical birds. A little train (*5 pesos*) can take you on a tour of the park.

The idea of building a mausoleum for Columbus was first suggested during the final years of President Trujillo's reign. In keeping with the famous explorer's character, a huge lighthouse was built. The **Faro a Colón** ★ (*10 pesos; on the east shore of the Río Ozama, in the Parque Mirador del Este*) took a number of years to build and was not completed in time for the 1992 celebrations marking the 500th anniversary of Columbus' arrival in the Americas. The project is said to have cost almost $250 million! The aim was to build a monument worthy of the great Genoese navigator. Unfortunately, despite its

impressive size, the cruciform, windowless concrete building is not particularly charming. The marble tomb in the heart of the building seems very small. It is guarded around the clock by four military guards. The building also contains a number of exhibition halls. The many tanks of **The Acuario Nacional** ★ (*Boul Sans Souci*) contain specimens of the colourful fish species and crustaceans that inhabit the waters around the island. One small room contains various species indigenous to Venezuela. There is also an ingenious display tank with a tunnel-like walkway right through it, allowing visitors to observe the fish from all sides. All explanatory texts are in Spanish only.

The Parque Nacional los Tres Ojos ★★★ (*every day 8am to 5pm; at the east side of Parque Mirador del Este, on Avenida de Faro a Colón*) is located on the outskirts of Santo Domingo, on the east bank of the Río Ozama. It has a few pleasant trails, but most visitors come for its enormous open-air grotto. Stone steps lead down into this cavern, which is home to a surprising abundance of tropical plantlife. A narrow path disappears into the vegetation, guiding visitors to the shores of

the three extraordinary but beautiful subterranean lakes, or "eyes", for which the park was named. Stalactites and other natural formations can be seen here as well. Outside the grotto, a trail leads to a fourth lake, which resembles a volcano crater. This is a truly extraordinary spot.

To reach the park from downtown, cross the Puente Duarte and continue along the Las Américas highway. Keep an eye out for the single small sign that points the way to the park.

Accommodations

The Zona Colonial

Though there are few hotels here, it is possible to stay in the Zona Colonial — and what a pleasure to sleep in a centuries-old building at the heart of old Santo Domingo.

The Hostal Nader
$56, ⊗;
At the corner of Duarte and Luperón
☎ 687-6674
≈ 687-7887
The Hostal Nader is an adorable old house that stands out for its beautiful stone façade. Upon enter-

ing you will find yourself in an interior courtyard surrounded by the balconies of the guest-rooms. The rooms themselves are all well kept and quite charming.

Palacio

$65, ≡, ⊗;
106 Calle Duarte
P.O. Box 20541
☎ *682-4730*
≈ *687-5535*

Not far from the Hostal Nader, and still on this relatively calm part of Calle Duarte, is The Palacio. This is another charming inn set up inside a beautiful old house, just a few steps from the alluring streets of The Zona Colonial. The wrought-iron light fixtures that adorn its façade make it easy to spot. Its tasteful decor makes this is an extremely pleasant place. The bathrooms in the hotel rooms are clean and spacious.

Hotel Frances

$90; ≡;
Calle Las Mercedes corner of Arzobispo Meriño
☎ *685-9331*

Situated in the Colonial Zone, this hotel occupies a pretty Spanish-style stone house that has just been completely renovated. It is a quiet place with a large square inner courtyard where guests can have breakfast or simply relax away from the bustle of town. The rooms are decorated with ochre-coloured walls and dark wooden furniture. The Hotel Frances' setting and location certainly make it one of this town's most charming establishments.

The Hostal Nicolas de Ovando

Calle Las Damas
☎ *687-3101*
≈ *687-5170*

The Hostal Nicolas de Ovando is situated in one of the most beautiful stone residences in the Colonial Zone. It was formerly the home of **Nicolas de Ovando**, the first governor of the colony (*1502-1509*). This establishment, however, was being fully renovated when we were there. The hotel has a lovely view of the Ozama River and will hopefully re-open soon for business.

Avenida George Washington and Surroundings

Avenida George Washington, which lines the Caribbean sea, offers exceptional views across the vast expanse of shimmering waves. It is therefore the perfect spot for a big hotel complex. Hotels ideal for those on a tighter budget can also be found close by.

The Palmeras del Caribe

$30, ⊗;
1 Cambronal, at the corner of Malecón
☎ *689-3872*

The Palmeras del Caribe offers small, sparsely furnished rooms. Though not incredibly comfortable, they are relatively well kept. The rooms run along either side of a long, open-air corridor, giving the place an unusual but appealing look.

The Hotel El Señorial

$36, ⊗, ≡,
58 Pte. Vicini Burgos
☎ *687-4359*
≈ *687-0600*

The Hotel El Señorial is an ordinary-looking white stucco building. It is located in front of a park near the sea, allowing visitors to enjoy some peace and quiet. The rooms are fairly large and attractively decorated.

Apart-hotel Sea View

$50, ≡, K,
Avenida Cambronal at the corner of George Washington
☎ *221-4420*

Behind the green and white façade of the Sea View are clean, comfortable apartments with well-equipped kitchenettes. Though the decor lacks style, rooms are functional.

The Napolitano

$80, ≡, ≈, ℜ, ♠,
Avenida George Washington
☎ 687-1131
≈ 689-2714

The Napolitano is a long building with a plain façade. It looks out on the sea, giving some rooms a beautiful view. The hotel is comfortable, though the decor is outdated.

The Melia Santo Domingo

$118, ≡, ≈, ℜ, ♠
365 Avenida George Washington
P.O. Box 1493
☎ *221-6666*
≈ *686-0711*

The Sheraton Santo Domingo faces the sea, so most of the rooms have wonderful views. The high standard of comfort and wide range of services are in keeping with the well-known chain. The spacious rooms are decorated with functional modern furniture. Unfortunately, the lobby is not very elegant.

The Ramada Renaissance Jaragua Resort
$140
≡, ≈, ℜ, ♠
367 Avenida George Washington, P.O. Box 769-2
☎ 221-2222
≈ 686-0528
The Ramada Renaissance Jaraqua Resort also faces the sea. A vast lobby adorned with flowers and elegant furnishings welcomes visitors. The rooms are tastefully decorated as well. Finally, the hotel has a lovely garden where visitors can escape the hurried pace of the city. In the evening, the Jaragua is a great place because of its good restaurants, excellent musical entertainment, large casino and one of the best nightclubs in town.

The Inter-Continental
$ 150, ≡, ≈, △, ♠, ℜ
218 Avenida George Washington
☎ 221-0000
≈ 221-2020
Formerly known as the Centenario V, The Inter-Continental is definitely one of the most chic hotels in town. Upon changing hands, the building was renovated and the lobby is now much more inviting. The rooms, as impeccable as ever, offer a superb view of the sea.

Elsewhere in Town

Maison Gautreaux
$38, ≡
8 Calle Félix Mariano Iluberes
☎ 687-4856
☎ 412-7837
≈ 412-7840
Situated in a quiet area not far from the Malecón, this small hotel has clean rooms, although they are a little bit shabby. The place can be a little noisy, however, especially the rooms on the ground floor near the reception area where the television is on night and day.

El Duque de Wellington
$ 37, ≡,
304 Avenida Independencia
☎ 682-4525
≈ 682-2844
This spruce little hotel is a perfectly decent place to stay in the Dominican capital without spending a fortune. The rooms are small but decorated with pretty wooden furniture, and the beds, with their white sheets, create an atmosphere of well-being. This establishment is on the pleasant Avenida Independencia and not far from the Malecón and the Colonial Zone.

Hotel Villa Italia
$48, ℜ
1107 Avenida Independencia corner of Alma Mater
☎ 682-3373
≈ 221-7461
This hotel is unpretentious and offers excellent quality for the price. Its rather soberly decorated rooms are well kept and not too small. The hotel is in a pretty white build-

ing near the beautiful Avenida Independencia and two steps from the sea. The guests have access to a lovely terrace with a whirlpool bath as well as a pleasant restaurant.

San Geronimo
$45, ≡, ≈, ℜ, ♠,
1067 Avenida Independencia, P.O. Box 15
☎ 221-6600
The decor at the 72-room San Geronimo Hotel is outdated and a bit unattractive, orange and brown being the dominant colours. Hardly elegant, the rooms are nonetheless well-kept.

The Delta
$75, ≡, ℜ, K
53 Avenida Sarasota, P.O. Box 1818
☎ 535-0800
≈ 535-5635
The Delta is a lovely pink building with a typically Caribbean air about it. It is ideally located in a peaceful part of the city. The rooms are decorated with distinctive modern furniture.

The Hispaniola
$160, ≡, ≈, ℜ, ♠
Avenida Independencia, at the corner of Abraham Lincoln
☎ 221-7111
≈ 535-4050
The five-story yellow building of The Hispaniola Hotel is easy to spot on the western edge of the city. Though this hotel is not in the most convenient part of town, it offers large, comfortable rooms, a big pool and a casino.

Santo Domingo

The Gran Hotel Lina

$111, ≡, ≈, ♠, ℜ

Maximo Gomez, at Calle 27 de Febrero

☎ *563-5000*

≈ *686-5521*

A handsome hotel with all the modern comforts, The Gran Hotel Lina is located downtown. It is a modern building that rises several stories high, looking out over this bustling part of the capital. Furthermore, some people are sure to consider it a plus that both a casino and a good restaurant (page?) can be found on its premises.

The Naco Hotel

$78, ♠, ℜ

22 Tiradentes

☎ *562-3100*

≈ *544-0957*

If you're looking for another good place to stay in Santo Domingo, you might consider the modern, comfortable Naco Hotel.

The Embajador Hotel

$85, ≡, ≈, ℜ, ♠

Avenida Sarasota

☎ *221-2131*

≈ *532-4494*

The chic Embajador Hotel was built under the Trujillo dictatorship. The rooms are decorated in a comfortable yet outdated fashion but have a certain charm. Guests also enjoy access to a vast and magnificent tropical garden, a rarity in the Dominican capital. This edenic spot, where you can enjoy a meal or take a dip in the pool, feels far from all the hubbub of the city. The huge, elegant lobby, where the hotel's casino and bar are located, at-

tracts a well-groomed crowd every night. One last little thing: take a good look at the trees around the hotel as there are *coticas* (page?) living in them.

Santo Domingo Hotel

$160, ≡, ≈, ℜ

Avenida Independencia, at the corner of Avenida Abraham Lincoln, P.O. Box 2112

☎ *221-1511*

≈ *535-1511*

The grand and luxurious Santo Domingo Hotel is located in a peaceful neighbourhood slightly removed from the downtown area. The rooms are spacious and attractively decorated.

Restaurants

The Zona Colonial

You are certain to find a good place for lunch among the restaurants that line the pedestrian street, El Conde. We suggest one of these:

Barriloche

$

Calle El Conde near Duarte

This restaurant is very popular with Dominicans at lunchtime. The cafeteria-style layout is quite simple; choose your meal at the counter, and sit down to eat it in the large nondescript room with the television. This place is ideal for a filling, inexpensive meal (*pollo, arroz and habichuela*).

La Cafeteria

$

Calle El Conde near 18 de Marzo

La Cafeteria is without a doubt one of the best places in town to have a good coffee. It is a modest but charming place that serves delicious espressos and cappuccinos.

Cafe de Las Flores

$

Calle El Conde near Sanchez

Continuing along the pedestrian street, El Conde, the Cafe de Las Flores is an unpretentious establishment that offers mainly Dominican food. There are also a few Italian and international dishes on the menu. On the terrace you can watch the hustle and bustle of town while listening to the latest merengue and batchata hits.

Petrus Cafeteria

$

Calle El Conde near 18 de Marzo

Right opposite the Cafe de Las Flores is the Petrus Cafeteria, a small nondescript kind of place where you can have a quick, inexpensive bite to eat (sandwiches, pizzas, hamburgers and ice cream).

Museo del Jamón

$

The charming little cafés that face the Alcázar de Colón offer a delightful setting in which to enjoy a drink and a bite to eat. Here you will find the Museo del Jamón, which serves delicious deli meats.

De Nosotros
$
Calle Hostos
For tasty *empanadas*,
head to De Nosotros.
Ready in minutes, they
are delicious and well-
garnished. Ask for a take-
out order and have a
picnic in Parque Duarte,
just around the corner.

Panadería Sum
$
The Calle Duarte has a
few restaurants where
you can go for a quick
lunch. Panadería Sum is a
good place for sand-
wiches and empanadas.

Meson D'Bari
$$
Calle Hostos corner of Salome Ureña
☎ **687-4091**
In the Colonial Zone,
Meson D'Bari is a pretty
neighbourhood restaurant
that serves Dominican
chicken, fish and meat
dishes. Located in an
elegant building, the two
small dining rooms are
charmingly decorated
with brick archways,
wooden beams and a
great many paintings by
Dominican artists. You
can also have a drink at
the bar.

🦐 La Crêperie
$$
Calle Atarazana
Plaza de España
☎ **221-4734**
Right opposite the Alca-
zar de Colomb, on the
Plaza de España, La
Crêperie serves sand-
wiches and salads as well
as excellent crêpes. The
shaded terrace on Plaza
de España is a good
place to go when it gets
hot, especially at midday.
It is also possible to sit in

the small dining room
located on the other side
of Calle Atarazana.

Café Galeria
$$
163 Isabel la Católica corner of
Luperón
☎ **688-7649**
Café Galeria is set slightly
back from Calle Isabel la
Católica. Its pretty little
shaded terrace is a very
good place to have a
light meal at noon (sand-
wiches, salads, etc.). In
the evening, the chef
concocts mainly French
specialities.

If you do not wish to eat
outside, this café also has
a bistro-style dining room
inside. After your meal,
you can go next door
and visit the charming
local handicrafts shop run
by the owners of the
restaurant.

L'Avocat
$$
Calle El Conde
☎ **688-1068**
L'Avocat is one of the
most pleasant areas of the
Colonial Zone, between
Las Damas and Isabel la
Católica. The restaurant
serves delicious fish and
seafood dishes, as well as
chicken and steak. Try to
get a seat in the courtyard
in back of the restaurant;
it is very quiet there but

there are only three tables.

The Brasserie Pat'e Palo
$$$
La Atarazana
☎ **687-8089**
Located inside a pretty
stone house that has
been completely reno-
vated, the Brasserie Pat'e
Palo has a comfortable
dining room with ex-
posed brick walls and
beautiful Spanish-style
wooden furniture. The
dining room has a long
bar that is especially
pleasant for cocktails. The
outside terrace with the
designer wrought iron
furniture is abso-
lutely beautiful
and from here
you can get a
great view of the
square and the
Alcazar just across the
street. This restaurant has
good selection of interna-
tional dishes, but you pay
more for the surround-
ings.

Coco's Restaurant
$$$
53 Calle Padre Billino
☎ **687-9624**
The superb Coco's Res-
taurant is located in a
beautiful house in the
Colonial Zone and has an
English pub-like setting.
Its charming dining room
is decorated with beauti-
ful wooden furniture,
attractive light fixtures
and interesting paintings.
You can also eat in a
small private room or
even in the interior courtyard where lively colours
contrast with the rest of
the restaurant. The menu

written on the blackboard offers quite original international dishes such as poached pears with stilton cheese and nuts. The excellent selection of whiskies on the wine list make Coco's an appropriate place to end the evening.

Retazos Restaurant
$$
Padre Billini
☎ 688-6141
An elegant white stucco façade that seems untouched by time conceals the charming Retazos Restaurant. The decor is hardly luxurious, but the dining room, laid out in a pleasant inner court, has a certain charm about it. It is in this relaxed atmosphere that guests select their meal from a vast choice of local and international specialties.

The Ristorante La Briciola
$$$
152-A Arzobispo Meriño
☎ 688-5055
By far the most beautiful restaurant and one of the best places to eat in Santo Domingo, the Ristorante La Briciola is just the place for special occasions. This is the place to savour Italian specialities prepared with flair, which are served in an elegant dining room or better still, under the stars in a magnificent interior courtyard surrounded by brick arches. The design of the place is absolutely magnificent. It is better to make reservations on weekends.

Fonda Atarazana
$$$
Calle Atarazana
☎ 689-2900
Housed in one of the many historic buildings on charming old Calle Atarazana, Fonda Atarazana is a very well-situated restaurant. This place is also very well decorated through and through. The first charming room in the house is the lobby, and the dining rooms, equally as charming, are upstairs. The menu offers local and international specialities, and what better setting could there be to enjoy them in?

Avenida George Washington

Opposite the fancy hotels that line Avenida Washington there are a number of food stalls and open-air bars. This lively, unpretentious area is popular with local inhabitants who come to enjoy an evening snack and the seaside.

Pizzeralli
$
Avenida George Washington
It is hard to miss the green and red façade of the Pizzeralli. This place is very popular with Dominican families, who arrive in large numbers and often become quite boisterous. The tasty pizza is served in large portions.

Vesuvio Pizzeria
$
Avenida George Washington
☎ 685-7608
The proprietors of the Vesuvio Pizzeria also own the chic Vesuvio restaurant. The atmosphere of the pizzeria is more relaxed, however. The menu features simple dishes, including, of course, a variety of pizzas.

La Parilla
$
533 Avenida George Washington
☎ 688-1511
La Parilla is a modest-looking restaurant that serves a good selection of deliciously prepared Creole dishes. You can sit on the terrace or in the small dining room with a gabled roof. Brochettes are the specialty of the house.

The Triomphe Café
$$
Avenida George Washington, next to the Ramada Hotel
The Triomphe Café is a pretty little seaside restaurant with an inexpensive and varied menu including succulent crepes. Comfortable cushioned benches lend themselves well to an intimate tête-à-tête meal.

Palacio de Jade
$$-$$$
José Maria de Heredia, close to George Washington
To savour Chinese food, head to the Palacio de Jade. The exterior, which vaguely resembles a medieval castle, may be a bit surprising, but the interior is beautifully decorated and the dishes are succulent.

Restaurante Vesuvio
$$$
521 Avenida George Washington
☎ 221-3333
This restaurant serves excellent Italian food, with seafood as the specialty. A friendly atmosphere adds to the charm of this elegant restaurant, which is definitely among the best in town.

Elsewhere in Town

The Comida del Pais
$
Avenida Jiménez Moya
The Comida del Pais is another typical Dominican cafeteria-style restaurant, where guests choose from a wide assortment of dishes to be enjoyed in a large adjoining dining room or as take-out. This inexpensive place is usually very busy.

La Pizza
$
Avenida Jiménez Moya
Right next door La Pizza serves great pizza. The restaurant has a pleasant terrace looking onto the street.

🌴 Mangiaridi
$$-$$$
302 Avenida Independencia
If you are craving linguini with crab or shrimp, or a delectable *tiramisu*, Mangiaridi serves a fine selection of dishes. To make things even better, you get to savour your meal comfortably seated in an air-conditioned dining room, attended by a courteous staff.

Jai Alai
$$-$$$
411 Avenida Independencia
Located on noisy Avenida Independecia, Jai Alai offers visitors an excellent chance to familiarize themselves with the local cuisine or treat themselves to one of the delicious seafood dishes for which the place is reputed.

Lina
$$$
Maximo Gomez, at Calle 27 de Febrero
☎ 563-5000
For years, the Lina Restaurant, in the hotel of the same name (see p88, 91) has been concocting Spanish dishes of a quality found nowhere else in Santo Domingo, winning over many fans of that cuisine. Each specialty served here, in particular the paella, is a delicious invitation to discover the culinary traditions of Spain.

Embajador
$$$
Avenida Sarasota
If there is one place that seems far from the frenzied activity in Santo Domingo, it is the garden of the Hotel Embajador, and it is in this peaceful spot that the hotel restaurant is located. The restaurant only takes up a small part of this vast stretch of land planted with trees and flowering bushes, letting guests enjoy an outstanding setting and serene atmosphere while eating. In addition to its location, the res-

taurant offers a varied menu and consistently good food.

🌴 Meson de la Cava
$$$
Avenida Mirador del Sur
☎ 533-2818
Meson de la Cava is definitely one of the most well known places in Santo Domingo, and merits a visit if only to admire its originality. Indeed, like its name indicates, the Meson de la Cava was built inside a large cave and the setting is spectacular. Of course, prices are high and the place is mostly frequented by tourists who come for the Dominican and international specialities.

Entertainment

Cultural Activities

In the last two weeks of July, when the **merengue festival** is in full swing, merengue fever reaches its peak in Santo Domingo. The Malecón is transformed into a huge, open-air stage, where some of the best bands in the country give free concerts. People from all over the country flock to the capital to party and kick up their heels to the rousing rhythms of

this music, which is na
tive to the Dominican
Republic. Merengue mu-
sic also sets the
mood at
many bars
and disco-
theques
during this
period.

The **Santo Domingo
Carnival** is a big event
in the pure Latin
American tradition of
carnivals. It overtakes
the city at the begin-
ning of February
each year and ends
with a parade on the
Malecon.

Dancer in Carnival Mask

Theatres

Teatro Nacional
Plaza Cultura
☎ 687-3191

The Teatro Nacional,
housed in a modern
auditorium that seats up
to 1,700 spectators, presents concerts and dance
shows in addition to
theatre productions. The
performances are gener-
ally good in quality and
spotlight local and international artists.

You can also attend
modern theatre produc-
tions at The Fine Arts
Theatre and experimental
productions at the Casa
de Teatro.

Fine Arts Theatre
corner of Maximo Gomez and
Avenida Independencia
☎ 221-5288

Casa de Teatro
14 Arzobispo Merino
☎ 689-3430

Baseball

Quisqueya Stadium
☎ 565-5565
From the month of Octo-
ber to the month of
January, which is profes-
sional baseball season in
the Dominican Republic,
you can attend a baseball
game at Quisqueya Sta-
dium. Games begin at
7:30pm during the week
and at 4pm on the week-
ends. Tickets run any-
where from $1 to $10 in
price. Fans wishing to
attend one of these
games are not likely to be
disappointed as the qual-
ity of the sport here is
quite elevated. In fact,
during the winter months,
several players from the
North American Major
Leagues come to com-
pete with Dominican
teams.

Casinos

The Hispaniola Hotel Casino
Avenida Independencia, corner of
Avenida Abraham Lincoln
☎ 535-9292
Santo Domingo has
several casinos, each the
more luxurious than the
last. The Hispaniola Hotel
Casino is one of the most
sumptuous in town and
is definitely worth the
trip. It has countless slot
machines and gaming
tables.

**The Ramada Renaissance
Jaragua Resort**
367 Avenida George Washington
☎ 221-2222
The Ramada Renaissance
Jaragua Resort is probably
the most luxurious hotel
in Santo Domingo, and its
casino definitely attests to
this. All kinds of gaming
tables and slot machines
are available to make
your fortune.

**The Melia Santo Domingo
Hotel Casino**
365 Avenida George Washington
☎ 687-8150
The Melia Santo
Domingo Hotel Casino
is very large, and "real
players" come to play
here.

**The San Geronimo Hotel
Casino**
1067 Avenida Independencia
☎ 533-8181
A little more modest than
the others, The San
Geronimo Hotel Casino is
a favourite of Domini-
cans.

Bars and Discos

Santo Domingo's night-life is very vibrant. Everywhere in the capital there are a number of bars and discotheques that are open until the wee hours of the morning.

Plaza España is *the* place to have a drink. It is pleasant and quiet with enchanting surroundings. **Calle Atarazana** has numerous outside terraces, cafés and bars and among them, the **Museo de Jamon** is a particularly friendly place.

Doubles Bar
154 Arzobispo Meriño
Located in a superb house in the Colonial Zone, the Doubles Bar was renovated in the colonial style and its harmonious design is just dazzling. It is an intimate, cosy bar and an ideal place for a drink before or after dinner. Light meals are also served. Entertainment staring local musicians is presented in the evening. The Doubles closes at 2am.

Coco's
53 Calle Padre Billini
Another good place to have a drink in the Colonial Zone is Coco's, with its calm and muted atmosphere. Primarily an English pub-style bar, this establishment has a charming and colourful interior courtyard. Coco's also has an excellent selection of cocktails and whiskies.

Plaza D'Frank
Avenida George Washington
Not far from the Jaragua Hotel, Plaza D'Frank is the place to go for a good cold beer, which is the specialty of the house. The ambiance is relaxed and friendly.

Bella Bleu
A little further west on Avenida George Washington

Similar to Plaza D'Frank, Bella Bleu is a good place to end the evening.

The Kokonos
523 Padre Billini
☎ 687-5624
This bar is very fashionable with the capital's wealthy young crowd who come here to party. You can sit in the pretty little open-air café or on the large exterior terrace. The club can be boisterous and very crowded on weekends. There is a make-shift dancefloor between tables and chairs where people move to the beat of the latest Dominican and international hits.

Merengue Bar
367 Avenida George Washington
☎ 221-2222
To hear Dominican and West Indian bands, visit the Merengue Bar at the Jarangua Hotel. Excellent shows are presented every evening, and what shows they are! The atmosphere is exhilarating.

Chez Drake
Arzobispo Meriño, corner of Portes
If, on the other hand, you have had enough merengue and want to spend the evening in a completely different am-

bience, go to Chez Drake where you can sip a drink to the soothing sounds of jazz and blues.

Guacara Taina
$10
Avenida Mirador del Sur
Guacara Taina will rock your soul! Built in an huge cave, this amazing nightclub has a very surrealist decor with stalactites and stalagmites as the backdrop. To get to the club's three dance floors, you have to walk down a flight of stairs. There, you can dance to Dominican and International music. Despite being underground, the place has an excellent ventilation system.

The Jubilee
367 Avenida George Washington
If all the nightclubs in town seem empty, go to The Jubilee at the Jaragua Hotel. After midnight, every night of the week, this nightclub always has action and people. The place is mostly frequented by the hotel guests, but also by a number of Dominicans. The music is West Indian and International.

Fantasy
Manaloa Hotel
Here is another good nightclub, although it is much smaller than the ones already mentioned. Mainly Dominican music is played and live musicians occasionally perform here.

Jet Set
Avenida Independencia
One of the most hip nightclubs in the capital, Jet Set has a chic decor

with many television screens and shiny steel furniture. Merengue music is mostly played here.

Shopping

The noisy, bustling downtown core extends from Calle 27 de Febrero to Calle Mella between Calle 30 de Marzo and Vincente Noble. This part of town is teeming with street vendors selling candies, fresh fruit and lottery tickets, and crowded with stores of every kind; if you look around a little, you can find almost anything!

There are several banks on Calle Mella where visitors can exchange their foreign currency for pesos (a branch of the Bank of Nova Scotia will change Canadian dollars). On the same street, the **Mercado Modelo** sells a variety of crafts, from wooden figurines and straw hats, to jewellery and t-shirts.

A panoply of other shops right next to the Mercado Modelo also sell all kinds of Dominican products. If you didn't find what you were looking for at the Mercado Modelo, take a stroll along Calle Mella. One shop you'll find is the **Casa del Café**, a good place to stock up on Dominican coffee.

Still in The Colonial Zone, you can also go to the **Café Galeria** (*63 Isabel la Católica*), an attractive two-floor shop with beautiful works by local artists, such as wood and stone sculptures with Taïnos themes, and painted furniture and antiques.

For a quieter shopping experience, stroll along **Calle El Conde**, a very pleasant pedestrian street with many small shops selling lovely local crafts and different types of clothing. Here are some of the more interesting ones:

A book and stationery store at the corner of Calle Hostos sells books on the Dominican Republic in Spanish and in other languages.

There are two sporting-goods stores, both with a good selection of snorkelling equipment and clothing (t-shirts, swimsuits, shoes):

Sporto
at the corner of Santome

El Molino Deportivo
at the corner of Duarte

For music, head to:

Disco Mundo
at the corner of Santome

Musicalia
at the corner of Santome

Several small souvenir shops selling local crafts can be found on Calle Arzobispo Merino, next to the cathedral. The quality of these items varies greatly, so choose carefully.

If you take Calle Arzopispo Meriño next to The Santa María la Menor Cathedral, you will soon come to **Mi País**. Perfect for visitors in search of Dominican souvenirs, this store is packed with great gift items: locally made handicrafts, amber and larimar jewellery, cigars, dolls, statuettes, books, etc. There is something here for everyone!Facing the cathedral, **Monte Cristi de Tabaco**, sells Dominican cigars and cigarillos.

On Atarazana, you'll find an unpretentious shop called **Ambar Tres**, which is another good place in town to buy amber.

On the ground floor of the **Museo del Ámbar** there is a large store, located in the last gallery of the museum. Jewellery, statuettes and scores of other amber items are available for purchase here. The pieces are of high quality and the salespersons are always right at hand, but not too insistent.

Sala de Arte Rosamaría
Calle Ataranza

Art lovers can stop by the Sala de Arte Rosamaría, where a small number of paintings by Dominican artists are exhibited and sold.

The Caribbean Coast

The miles of beautiful coastline in the southeastern region of the Dominican Republic are popular with visitors from around the world.

Numerous hotel complexes have been built to accommodate all of these visitors. Tourist complexes, like Juan Dolio and Casa de Campo, have sprung up in previously uninhabited areas, near beautiful sandy beaches. Luxurious modern complexes have also been built in the centre of typical Dominican villages, alongside modest Creole cottages.

Although the juxtaposition is at times disquieting, these hotels have the advantage of being right in the thick of the island's daily hustle and bustle. The coastline features some outstanding attractions as well, including Altos de Chavón, a reconstruction of a 14th century Italian village. The southeast has also attracted rich Dominicans, who have built magnificent houses here to escape the hectic pace of Santo Domingo.

This whole coastline, from Boca Chica to Boca del Yuma, is lapped by the shimmering waters of the Caribbean Sea. The vegetation is sometimes lush, a patchwork of palm groves and fields of sugar cane, other times sparse, as in the region of Bayahibe. Just off the southern shores lie charming little islands like Catalina and Isla Saona, each a veritable paradise of sand and palm trees where horseback riding is enjoyed on daytime excursions.

Finding Your Way Around

It is easy to reach the coast by car or guagua (public bus) from the capital. This last mode of transport is the least expensive; for example, it costs 10 pesos to get to Boca Chica.

A single highway leads to the southeastern part of the island. It begins in Santo Domingo and follows the Caribbean coast to the town of La Romana. The importance of tourism to the area and the recent development boom ensure that the highway is well maintained. The section between Santo Domingo and the Las Américas airport even has a special installation of concrete columns (in bad shape these days), each representing a South American country. Tourist destinations are often off the highway, so visitors must keep an eye out for billboards advertising specific destinations. This is an interesting region and well worth a visit.

To reach the southwestern coast from Santo Domingo, take the highway over the Puente Duarte and continue straight along Avenida Las Américas.

Boca Chica

Boca Chica is about 30 kilometres from the capital. Avenida Las Américas follows the sea all the way to and through the town. To reach downtown Boca Chica from the highway, take Calle Juan Bautista Vicini or Avenida Las Caracoles and then turn on Calle Duarte.

The car rental agencies in Boca Chica tend to have older vehicles on hand. A better alternative is renting a car at the Las Américas airport. The following agencies have offices at the airport:

Avis
☎ *549-0468*

Hertz
☎ *549-0454*

Budget
☎ *544-1244.*

There are many guaguas between Santo Domingo and Boca Chica. They pick up passengers along Avenida Los Caracoles.

Juan Dolio

A few kilometres from Boca Chica, the village of Juan Dolio is composed almost exclusively of large resort complexes and a few restaurants. Although the village is off the highway and you won't see many signs for it, it is easy to find: watch for a shopping centre and two large hotels near the two beach entrances.

There is a guagua to Juan Dolio; just head out of town and wait for it to come along the highway.

There is a car rental agency in front of the casino.

Budget
☎ *526-1907*

San Pedro de Macorís

The highway passes through the village and traffic can be heavy at peak times. Be careful, because people drive very fast and there are many pedestrians.

The guagua station is next to the Iglesia San Pedro.

La Romana

The highway runs alongside the village. To reach the seashore or Casa de Campo, you must head south across town to join up with the road along the coast.

Casa de Campo lies on a vast property east of La Romana. As you leave La Romana by the road along the coast, you'll easily spot the signs for both the tourist complex and Altos de Chavón, which is located on the grounds of Casa de Campo.

Bayahibe

The highway, a narrow strip of asphalt snaking through the shrubs and undergrowth, goes all the way to the village of Bayahibe. It might seem odd that a highway in such excellent condition

Sun-drenched pastel-coloured houses line the length of Santo Domingo's Calle Hostos.
- *Claude Hervé-Bazin*

Dominican painting depicting everyday life.
- *Dugast*

Close-up of Santo Domingo's Panteon Nacional, a memorial to Dominican heros.
- *Claude Hervé-Bazin*

Altos de Chavón in La Romana.
- *Claude Hervé-Bazin*

Simple sun-lit cabins in a picturesque Dominican village, like those seen all across the country.
T. Philiptchenko

Creole cabin in the shadow of a palm tree.
- Claude Hervé-Bazin

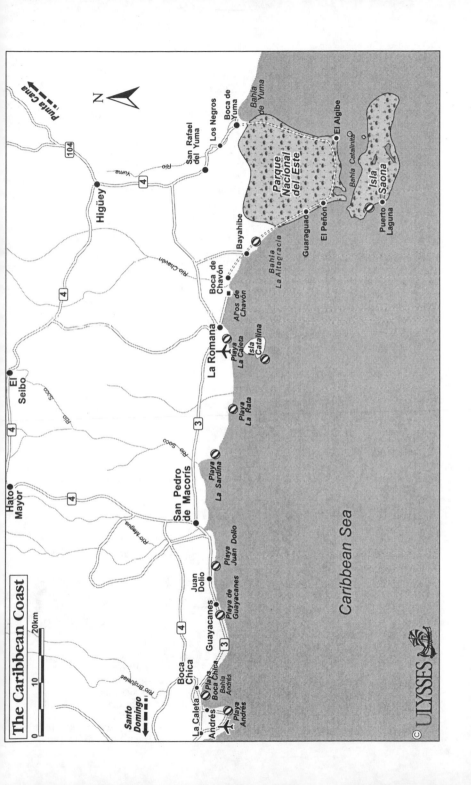

serves such a small village; in fact, the road was built mainly for the Club Dominicus hotel complex, not far from the village.

Boca de Yuma

To get to Boca de Yuma from La Romana, continue on the main road. Don't take the little road leading to Bayahibe. After about 30 kilometres, you'll come to an intersection; the road heading left goes to Higüey, the one to the right to Boca de Yuma, passing through the villages of San Rafael del Yuma and Los Negros along the way.

Practical Information

Boca Chica

In the downtown area of Boca Chica, essentially limited to the section of Calle Duarte between Juan Bautista Vicini and Caracoles, you will find a number of little shops and restaurants, some of which sell attractive local crafts. The Banco Popular will exchange American and Canadian money. The post office (*at the corner of Juan Bautista Vicini*) and the **Codetel** (*at the corner of*

Caracoles) are located on the same street.

Tourist Information Office
Boca Chica
Calle Juan Rafael
Plaza Comercial
☎ *523-5106*

San Pedro de Macorís

The highway crosses through the heart of San Pedro de Macorís. The town is centred around a park located at Avenida Independencia and Calle Gran Cabral. This area contains many shops and restaurants. The **Codetel** is on *Avenida Independencia*.

Tourist Information Office
San Pedro de Macorís
Avenida Circunvalación
Oficinas Gubernamentales
☎ *529-3967*

La Romana

The main streets in downtown La Romana are Calle Santo Rosa and Avenida Libertad. Several banks can be found near the park along Calle Duarte. You can catch a guagua out of the city on this last street. The **Codetel** is on *Avenida Padre Abreu, at the corner of Calle Santo Rosa*.

Exploring

Parque Nacional La Caleta

On the Autopista Las Américas, just before the road to the airport, you will come across Parque La Caleta. This green space along the highway consists essentially of a few trees, some benches and a beach often overrun with young Dominicans. Somewhat surprisingly, it is also home to the **Museo la Caleta**, a little house containing the remains of the Taino tombs discovered during construction of the airport. This museum makes for a short but interesting visit.

Created to protect a small part of this coastal region, The Parque Nacional La Caleta has an underwater area of 10km².

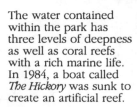

Moorish Idol Fish

The water contained within the park has three levels of deepness as well as coral reefs with a rich marine life. In 1984, a boat called *The Hickory* was sunk to create an artificial reef.

Some Dominican Heroes

When travelling though the Dominican Republic, you will soon notice that the names of streets and parks are much the same from town to town. Very often, they are named for historical figures who played a central part in the fight for Dominican or Cuban independence.

Juan Pablo Duarte (Santo Domingo 1813 – Caracas 1876) was the leader of a rebel group that drove Haitian invaders out of the Dominican Republic in 1844. Soon after the country regained its independence, a civil war broke out; Duarte was ousted from power and went into exile in Venezuela.

José Martí (Cuba 1853 – Cuba 1895) is considered the father of Cuban independence. His zeal to see the country throw off the yoke of colonialism landed him in exile. Martí nevertheless remained an influential figure throughout Latin America. He was also a respected author.

Máximo Gómez (Baní 1836 – Havana 1905) fought Haitian and Spanish attempts to take over the Dominican Republic. When Spain annexed the country again, he fled to Cuba, where he became the leader of the revolutionary forces. In 1895, he fought Spain once again, this time in a successful bid to liberate Cuba.

★★

Boca Chica

Boca Chica is a bustling town popular with both foreign and Dominican visitors. Its main street is lined with hotels, restaurants and boutiques ready to serve the needs of tourists. Indeed, the whole town is geared toward tourism, and suffers as a result from an aesthetic standpoint. However, the beach — a magnificent long stretch of white sand caressed by the turquoise waters of the Caribbean — is suffi-ciently breathtaking to make up for the jumbled architecture of the town, where little hotels are crowded in with big ones. The bay at Boca Chica is sheltered from rough seas by coral reefs making it great for swimming. In fact, this magnificent beach, located close to Santo Domingo, has been attracting residents of the capital for weekend visits for several decades.

Although Boca Chica is no paradise lost, and prostitution is unfortunately very evident, it is an enchanting spot for visitors in search of a beautiful beach where they can enjoy all sorts of exciting water sports. Many foreigners have opened small businesses here, and you may often find yourself in a hotel or restaurant run by Italians or Canadians.

Boca Chica is practically a suburb of Santo Domingo. Getting to the capital from Boca Chica to do some sightseeing is easy; the distance can be covered in about 30 minutes and the route is beautiful. Quieter than Santo Domingo, Boca Chica nevertheless offers all the same services and comforts. A popular option is to spend the day in Santo

The Caribbean Coast

Domingo and sleep in Boca Chica.

Take a ten-minute walk along the beach in Boca Chica and you will find yourself in the neighbouring village of **Andrés**, where several attractive marinas organize deep-sea fishing and scuba diving expeditions. Be careful walking along here at night, since it is not lit.

The waters at the **Boca Chica Bay** are very deep. In order to make the most of this calm spot, you can take a stroll along the two islands of the bay: **La Matica** and **Los Pinos**.

Juan Dolio

Juan Dolio is located about 40 kilometres east of Santo Domingo. A small shopping centre and several hotels line the highway near the beach. The road to the beach is indicated by commercial signs (rather than regular road signs), so watch carefully. All the local hotels lie on either side of the only road that passes through Juan Dolio.

The resort town of Juan Dolio is located on a long beach, which is quite beautiful, but less spectacular than some in other parts of the country. The village, once just a few fisherman's huts, has only recently sprung up in response to the growing tourist boom. To-

day, Juan Dolio lives by tourism alone. Each hotel occupies a vast property and most have direct access to the beach. Unfortunately, the lots between these hotels are often empty save for a few shrubs growing here and there. If you stay in one of these hotels, you will enjoy superb tropical gardens and a safe environment. Nevertheless, be careful if you explore the area, as there have been reports of thieves.

These hotel complexes offer a panoply of services. You may also notice the luxury apartment buildings of rich Dominicans. A few shops and restaurants have also opened for business. As a result of the still ongoing construction in Juan Dolio, the road is not in the best condition. Nonetheless, this is an attractive spot.

San Pedro de Macorís

By taking The Las Americas Highway eastbound, it is easy to get to San Pedro de Marcorís as this highway goes right across the city.

San Pedro de Macorís was founded near the end of the 19th century by Cubans fleeing the terrible war of independence that was ravaging their country. The immigrants, many of whom were wealthy, had extensive experi-

ence in sugar-cane farming. They began to cultivate the crop throughout the region, thus developing a sugar industry that boosted the local economy. Even today sugar-cane cultivation predominates in this region.

At the beginning of the 20th century, San Pedro de Macorís was a prosperous town with handsome buildings that are still possible to admire today. Among the most interesting is the **fire station** (*Calle Duarte, corner of Calle Rafael Deligne*), which was built back in 1907 in the republican style and which can be easily toured by asking the permission of one of the firemen on duty.

The Catholic Church of San Pedro Apostol (*Avenida Independencia, corner of Colón*), executed in an English Gothic style, is another fine example of an architectural accomplishment from this period and merits a visit. Although the downtown architecture incontestably possesses a certain charm, a visit to this typically Dominican city can not be considered complete until one ventures out beyond the bustling downtown core to stroll on the **Malecón**. This beautiful lane at the border of the ocean, has everything to make one forget the incessant movement of the city and lose oneself in the pulse of the of blue waves.

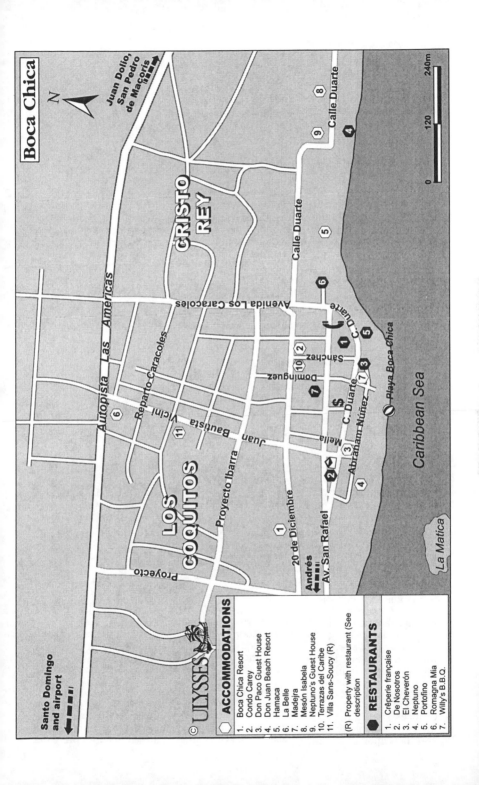

Boca Chica

Santo Domingo and airport

Juan Dolio, San Pedro de Macorís

N

LOS COQUITOS

CRISTO REY

Autopista Las Americas

Reparto Caracoles

Proyecto Ibarra

Juan Bautista Vicini

Proyecto

20 de Diciembre

Andrés

Av. San Rafael

Abraham Núñez

Mella

C. Duarte

Domínguez

Sánchez

Avenida Los Caracoles

Calle Duarte

Calle Duarte

C. Duarte

Playa Boca Chica

Caribbean Sea

La Matica

© ULYSSES

0   120   240m

ACCOMMODATIONS

1. Boca Chica Resort
2. Condo Carey
3. Don Paco Guest House
4. Don Juan Beach Resort
5. Hamaca
6. La Belle
7. Madejra
8. Mesón Isabela
9. Neptuno's Guest House
10. Terrazas del Caribe
11. Villa Sans-Soucy (R)

(R) Property with restaurant (See description

RESTAURANTS

1. Crêperie française
2. De Nosotros
3. El Cheverón
4. Neptuno
5. Portofino
6. Romagna Mia
7. Willy's B.B.Q.

From this vantage point, you can also see the animated port of San Pedro.

San Pedro is also known to baseball fans as the birthplace of some of that sport's biggest stars, most notably Sammy Sosa. In fact, San Pedro de Macorís has contributed more players per capita to the American professional leagues than any other town. If you like baseball, you might be interested to know that the town's team is a member of the Dominican league, and that games are regularly held here.

La Romana

When arriving from the northern part of the country (Seibo), enter La Romana on Calle Santa Rosa; from the west (Higüey, Bayahibe, San Pedro), turn onto Avenida Libertad from the Las Américas highway to reach downtown.

With a population of nearly 100,000, La Romana is the biggest urban centre in the southeastern part of the Dominican Republic. The economy of the city prospered for much of this century, fuelled by sugar production at the Puerto Rica Sugar Co. refinery. However, in the seventies, a drop in sugar prices brought a period of recession. To help the economy of the city and the region, the tourist industry was developed, since La Romana had the right resources — beautiful beaches on the Caribbean Sea — for promoters to undertake such a project. In order for the plan to be successful, hotels able to comfortably accommodate guests from all over the world had to be built. The first step was to renovate the Hotel La Romana, just outside the city. This was a success; the hotel became the gigantic

The Casa de Campo Complex, which now wel-

comes thousands of wealthy visitors a year. It has become the biggest holiday resort in the southeastern Dominican Republic.

While tourism has become very important to La Romana, the city retains a typically Dominican downtown area characterized by rows of simple wooden houses. There is also a much more opulent neighbourhood by the sea, just outside the centre of the city, where affluent Dominicans have built luxurious houses.

The region is flat and is dotted with palm trees, sugar-cane fields and scrub growth. Excursions inland on the **Río Chavón** are a good way to see the countryside up close. The La Romana region also includes several surprises; for example, just

Altos de Chavón

off the coast lies **Isla Catalina ★**, with its cache of idyllic beaches. **Altos de Chavón** (*free admission; Avenida Libertad*), located to the east of La Romana, is a surprisingly beautiful reconstruction of a late 14th century Italian village. It was built by ambitious entrepreneurs

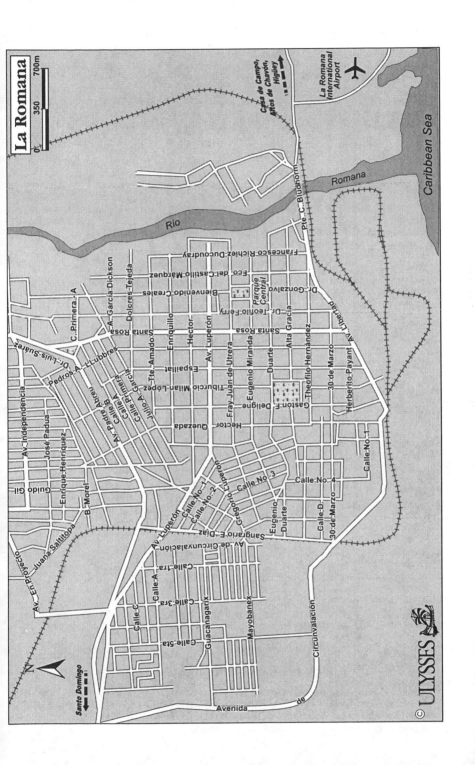

La Romana

0 350 700m

N

Santo Domingo

Caribbean Sea

Rio Romana

Casa de Campo, Altos de Chavón, Higüey

La Romana International Airport

Pte. C. Blandborn

Francesco Richiez-Ducoudray
Fco. del Castillo-Márquez
Bienvenido-Creales
Dr.-Teófilo-Ferry
Parque Central
Dr.-Gonzalvo
A.-García-Dickson
Dolores-Tejeda
Santa Rosa
Héctor
Enriquillo
Tte.-Amado
Av.-Luperón
Santa Rosa
Alta Gracia
Duarte
Theófilo-Hernández
Av.-Libertad
30-de-Marzo
Herberito-Payant
Calle-No.-1
Gastón-F.-Deligne
Eugenio Miranda
Fray-Juan-de-Utrera
Tiburcio Milán-López
Espaillat
Fte.-Primera-A
C.-Primera-A
Dr.-Luis-Suárez
Pedros-A.-L'ubbres
Julio-A.-García
Calle-Primera
Calle-A
Calle-B
Av.-Padre-Abreu
Av.-Independencia
José-Padua
Enrique-Henríquez
B.-Moreí
Guido Gil
Juana-Saltitopa
Av.-En-Proyecto
Héctor-Quezada
Calle-No.-3
Calle-No.-2
Calle-No.-1
Av.-Luperón
Gregorio-Luperón
Sangrario-E.-Díaz
Av.-de-Circunvalación
Eugenio Duarte
Calle-D
30-de-Marzo
Calle-No.-4
Calle-1ra.
Calle-A
Calle-3ra.
Calle-C
Guacanagarix
Mayobanex
Calle-5ta.
Avenida de Circunvalación

© ULYSSES

from Casa de Campo in order to add a major tourist attraction to the region. This replica is faithful in many ways to the original village, due to an incredible attention to detail. Built entirely of stone, Altos de Chavón includes a fountain, a small museum of pre-Hispanic art, period houses containing several shops and restaurants, a small church and an amphitheatre. Because of its size, the amphitheatre is the most impressive structure in the village; renowned artists occasionally play here. Built on a hill overlooking the sea, the village also has a terrace with a spectacular view of the region. To really get a feel for Altos de Chavón, also known as the "artist's village", take the time to explore its narrow streets, each more charming than the last. Altos de Chavón is part of the Casa de Campo hotel complex. Small buses shuttle hotel guests between the hotel and the village. As you enter the village you will be met by people offering to act as your guide, for a fee of course. Keep in mind, however, that the narrow streets of the village are easy to explore on your own.

To build the section of road heading east, high cliffs had to be dug out. On the way to Bayahibe, motorists now pass through an impressive other-worldly canyon known as **The Boca de Chavón Canyon**.

Bayahibe

The road from La Romana to Bayahibe is in relatively good shape, considering that it leads to a simple small isolated village. It passes through a landscape of shrubs and undergrowth, with not a soul in sight for several kilometres before reaching Bayahibe.

Bayahibe is a charming little fishing village made up of modest wooden houses. Everything seems to depend on the sea here, and while there are more and more businesses dedicated to tourism, including a few hotels in the centre of the village, nothing has marred the authenticity of the setting. The main attraction is a superb fine-sand beach washed by the Caribbean Sea with colourful little boats dotting the horizon. This is a peaceful, attractive place far from big towns and major tourist developments.

A large-scale hotel complex, the Club Dominicus, has been built on a beach neighbouring Bayahibe. This huge, luxurious place, which already attracts a lot of visitors, never seems to stop growing, surrounding construction sites indicate that it is to be substantially enlarged.

Excursions to **Isla Saona** ★ (see p108) and **Isla Catalina** ★ (see p108) are organized from Bayahibe. Both islands have magnificent white-sand beaches and palm trees. **Isla Saona** has only a small number of residents divided between two hamlets. Life on the island is as peaceful as can be when it is not overrun by visitors. These quiet periods are becoming rare as more and more people discover the charms of this lush island. The Parque Nacional Del Este, which also includes the southeastern point of the Dominican Republic was created to protect. Isla Saona's exceptional flora and fauna, featuring a wide variety of birds

Pelican

The Manatee

The manatee is a mammal found along the Dominican coast. It is a sirenian species like the dugong. These two marine mammals are found in various places in the world, but because they are cold-blooded, the manatee and the dugong life in warm waters. Two kinds of manatees live in the Americas: the Amazon manatee (*Trichechus inunguis*), in the Amazon and Orinoco rivers in South America, and the Florida manatee (*Trichechus manatees*), in the Gulf of Mexico and the Caribbean Sea. In the Dominican Republic the manatee makes its home in the southeastern part of the island, particularly in the Parque Nacional del Este (see p 58). The third kind of manatee is the African manatee (*Trichechus Senegalensis*). The dugong looks like the manatee and can be found in Asia, on the coast of East Africa and in Australia.

Despite their considerable size, measuring as much as 2.5 to 3 metres in length and weighing up to 400 kilograms, few of us ever have the opportunity to see one of these harmless creatures. They live in shallow water, never more than 12 metres deep, usually at the mouth of a river or the shoreline. This preference puts the species' survival at risk as shallow waters are particularly susceptible to pollution from human refuse. In addition, manatees often fall victim to motorboat propellers.

Herbivorous, the manatee eats mostly floating vegetation and occasionally nibbles on underwater plants. The poor nourishment value of this food forces it to consume large quantities and to spend most of its time eating. This animal lives in groups and the females and their babies have a strong bond. The female has only one offspring every two years because it nurtures the young for two years following its birth. She nurses her young for about three months with her teats which like elephants are situated under her axilla (forelimb or flipper). After three months the baby begins to find food for itself. It reaches adulthood between four and six years.

Parque Nacional del Este

The Parque Nacional del Este protects the southeastern peninsula of the Dominican Republic. It encompasses most of the peninsula as well as Isla Saona, located at the southeastern extremity of the country. This immense peninsula of about 300 square kilometres emerged from the water about one million years ago, receiving its current form from the ancient movements of the ocean. Consisting of very porous marine rock, the terrain has no rivers or streams. Nonetheless, a wealth of plant life has managed to spring forth from this base: the coastal forest being wet and tropical;

the inland forest giving rise to a drier, tropical vegetation. Some of the trees that bloom in the park are: the Dominican mahogany tree, the common palm tree, the mesquite tree and the dune grape tree.

rate the walls of several caves, opening the doors to exploration of the Amerindian culture that initially occupied the region.

The park is accessible from the coastal road that connects Bayahibe and Boca del Yuma.

Manatee

subtropical forest covers a large portion of the territory and is home to a multitude of bird species. The park is also a stop along the migration path of some birds. If you're lucky, you'll spot some manatees along the coast; these large aquatic mammals usually live at the mouths of rivers. Unfortunately, the manatee population has dropped considerably and the animal is quite rare.

Work is underway to improve access to the park (the peninsula region); it is unknown when the project will be completed.

Renowned for its fauna, the park is home to over 112 species of birds, 8 of which are exclusive to its borders. If one is equipped with a small dose of patience and a good pair of binoculars, the colours and sounds of the brown pelican, the frigate bird, the red-footed gannet and the Dominican parrot are all there for the taking. A larger dose of patience and a little bit of luck may unveil two rarely-seen water mammals that inhabit the coastline: the manatee and the large-nosed dolphin. Lizards, marine turtles and the rhinoceros iguana are some of the reptiles that one may see during an excursion on the magnificent wild beaches of the coastline.

On the eastern side of the park, ancient Tainoan pictograms and petroglyphs deco-

The entrances to the park are a few kilometres south of Bayahibe (near Guaraguao), and south of Boca de Yuma. Before heading off, be reminded that the road is not much more than a narrow, sandy trail, only accessible with an all-terrain vehicle. There are no villages or gas stations along the road so make sure you fill your tank beforehand. If your vehicle gets stuck, use a palm leaf to dig it out of the sand.

The park's coastline is dotted with magnificent wild beaches; the isolated beach at **Puerto Laguna**, for example, will make you feel like you are the only person on earth.

Besides these oases of white sand, the peninsula and island feature a wealth of tropical plant and animal life. A

Covering almost 100 square kilometres, **Isla Saona** ★★, is a haven of tranquillity. The only human inhabitants of this vast palm grove are a few families of fishermen; in the high season, however the island's beaches come under siege. To reach Isla Saona, you can take part in the excursion from Bayahibe (1,500 pesos for 10 people).

These are organized at restaurants along the beach, in particular the La Bahia restaurant. Theoretically, visitors require a permit to enter a Dominican park (*Santo Domingo*, ☎221-5340), but surveillance is virtually nonexistent. The companies that organize excursions to Isla Saona usually arrange for permits.

San Rafael de Yuma

This small village dating back to the 16th century and composed of quaint Creole cabins, is the home of the **Casa de Juan Ponce de León** (*from the centre of the village, go east for about one kilometre*), named after the conquistador Juan Ponce de Leon who colonized Puerto Rico and was made its governor in 1509. Leon resided in this stone house for some time. It was completely refurbished in 1972 in order to accurately reproduce the style of housing that was in fashion in the 16th century. Furniture and weapons dating from this time period are also on display.

Boca de Yuma

The village of Boca de Yuma sits atop steep cliffs that plunge into the Caribbean at the mouth of The Boca de Yuma River. The cliffs offer a fascinating view of the waves crashing against the rocks below. The area is rich in aquatic bird life, attracting interesting species such as the pelican. The town is perhaps best known for the **natural pools** the ocean has formed in the cliffs along the shore. There is a small half-moon shaped beach at the mouth of the river, but the most impressive stretch of sand is the one circled by cliffs. A hole in the rock wall allows the water to enter this spectacular pool.

There is an underground cave located about 500 metres away from the natural pool

The village of Boca de Yuma does not have a beach, but there is a magnificent stretch of fine sand on the other side of the Yuma River which can be easily reached with a small fishing boat. Because it is located somewhat off the beaten path, this beach is not frequented by a lot of tourists, leaving it virtually open for those who seek a more intimate place to enjoy the sun.

Outdoor Activities

Swimming

La Caleta

The craze for the minuscule beach at **La Caleta** is quite strange indeed. The sea rushes into a tiny bay formed by the coastal cliffs, and hordes of young people come here to go swimming. Space is so limited that they appear to be swimming on top of each other.

Boca Chica

The Boca Chica Beach ★★ is magnificent: large coral reefs have developed offshore, forming a natural breakwater; as a result, the waters are always calm. Swimmers must venture out several metres before the shallow waters of Boca Chica bay drop off to any considerable depth, creating a natural swimming pool. The sea holds its share of treasures as well: scuba divers and snorkellers can observe the multitude of tropical fish that gravitate around the coral reefs.

In an effort to beautify the area, the countless wooden stalls that used to line the beach have been torn down. However, crowds of vendors now roam the beach hawking anything and everything, often very aggressively. If you aren't interested, avert your gaze from the merchandise and make your refusal clear. Despite this inconvenience, which is all too common in touristy areas, the beach is very pleasant, since much care is taken to maintain it; it is cleaned every day. Beach-goers can thus enjoy the best this natural site has to offer.

Following the shoreline towards Andrès, you'll come upon another portion of the **beach ★**, which is literally over-run on Sundays by crowds of Dominicans relaxing with friends and family. This is the peak time, and finding an empty spot is no picnic, not to mention trying to spread out a towel. This part of the beach is not bordered by the village, but that doesn't stop vendors from coming here. Though the beach is pleasant, it is not as nice as the one near the centre of town.

Juan Dolio

The long **Juan Dolio Beach ★** is trimmed by a beautiful ribbon of sand, which is unfortunately not as fine as at Boca Chica, but is much less crowded. Palm trees offer welcome shade from the noonday sun and frame the beach nicely. Furthermore, there are none of those shabby wooden stalls displaying all sorts of merchandise, which all too often cheapen touristy beaches. Instead, there are a few inconspicuous water-sports centres.

La Romana

The very private grounds of the Casa de Campo include a magnificent beach, which is only accessible to guests of the complex. Just outside of town is another beach, **Caleton**,

which is pretty average.

Isla Saona

The island, protected as part of Parque Nacional del Este, is ringed by a magnificent strip of golden sand and the warm, shimmering waters of the Caribbean Sea. The **beach ★★** is so lovely that many hotel complexes arrange daytrips to it, arousing concern about the area's ecological equilibrium. For this reason, certain precautions aimed at protecting this remarkable natural site should be taken.

Boca de Yuma

Boca de Yuma has no beach all to itself. However, on the other side of the river, a short distance from the village, there is a lovely sandy beach where you can relax or go for a swim. It is easy to get

there, as the local fishermen will take you across the river for a few pesos.

Isla Catalina

Less popular than neighbouring Isla Saona, lush **Isla Catalina ★** is no less enchanting. It boasts superb white-sand beaches, perfect for a relaxing swim and catching some rays. More and more people are making their way here, as the island is an interesting dive site. Boats bring visitors from Bayahibe (*1,300 pesos for 10 people*).

Bayahibe

A long, tree-studded crescent of soft sand at the border of a peaceful village lined with trees are the essential elements of this magnificent **beach ★**, one of the most beautiful in the region. This beach is still wild and not as well-maintained as those that belong to the neighbouring tourist villages, but it has its own unique charm. The section of beach right next to the Club Dominicus is better maintained and more frequented.

Parque Nacional Del Este

By following the road along the water through the Parque Nacional Del Este (assuming your vehicle does not get stuck), you'll discover a series of unspoiled, isolated little beaches great for sunning or swimming. Be careful though: these beaches are very remote, and you will be far from help if problems arise.

Scuba Diving and Snorkelling

Boca Chica

The coral reefs offshore in Bahía de Boca Chica make this an ideal spot to observe underwater life, and several diving excursions are available.

Don Juan
☎ *523-4511*
Don Juan rents snorkelling equipment for about *$6 US* per hour. Its diving centre, Treasure Divers, organizes excursions and diving courses. Beginners can try a day of lessons and a dive for *$75 US*.

The Boca Chica Resort
☎ *223-0622*

This resort offers a day-long (*10am to 5pm*) package deal that includes access to the pool, tennis courts,

snorkelling equipment and a windsurfer for *300 pesos*.

Juan Dolio

The beach at Juan Dolio is another good diving site with an abundance of underwater attractions. The diving centre at the entrance to Juan Dolio organizes excursions, and many of the larger hotels also have snorkelling and scuba diving equipment on hand. Those wishing to go scuba diving can head to the **REEF Marena Beach Resort** (see p113), which has a diving centre.

Bayahibe

Bayahibe also has a diving centre.

Casa Daniel
☎ *223-0622*
Here excurssions are offered for both experienced and novice divers.

Sailing and Windsurfing

Boca Chica

The Don Juan Hotel in Boca Chica rents windsurfers for *$12 US* an hour. The gentle waters in the bay off Boca Chica are perfect for novice wind-surfers. Small sailboats are available from the same hotel.

The Boca Chica Resort
☎ *223-0622*
also rents out windsurfers.

Deep-Sea Fishing

Boca Chica

Several species of fish, including sea-bream, swordfish and some times barracuda, might be your catch of the day after partaking in one of the deep-sea fishing excursions offered by the **Hamaca** and **Don Juan** hotels. While prices vary depending on the length of the trip, you can expect to pay about *$50 US* per person.

Cruises

Bayahibe

Cruises to Isla Saona and Isla Catalina are organized and depart from Bayahibe.

Madrugadora Tours
☎ *556-5055*
Isla Saona
$100 for 10 people
Isla Catalina
$90 for 10 people

Bicycling

Boca Chica

For those looking to tour around the vicinity of Boca Chica the following locations offer bike rentals:

The Hotel Hamaca
$8 US per day

Alpha 3000
$5 US per day

Motorcycling

Boca Chica

To explore the area beyond the reaches of a bicycle, consider renting a motorcycle (but watch out for dangerous drivers). Motorcycles can be rented at:

Alpha 3000
Calle Pimera
☎ *523-6059*
$22 US a day for a scooter and $35 US a day for a motorcycle.

Harley Davidsons are also available for real enthusiasts.

Juan Dolio

Motorcycles can also be rented in Juan Dolio:

Alpha 3000
$35 US per day

Bayahibe

In Bayahibe, at the centre of town, **Tom M.** rents motorcycles.

Golf

Boca Chica

A nine-hole golf course, has been set out 5 kilometres west of Boca Chica. Several hotels in Boca Chica offer package deals that include greens fees.

San Andres Country Club
☎ *545-1278*
150 pesos per round and 150 pesos for clubs.

La Romana

The Casa de Campo Hotel in La Romana possesses not one, but four golf courses which number among the most beautiful in the Caribbean. They are spread out along the Caribbean coastline enabling golfers to enjoy some stunning views.

The Casa de Campo Hotel
☎ *523-3187*

Horseback Riding

Bayahibe

The surroundings of Bayahibe can be explored on horseback. Casa Daniel provides well-cared-for horses for pleasant tours of the area.

Casa Daniel
☎ *223-0622*

Accommodations

All sorts of accommodations, from modest hotels to the grand resort complexes, dot the southeastern coast. Since these places are always located near one of the many beautiful sandy beaches along this coast, visitors have many options to choose from.

Boca Chica

All of the hotels in Boca Chica have been built near the centre of town. Some lie on pretty streets in quiet neighbourhoods, while others are right by the water downtown. Boca Chica definitely has the largest choice of accommodations in the region, and it doesn't take long to find what you are looking for.

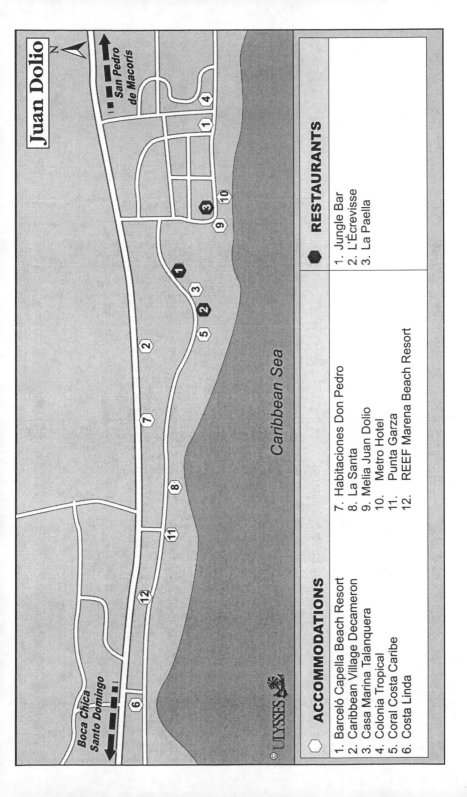

Juan Dolio

N

Boca Chica
Santo Domingo

San Pedro de Macoris

Caribbean Sea

© ULYSSES

ACCOMMODATIONS

1. Barceló Capella Beach Resort
2. Caribbean Village Decameron
3. Casa Marina Talanquera
4. Colonia Tropical
5. Coral Costa Caribe
6. Costa Linda

7. Habitaciones Don Pedro
8. La Santa
9. Melia Juan Dolio
10. Metro Hotel
11. Punta Garza
12. REEF Marena Beach Resort

RESTAURANTS

1. Jungle Bar
2. L'Écrevisse
3. La Paella

The Don Paco Guest House
$25, ⊗
☎ *523-4816*
Located in the heart of the city, this hotel offers good value for the money. The rooms are rather spartan in their decor, but they are clean and come with a friendly welcome.

The Apartment-Hotel Madejra
$50, K
☎ *523-4434*
↹ *523-4532*
Not far from the beach, the Hotel-Apartment Madejra offers modest but comfortable rooms equipped with kitchenettes.

🦎 Meson Isabela
$38/$48, ⊗, ≈, *K*
Calle Duarte, behind the Hamaca Hotel
☎ *523-4224*
↹ *523-4532*
Some inns make you want to return to a particular village. This is certainly the case with the Meson Isabela, where a Dominican and a Québecer are your friendly hosts. This isn't the place for late night carousing; instead, guests enjoy a magnificent, peaceful garden, a pool rarely used by more than two swimmers at a time, and rooms in well-maintained buildings. The owners can also help familiarize you with the country. Finally, for those wishing to avoid the hustle and bustle of the town, there is private access to the beach. Golf packages and rooms with equipped kitchen-

ettes are also available here.

Villa Sans-Soucy
$45,1/2 b, ≡, ≈, ℜ
48 Calle Juan Bautista Vicini
☎ *1-800-463-0097*
☎ *523-4461*
This well-maintained property is set back from the street for added peace and quiet. The pleasant rooms open onto a inner courtyard with a pool.

La Belle
$40, ≈,
9 Juan Bautista Vicini
☎ *523-5959*
↹ *523-5077*
This property is located by the side of the highway on the way into the village, but manages to offer a relatively peaceful atmosphere. Though hardly a tropical paradise, this hotel is new and well maintained. Its small, clean rooms are equipped with balconies. Perfectly acceptable for the price.

Neptuno's Guest House
$60, ≈, *K*
12 Duarte
☎ *523-6534*
↹ *523-4251*
For many people, the name "Neptuno" refers to one of the finest restaurants (see p 118) in Boca Chica. The restaurant now operates a small inn that is located in the residential part of town across from the Hamaca Hotel. A former Dominican home that has been enlarged to an establishment spread out on a few level , it

has comfortable rooms, each of which is equipped with a kitchenette. The place is well kept and inviting, but unfortunately has no garden.

Terrazas del Caribe
$45, ≈, ⊗, *K*
7 Calle Sanchez
☎ *523-4488*
↹ *523-4444*
The green balcony of the Terrazas del Caribe is easy to spot behind the downtown area. The buildings stand next to an uninteresting empty lot, but the rooms, equipped with kitchenettes, are perfectly adequate.

The Condo Carey
$50, ≡, *K*
8 Calle Francisco del Rosario Sánchez
☎ *523-5436*
↹ *523-5435*
Set back from the beach, The Condo Carey has large, relatively comfortable rooms, each with a private bath, a kitchenette and a dining nook.

The Don Juan Beach Resort
$190 all-inclusive
≡, ≈, ℜ
Abraham Nunez
☎ *523-4511*
↹ *523-6422*
This property consists of several buildings on a large piece of property right on the beach. The owners have made the most of the available space. The restaurant was recently expanded, and there are two gardens giving onto the beach, one of which looks a little neglected. The place is quite com-

fortable and offers easy access to the sea. Some rooms afford a view of the shimmering waves. Finally, there is a water sports centre right on the property, enabling guests to enjoy a variety of activities.

The Hamaca
$250, all-inclusive
≡, ≈, ℜ, ♠
Calle Duarte
☎ *523-4611*
⇰ *566-2354*

In order to be close to the sea, The Hamaca had to build right over the main road. The back of this large pink building, at first sight hardly inviting, is easily spotted from downtown, and you have to drive around it to get to the other side of Boca Chica. The lobby, restaurants and guest rooms, are all tastefully decorated. There is also a splendid beach nearby. The Hamaca has expanded recently, and now extends to the other side of the street. The changes have resulted in the creation of a well-balanced arrangement that unites the pool, tennis courts, and guest rooms under one roof.

The Boca Chica Resort
$150 all-inclusive
≡, ≈, ℜ
20 Calle Juan Bautista Vicini
☎ *567-9238*
⇰ *686-6741*

This large hotel complex stands on a vast piece of property, well protected from intruders. Although the hotel is a short distance from the sea, the range of

services offered here is extensive and makes up for this inconvenience. The location, furthermore, ensures a relaxing, peaceful stay. Some of the rooms could be better kept up, and the staff, while ever-courteous, is not always friendly. Golf packages are available.

Juan Dolio

This tourist village consists essentially of large, luxurious hotel complexes. Most guests reserve ahead of time, and opt for an all-inclusive package. Because smaller hotels have sprung up next to the larger complexes, you can easily find accommodations in Juan Dolio without paying a fortune.

The Habitaciones Don Pedro
$16
50 Calle Marina
☎ *526-2147*

The Habitaciones Don Pedro is one of these low-budget hotels offering clean and decent rooms without the flashy amenities of some of the bigger hotels.

La Santa
$40, ≈, ≡, ℜ
☎ *526-1011*
⇰ *526-1706*

This is the only small inn in Juan Dolio. It is a charming, quiet place with pretty rooms and a lovely garden with flowering shrubs and plants. A good choice

for those who prefer a pleasant inn to a large, often impersonal hotel complex.

Punta Garza
$ 100 all-inclusive
≈, ≡, ℜ
☎ *687-6686*
⇰ *526-3814*

A lovely complex looking out onto the sea, The Punta Garza has a few pretty villas, as well as several pink buildings adorned with balconies with white friezes. These take up the larger part of the garden, but the property has been carefully landscaped so that lovely flowering plants grow all over, lending the place a remarkably calm atmosphere. The pool and restaurant are located on the part of the property facing the sea, thus offering a magnificent view of the waves.

The Marena Beach Resort
$100 all-inclusive
≈, ≡, ℜ
☎ *526-2121*
⇰ *526-1213*

This property is divided into two sections. The first is a big white building containing the reception desk and the guestrooms; the other, across the street, by the sea, consists of several outbuildings scattered across a pleasant garden. The outbuildings definitely offer a more beautiful setting, but all the rooms are decorated with pretty wood furniture.

The Caribbean Coast

Colonia Tropical
$75, ≈, ≡, ℜ
☎ 526-1660
≈ 526-2538
Although the Colonia Tropical does not have the benefit of being at the water's edge, it is sure to please those who prefer more intimate hotels as it is stands within a peaceful setting far from all the hustle and bustle of the city. The rooms, brightened up with pretty tropical colours, are divided up among several Spanish-style buildings laid out around a pretty cobblestoned courtyard with a pool in it.

The Metro Hotel
$200, ≡, ≈, ℜ
Juan Dolio
☎ 526-2811
≈ 526-1808
The Metro Hotel stands right on the beach, and stretches along the sea. As a result, many of its rooms profit from a splendid view. On first impression, the building seems less handsome than the more recently built hotels nearby that benefit from attractive gardens, but the rooms are pleasant, and the back of the hotel, opening onto the beach, is certainly the envy of the neighbours.

The Melia Juan Dolio
$200 all-inclusive
≈, ≡, ℜ, △
☎ 526-1521
≈ 526-2184
The Melia Juan Dolio occupies a long, ochre-coloured building, that is five storeys high and stretches along the azur borders of the ocean in such a way as to ensure that a maximum of the rooms have a view onto the seascape. What's more, each room is equipped with a balcony, allowing guests to take full advantage of the elements. The golden ribbon of the beach is the place of preference, of course, and it includes a small, tropical garden.

Caribbean Village De Cameron
$200 all-inclusive
≡, ≈, ℜ, ☺
Juan Dolio
☎ 526-2009
This gigantic hotel complex sits on a vast terrain in the centre of town. It is almost a world unto itself, complete with exercise rooms, a casino, and a selection of bars and restaurants to satisfy any and all its guests needs.

Part of the garden is taken up by a huge swimming pool, where nonstop music creates a festive atmosphere for fun-seekers. The rooms are distributed among eight different buildings, all of which surround a garden. Some have a beautiful view onto the flowers below, while others, have the luxury of an ocean-view. All rooms offer a high standard of comfort.

Barcelo Capella Beach Resort
$200 all-inclusive
≈, ≡, ℜ
☎ 526-1080
≈ 526-1088
This hotel complex stretches over a vast and beautiful garden. In addition to this wonderful, verdant setting, the hotel offers a number of amenities including a large swimming pool.

Coral Costa Caribe
$240 all-inclusive
≡, ≈, ℜ, ♠
☎ 526-2244
≈ 526-3141
Juan Dolio is basically a succession of large hotel complexes each trying to outdo the other by offering a extensive array of services. There is one complex, however, that distinguishes itself from the others by the beauty of its design. The Coral Costa Caribe consists of several, stunning salmon-coloured buildings on vast grounds, arranged in such a way to allow a good number of the rooms to look out onto

most impressive of these is the main building, consisting of rooms whose mezzanines open out onto the hall. Offering excellent comfort and an incredible range of sports activities,this is definitely an address to keep in mind when in the village.

The Casa Marina Talanquera
$130 all inclusive
≡, ≈, ℜ, ☺
☎ *526-1511*
The Casa Marina Talanquera is a handsome ensemble of cottages of various styles, arranged in a free-spirited manner around the site. Whether you like a sojourn in a small room of moderate comfort or prefer the more luxurious setting of an apartment, a diverse range of options are available.

The charm of this motley arrangement is further enhanced by a splendid garden which enthrones an astonishingly attractive pool composed of different levels of water that are linked together by wooden bridges. The combination of all of these elements gives the spot the allure of a quaint village.

The Costa Linda
≡, ≈, ℜ;
☎ *526-3909*
This hotel has long buildings running along the sea, but not quite on the beach. Although the main attraction is a lovely flowering garden

where guests can stroll about, the carefully chosen decor adds to the charm of this hotel. In the summer of 1999, the hotel was ravaged by the passage of Hurricaine George and has not yet been renovated.

San Pedro de Macorís

San Pedro has few luxurious hotels. Though there are some simple inexpensive places, we suggest staying in Boca Chica, where you'll have a wider choice, or in Bayahibe, where the hotels have more charm.

Howard Johnson
$55
Calle Gaston Deligne
☎ *529-2100*
☎ *529-9239*
If you've yet to find a room and the night is rapidly approaching, there is always the Howard Johnson. Here you can rely on receiving a decent standard of lodging.

La Romana

La Romana offers two very different types of accommodations: low-budget, low-comfort hotels and a gigantic hotel complex that is definitely the most luxurious on the island, Casa de Campo.

The Tío Tom Hotel
$35
≡, ≈, ℜ
on the highway to San Pedro de Macorís, at the edge of La Romana
☎ *556-6211*
≈ *556-6201*
The Tio Tom Hotel is located on the highway on the outskirts of town. The surroundings are not particularly interesting but the rooms are functional, if not the most comfortable. Next door is the Adamaney Hotel, offering a similar level of comfort. Besides these two, there are few budget hotels in the city.

Casa de Campo
$230 all-inclusive
≡, ⊗, ≈, ℜ
☎ *523-3333*
≈ *523-8548*
www.casadcampo.com
Without a shadow of a doubt, The Casa de Campo Hotel Complex is among the most luxurious and seductive on the island. It stretches across a gigantic site of 2800 hectares of immaculately kept grounds upon which a series of villas have been erected. Some of these are equipped guestrooms, others apartments, but all are decorated with gorgeous wood furniture, tile floors, impeccable bathrooms, and large windows with shutters - all of which open onto a balcony. Whether you choose a simple guestroom or an apartment, the superior comfort to be experienced here carry the promise of a memorable holiday.

Of course, the site does not limit itself to accommodation, for it includes, among other things, four magnificent golf courses, an equitation centre, tennis courts, and a superb beach where one can participate in a wide array of water sports.

Careful attention has been paid to a number of other details to ensure that vacationers are fully satisfied; the presence of delectable restaurants, and a shuttle service are just a couple worthy of mention. To top it all off, there is a private airport located right on-site equipped to receive private jets and certain flights coming from the United States.

Bayahibe

This tiny hamlet hidden on the shores of the Caribbean has a few hotels to satisfy the needs of the still small numbers of visitors who come here.

Villa Bayahibe
$15, ⊗
The very basics (no electricity or hot water) in non-luxurious but nonetheless pleasant rooms are offered at the Villa Bayahibe, a green and white building in the centre of town.

Trip Town Bungalow
$15, ⊗
This property, located in the centre of town next to the Villa Bayahibe, offers rooms in modest pink and white cottages, which are more than adequate for those looking for budget accommodation. The rooms are well maintained, and the beach is just a few steps away.

Club Dominicus Beach
$200 all-inclusive
≡, ≈, ℜ
☎ 686-5658
✉ 687-8583
Located on a beach next to Bayahibe, you will not want to miss these buildings made from marine stone, which give this spot its unique style.

While touring around this site, you will have ample opportunity to admire some of the colourful and well-tended gardens that artfully border the series of cute, palm-thatched cabins housing the comfortable rooms that will serve as your shelter. A stroll will undoubtedly lead you to the pool, the bar, and the theatre all of which are found on the grounds of this property. Finally, extending out along the very edge of the site, is the beach, a long crescent of gentle sand, bordered by the azur waves of the Caribbean Ocean.

Ventana Gran Dominicus
$150 all inclusive
≈, ≡, ℜ
☎ 221-6767
✉ 221-5894
Close by looms a newly-built complex, The Ventana Gran Dominicus where coloured buildings of blue, yellow, and orange give the spot the allure of a hacienda. The hall decorated with a towering fountain may seem pretentious to some, but the general atmosphere of the site is warm and peaceful. The buildings housing the rooms are a bit close to each another, but they still provide a good level of comfort and are equipped with pleasant patios.

Boca de Yuma

The Club El 28
$18 or $35 fb
≈, ⊗
☎ 476-8660
The Club El 28 is one of those small, family hotels that don't have luxurious facilities but offer warm hospitality, a peaceful setting and well-kept rooms, which are basic but perfectly acceptable for the price. Packages including three delicious meals at the hotel restaurant are available—an excellent option for those looking to spend a few days of peace and quiet without breaking their budget.

The Hotel Saina
$ 35
☎ *223-0681*
If you'd rather stay in a hotel that's not quite as hospitable but offers a more majestic setting, head to the Hotel Saina, which stands atop a cliff alongside the natural pool in Boca de Yuma, offering up this impressive natural site, as well as the Caribbean. At the moment of our passage through town this hotel was in the process of being renovated.

Restaurants

Boca Chica

Many food stalls downtown sell grilled and breaded fish. One of the best spots for chicken is the stall next to the Boca Chica Gift Shop. While De Nosotros, across from the central park, at the corner of Calles Juan Bautista Vicini and Duarte, sells delicious empanadas. As well, the restaurant at the corner of Calle Abraham Nuñez and Juan Bautista Vicini serves good breakfasts.

Villa Sans-Soucy
$
Calle Juan Bautista Vicini

The menu at the Villa Sans-Soucy lists simple but delicious Québec dishes like roast chicken and hot chicken sandwiches. There's nothing refined about these meals, but they are always good and the portions are generous. Courteous service.

El Cheveron
$
Calle Duarte

This little restaurant has a good location near the beach and an attractive terrace looking out onto the street. The menu features deliciously prepared Dominican specialities from a menu based mainly on fish and seafood. This is a good and inexpensive place to sample the local cuisine. The restaurant also serves pizza and pasta dishes.

Creperia Française
$-$$
Calle Duarte

If you're overtaken with a sudden craving, few things will satisfy you more than the Creperia française, a charming little restaurant embellished with a simple palm-thatched roof. If you have a fancy for chocolate-filled or butter croissants a breakfast here will surely delight your taste-buds. For lunch, a dazzling array of crêpes and pancakes steal the spotlight on the menu.

Portofino
$$
Calle Duarte

For good Italian food, try the lively Portofino, located by the water. The menu lists a wide variety of tasty pasta and meat dishes. Breakfast is also served.

Willy's B.B.Q
$$

Countless signs lead the way to Willy's B.B.Q. , located behind the main street. The succulent ribs cooked over a wood fire alone are reason enough to go. The setting is pleasant as well, featuring a garden filled with bird cages, where all sorts of birds flutter about. The cordial service and the cheery ambiance round it all off, making for a most satisfying evening.

Romagna Mia
$$
Calle Duarte
At the very end of Calle Duarte, steps away from the Hamaca, you'll find an Italian restaurant

Caribbean Coast

called Romagna Mia. The first thing that will catch your attention is the ice cream counter, but don't just think about indulging your sweet tooth, as the restaurant offers a good daily selection of Italian specialties that are invariably delicious.

Neptuno
$$$
Calle Juan Bautista Vicini
at the corner of Calle 20 de Diciembre

Neptuno is without a doubt the best place in town for fish and seafood. Everything from traditional Dominican food to paella is prepared with great flair and served on a beautiful seaside terrace. At the quay, a small pirate ship is docked, enticing us to climb aboard for a meal. Because this restaurant has been very successful in attracting clientele, it is advisable to reserve in advance if one wants a table that looks out over the water. Something worth noting: Le Neptuno is a meeting place for Dominican and international stars.

Juan Dolio

The Jungle Bar
$-$$
about 50 metres from Casa Marina

For those of you that are plant-lovers there is a welcoming restaurant, The Jungle Bar which is nested in the midst of an Epicurean garden. Plants and bushes of all kinds grow around tables that are neatly arrayed with parasols, creating a pleasant and relaxing atmosphere for enjoying the specialty of the house: grilled brochettes.

La Paella
$-$$

Across from The Metro Hotel stands a charming little restaurant La Paella, perfect if you feel like pasta or a seafood specialty (grilled sea bream, coconut fish, lambi, etc.). A sampling of these plates is to be had in one of two open-air dining rooms that are covered by thatched palm canopies.

L'Écrevisse
$$-$$$

Occupying a pretty building facing the street, right next to the De Cameron Hotel Complex is one of the few good restaurants in town that is not located in a hotel. In addition to its attractive decor, it offers succulent dishes that are a pleasant change from the food served at the hotel buffets, which is often not hot enough.

La Romana

Calle Santa Rosa has several small restaurants serving simple, inexpensive fare such as sandwiches and hamburg

El Pici
$

El Polo
$

The El Pici Pizzeria is located on Calle Duarte, along with the El Polo which serves pica pollo.

Trigo de Oro
$
8am to 12:30pm and 3pm to 8:30pm
Calle Trinitaria

It's breakfast time and you're craving a thick, delicious sandwich made with French bread with a nice crispy crust. Or perhaps you're in the mood for a croissant... In any case, head to the café-cum-bakery Trigo de Oro, where you can enjoy your meal on the terrace.

Piazzeta
$

Giacosa
$$

El Sombrero
$$

There are a number of pleasant, quaintly decorated restaurants at **Altos de Chavón**. Particularly noteworthy are the pizzeria, the Italian restaurants **Piazzeta** and **Giacos**a, and the **Sombrero**, a Mexican restaurant. Prices are a bit high, but the beautiful setting makes it all worthwhile.

Bayahibe

The Bar Billard
$

This bar doesn't look like much, but it is a good, friendly spot for a quick bite. The menu offers sandwiches and burgers.

La Punta
$$

Besides a great location right by the sea, La Punta offers mouthwatering seafood dishes. The interior is simply decorated, but very pleasant.

La Bahia
$$

Right by the water as well, La Bahia is another place to remember for Dominican specialties, including great fish and seafood dishes.

Boca de Yuma

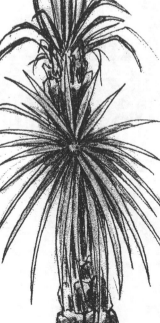

Le Club El 28
$$$
☎ *476-8660*

Le Club El 28 is a wonderful surprise in this tiny Dominican village. Run by an Italian family that recently immigrated to the country, this restaurant is the place to go if you feel like dipping into some delicious Italian

specialties—something hard to come by in this area. You'll enjoy your meal beneath a big wooden roof, in a big dining room that opens onto the street. Unpretentious and as pleasant as can be.

Brisas del Mar
$$
You can enjoy a good meal while taking in la Boca de Yuma at the Brisas del Mar Restaurant, where seafood is served, among other things. The place really comes alive at night, becoming both a bar and a discotheque where people flock to the dance floor.

Entertainment

Boca Chica

If you're willing to brave the hustle and bustle of a noisy street, then head for one of the many terraces along Calle Duarte, from late afternoon into the night. Among these, **The Route 66 Bar** is definitely worth mentioning.The bigger hotels, such as **The Hamaca** and **The Don Juan**, have good discos.

The Hamaca Hotel now houses the only **casino** in town. You can try your luck at slot machines and various games such as roulette.

Juan Dolio

At present **The De Cameron Hotel** has the most noteworthy **casino** in town. Give it a whirl! For dancing, try **The Caligula**, also in The De Cameron. Many little bars open in the afternoon and evening are spread along the beach. About fifteen metres from The Casa Marina Hotel, at the end of a walkway of tropical plants, is nestled **The Jungle Bar**, a nice spot for enjoying a great drink in the company of friends. Good meals are also served here.

Shopping

Boca Chica

In Boca Chica, Calle Duarte is the main drag and the best place to find souvenirs. The quality of the goods sold varies, however, so choose carefully.

La Romana

There are boutiques and small markets in downtown La Romana, along Calle Santa Rosa and Avenida Libe

Alto de Chavón

At **Altos de Chavón**, a few shops sell good local arts and crafts, but the prices are high. There is also a little bookstore, which sells books written in a number of different languages.

Bayahibe

The entrance of the Club Dominicus Beach is lined with several warmly coloured cottages that sell lovely arts and crafts.

Barnes & Noble
1231 NE Broadway
Portland, OR 97232
503-335-0201 10-20-00 S01964 R005

Ulysses Travel Guide: Do   17.95N
2894642091
Magazine +   5.99N
725274868971

SUB TOTAL   23.94
TOTAL   23.94
AMOUNT TENDERED
CASH   23.94

TOTAL PAYMENT   24.00
CHANGE   .06
        Visit us online.
    www.bn.com   AOL Keyword: bn
Thanks for shopping at Barnes & Noble!
#61516 10-20-00 01:37P Bonnie

        Booksellers since 1873

14 days with a receipt from any Barnes & Noble store.
Store Credit issued for new and unread books and unopened music after
14 days or without a sales receipt. Credit issued at lowest sale price.

Full refund issued for new and unread books and unopened music within
14 days with a receipt from any Barnes & Noble store.
Store Credit issued for new and unread books and unopened music after
14 days or without a sales receipt. Credit issued at lowest sale price.

Full refund issued for new and unread books and unopened music within
14 days with a receipt from any Barnes & Noble store.

Punta Cana and its Surroundings

T he Dominican Republic's eastern point is characterized by an almost unbroken succession of sugar cane fields and orange groves.

Picturesque, pastel-coloured villages pop up here and there on the landscape. It is common to see people travelling by horse, a much more popular means of transport than the car in some villages. In fact, Higüey is the only sizeable urban centre in this sparsely populated region, where you can drive for tens of kilometres without encountering any towns. The eastern point thus offers curious travellers an intriguing look at the traditions and customs of the Dominican countryside.

Most travellers, however, come to this region for another reason: its beaches are among the most beautiful in the country, if not the whole Caribbean.

For over a decade now, the once nearly uninhabited northeastern shore of the Dominican Republic, known as the Coconut Coast, has become a major holiday destination. Most developers have followed the same general plan, building grand luxury hotels on large properties, at the edge of breathtaking and completely isolated beaches. Relaxation, the beach and outdoor activities are what attract vacationers to Punta Cana and the surrounding area.

Finding Your Way Around

A network of excellent roads connects all of the hotels complexes. Getting from Santo Domingo to Punta Cana is easily accomplished on the road that passes through

Romana, San Rafael de Yuma and Higüey. Other roads in the region are in poorer condition. The section along the coast north of Higüey is particularly bad.

Punta Cana Airport

Punta Cana's small airport is the point of arrival for most guests who have reserved ahead for a room in one of the region's resort complexes. The airport is located

near most of the big hotels (*just a few kilometres north of Club Med*). The waiting room has a small restaurant that serves light meals, and accepts both American dollars and pesos.

From Punta Cana airport, **Air Santo Domingo** (☎ *683-8020*) has four flights a day to Santo Domingo, two to El Portillo on the Samaná Peninsula, and one to Puerto Plata and La Romana respectively.

Sabana de la Mar

The road between Hato Mayor and Sabana de la Mar has been recently widened and repaved for about half its length. Sabana de la

Mar can also be reached by boat from Santa Barbara de Samaná, on the other side of the Bahía de Samaná. The **Codetel** is located at *47 Calle Diego de Lira.*

Miches

From Sabaneta de la Mar, a road that is in good condition for about 30 kilometres will get you to Miches from Higuey. It is also possible to get to Miches from Higuey by taking Highway 104, which has recently been repaved.

Higüey

The road from Romana provides quick access to Higüey. Higüey's **Codetel** is on *Avenida Bertilio.*

The Coconut Coast

To reach Punta Cana, the main tourist area of the region, drive along the full length of the basilica in Higüey, then turn right.

Continue along the main road to reach the Club Med or the Punta Cana Beach Resort (*about 40 km from*

Higüey). To reach the other large hotel complexes, turn left at Kilometre 27.

As public buses (*guaguas*) in this area is not very efficient, visitors who want to explore the countryside are better off renting a car or motorcycle, or taking taxis. Taxis wait outside some of the major hotels, and can take you just about anywhere (fares are always posted).

Car Rentals

National Car Rental
Plaza Bávaro
☎ *221-0286*

By Taxi

There is a taxi service every hour to all the hotels on the Coconut Coast:

Taxi-Service Sitratural
☎ *552-0617*

Practical Information

Higüey

Most shops and restaurants are located in the heart of the city, near the Basilica.

Tourist Information Office
Calle Augustin Guerrero
Edificio de la Gobernacíon
☎ *554-2672*
Punta Cana and Surroundings

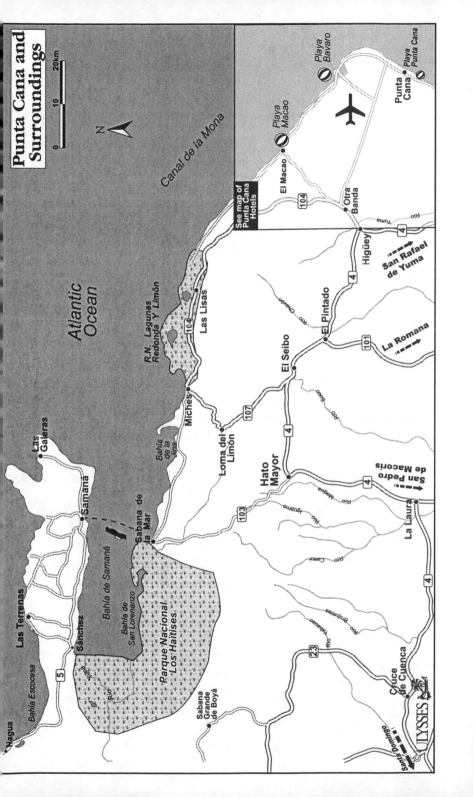

Punta Cana and Surroundings

0 10 20km

N

Atlantic Ocean

Canal de la Mona

See map of Punta Cana Hotels

Playa Bavaro

Playa Macao

Playa Punta Cana

Punta Cana

El Macao

Otra Banda

104

Río Yuma

4

Higüey

San Rafael de Yuma

El Pintado

101

La Romana

El Seibo

Río Seco

4

107

Miches

Las Lisas

R.N. Lagunas Redonda Y Limón

104

Bahía de la Jina

Loma del Limón

Hato Mayor

San Pedro de Macorís

4

103

Río Magua

Río Iguamo

La Laura

4

Río Casuí

Río Brujuelas

23

Río Yabacao

Santo Domingo

Cruce de Cuenca

Sabana Grande de Boyá

Parque Nacional Los Haitises

Río Yabón

Bahía de San Lorenazo

Sabana de la Mar

Bahía de Samaná

Sánchez

5

Las Terrenas

Bahía Escocesa

Nagua

Samaná

Las Galeras

© ULYSSES

Exploring

Sabana de la Mar

Sabana de la Mar is an isolated and rather uninspiring little fishing village, on the southern shore of Bahía de Samaná. Dominicans attempt to enter Puerto Rico illegally from here and then continue on to the United States.

From the port, boats take visitors to the superb **Parque Nacional de los Haitises ★★**. (See p 222) However, departures are more frequent and better organized from Sanchez and Santa Barbara de Samaná, on the Samaná peninsula.

A ferry links Sabana de la Mar to Santa Barbara de Samaná, departing three times a day, but only pedestrians and motorcyclists are allowed on board. Since the captain sometimes has difficulty docking the ferry in Sabana de la Mar's port, it is sometimes necessary to have recourse to fishing boats (*at about 5 pesos*) in order to make it to shore.

Heading east from Sabana de la Mar, you will come across a nice long stretch of coast with deserted beaches just waiting to be discovered by the adventurer.

Miches

This little town on the coast of the Samaná Bay is known above all as the main departure point for Dominicans attempting to enter Puerto Rico illegally before making their way to the United States. The city itself has only a few attractions, but it has some hotels and is a good place to stop over for those who want to explore the Northeast part of the country. On the route from Miches to Higuey you will discover numerous beaches and picturesque hamlets that are rarely visited.

La Reserva Cientifica Laguna Reconda y Limón

This scientific reserve is situated about 20 kilometres east of Miches, on the Atlantic Ocean. It protects two of the largest fresh-water lagoons in the country, the Redonda and Limón lagoons. The reserve contains a mangrove swamp sheltering many different kinds of birds, as well as beaches providing nesting grounds for several species of sea turtles.

Higüey

Founded in 1502 by order of **Nicolás de Ovando**, the town of Higüey is one of the cradles of Spanish civilization in America. It became an important economic centre early in its history and, more importantly, the principal religious site in the country.

Even today, Dominicans come from all over the country to pay their respects to the sacred image of la **Señora de la Altagracia**, the country's patron saint, who is said to have performed several miracles. The basilica that houses the tiny painting is Higüey's focal point; without it, the place would be of little interest.

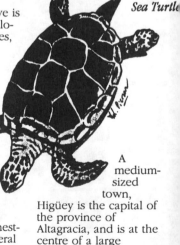

Sea Turtle

A medium-sized town, Higüey is the capital of the province of Altagracia, and is at the centre of a large orange-producing area.

The **Basílica de Nuestra Señora de la Altagracia** ★ (*right in the centre of town*) is striking from an architectural standpoint, with its 80-metre high arches. Construction of the church, built in honour of the patron saint of the region, began in 1954. The painting of the highly-venerated saint hangs inside. There is an impressive annual pilgrimage to the site each year on January 21. Visitors wearing shorts or miniskirts are not allowed inside.

however, is to head southeast from Otra Banda.

Basilica de Nuestra Senora de la Altagracia

Otra Banda

With its array of creole pastel-coloured cabins, the hamlet of Otra Banda, about 5 kilometres east of Higüey, is quite a sight. It is definitely one of the prettiest villages in the country. You'll come to a fork a few kilometres along the road heading north from Otra Banda. Keep right to reach the Coconut Coast via Playa Macao. The left fork heads through beautiful scenery and isolated villages, where people on horseback are as common as those on motorcycles. The quickest way to the Coconut Coast,

★★

The Coconut Coast

Punta Cana, Playa Macao and Playa Bavaro ★★
An almost unbroken string of white-sand **beaches** ★★★ extends as far as the eye can see along the turquoise waters of the **Canal de la Mona**, which separates the Dominican Republic from Puerto Rico. Although a few of these beaches belong to large hotels, you won't have much trouble finding some wilder more scenic spots. As the name indicates, the vegetation of the region consists mostly of coconut palms. In fact, these trees line the entire strip of beaches, adding a certain idyllic

cachet to the region. The area around Punta Cana has some of the most stunning beaches in the country. The local population is scattered amongst a few charming hamlets including **Cabessa de Toro**. This fishing village is known for its annual world fishing tournament.

Manatí Park (*$21*; ☎ 552-0807) is a large zoo not far from the hotels in Punta Cana. Strolling through the beautiful grounds, you can observe various tropical animals like crocodiles, iguanas, butterflies, pink flamingos, parrots, as well as dolphins swimming and playing in the large basin.

Outdoor Activities

The big hotel complexes in Playa Bavaro and Punta Cana all organize activities. Because most of these hotels offer all-inclusive packages, these activities are usually offered to guests free of charge. Their prime locations mean that guests can enjoy scuba diving, snorkelling, sailing, windsurfing, horseback riding and many other sports, including tennis. There is only one golf course in the region, the one at the Hotel Bavaro.

Swimming

The Coconut Coast boasts some of the most beautiful **beaches ★★★** in the country, if not in all of the Caribbean. Whether it be the **Playa Macao, the Playa Bavaro, the Playa Punta Cana**, or - for a beach a little more on the wild side- at the **Playa Juanillo**, these vast stretches of fine white sand are thriving with coconut palms. All of the hotel complexes in Playa Bavaro and Punta Cana offer direct access to the beach. More adventurous types can head off in search of countless deserted beaches lining the road between Playa Macao and Sabaná de la Mar.

These long expanses of fine-white sand gradually give way to the calm, turquoise-blue waters of the Caribbean Sea. Here, not a single rock sticks out of the water, nor are there any sudden drops in the water level as you head out to sea, making this beach a pleasant place to swim. The sands, in fact, ideal for pleasant swimming.

The tall palm trees lining these beaches provide some much-appreciated shade when the sun hit its peak.

Marlin

Golf

Bavaro Golf Club is one of the most beautiful courses in the country, and is part of the hotel complex of the same name, therefore guests staying in any of the five buildings that make up the complex have easier access to it. The well-groomed 18-hole winds its way through a vast garden with ponds. There is also a shop (☎ **686-5797**) on site that sells golf equipment.

Deep-Sea Fishing

Punta Cana is renowned for its excellent deep-sea fishing.

Each year, an international deep-sea fishing tournament takes place here to see who can catch the biggest fish. Hotels in the region also offer deep-sea fishing excursions throughout the year, so you can practise casting your line in time for next year's tournament.

The Marlin Fishing Center also offers deep-sea fishing excursions.

The Marlin Fishing Center
☎ *552-0729*
Cost per person is about $50.

Accommodations

Miches

Punta El Rey Beach Club
$43, ½b
9 km east of Miches
☎ *248-5888*
≈ *248-5887*
About 30 kilometres from Sabana de la Mar, past the tiny village of Miches, The Punta El Rey Beach Club is a peaceful hotel off the beaten track. This small family-owned establishment offers six cabañas right on a beautiful beach that will make you feel like you're in paradise. This is the perfect place to just relax and watch time go by. The reception is very friendly. One

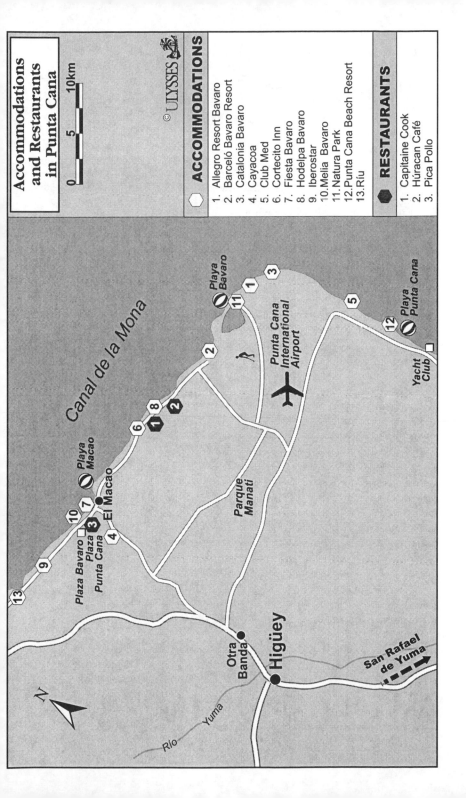

Accommodations and Restaurants in Punta Cana

© ULYSSES

ACCOMMODATIONS

1. Allegro Resort Bavaro
2. Barceló Bavaro Resort
3. Catalonia Bavaro
4. Cayacoa
5. Club Med
6. Cortecito Inn
7. Fiesta Bavaro
8. Hodelpa Bavaro
9. Iberostar
10. Melia Bavaro
11. Natura Park
12. Punta Cana Beach Resort
13. Riu

RESTAURANTS

1. Capitaine Cook
2. Húracan Café
3. Pica Pollo

Palm Trees

Tall and stately, palm trees dot the landscape of the West Indies and other parts of world. There are more than 2,779 varieties of this tree, which belongs to the monocotyledonous family: 837 species grow in South America, 339 can be found in North America and only one in Europe. There are six genuses of palm trees: the coryphoides, calami, nypoides, ceroxyloides, areca and phytelophantoides.

Palm trees grow in the most diverse environments, from rainforests and coastal regions to deserts and mountains. In the Dominican Republic, there are several kinds of palm trees, including the Royal palm, the Latania and the Coconut palm, which have many uses. Take the coconut palm, for example: its stalk is used as building material; its fruit (coconut) as well as being a popular food is used to produce coconut oil; its leaves are used in roofing and its fibres to create hats, baskets and other woven items.

Except for lianas, all palm trees are similar. Their stalks, which are almost the same in diameter at the base as at the top, are not trunks but rather stipe that end in a fountain of leaves. The new leaves grow out of the middle of this "bouquet", while the old leaves fall off, revealing the stalk. Some palm trees adapt easily to difficult environments because their roots are not very deep and grow parallel to the ground.

word of advice – the mosquitoes are especially voracious at night, so bring along the best insect repellent available.

Higüey

The Hotel San Juan
$11, ⊗;
at the corner of Colón and Juan Esquivel
The Hotel San Juan has a few clean, moderately comfortable rooms. Find out precisely which nights the disco is open before booking a room here, though.

The Topacio
$25 ⊗, ℜ
at the corner of Duarte and Cambronal
☎ 554-5892
The Topacio offers clean, quiet rooms, decorated with outrageously bad taste. This is nevertheless a very popular hotel, and it can be hard to get a room here on holidays and weekends. The restaurant on the ground floor is the preferred meeting place of prominent townsfolk.

The El Naranjo
$32 ≡, ℜ
corner of Altagracia and Juan XXIII
☎ 554-3400
⌨ 554-5455
The El Naranjo was a recently built and is conveniently located close to the Basilica and the centre of town. The rooms are clean and comfortable, making the El Naranjo one of the best hotels in the city.

Coconut Coast

If you plan to stay in one of the large hotel complexes in Punta Cana, Playa Macao and Playa Bavaro, reserve well in advance and do not arrive after nightfall, as you may be denied access. All of these establishments offer high-quality accommodation. Most offer all-inclusive packages, which include two or three meals a day and in some cases drinks and activities; such hotels include the mention "all-inclusive" after the price.

The Hotel Cayacoa
$32, ℜ, ⊗, ≈
Carretera Melia
☎ 552-0622
✉ 552-0631
Those wishing to visit the region without the big hotel bill usually associated with it should try the Hotel Cayacoa, which offers clean, reasonably priced rooms. Located next to the road, the setting might not be the most enchanting, but it is still close enough to the beach (not far from the Melia Bavaro). The facilities are adequate and there is a pretty pool.

The Cortecito Inn
$60, ≈, ≡, ℜ
☎ 552-0639
✉ 552-0641
The Cortecito Inn is not located right on the beachfront, but the rooms are comfortable and offer good value for the money.

The Melia Bavaro Resort
$160, all-inclusive,
≡, ≈, ℜ
Playa Bavaro
☎ 221-2311
The Melia Bavaro Resort has 500 pleasantly furnished rooms in more than fifty beautiful little buildings surrounded by lush tropical vegetation. The huge grounds of the Bavaro Resort, part of the Spanish Melia chain, have been tastefully designed, and overlook an excellent beach. At the moment of your arrival you are greeted in a large, airy lobby graced with large pools of water. Not only can all water sports be enjoyed here, but the place also organizes a host of evening activities and regional excursions. Taxis wait by the entrance, making it very easy to explore on your own.

The Riu Hotels
Playa Macao
☎ 221-2290
☎ 221-7515
✉ 221-1645

The Riu Taino
$160, all-inclusive
tv, ℜ, ⊗, ≡, ≈

The Riu Naiboa
$180, all-inclusive
tv, ℜ, ⊗, ≡, ≈

The Riu Melao
$190, all-inclusive
tv, ℜ, ⊗, ≡, ≈

Bambi
$240, ℜ, ≡, ≈

The Riu Palace Macao
$210 all-inclusive
tv, ℜ, ⊗, ≡, ≈

The Riu Hotels form an immense complex with five different luxury hotels all near a superb beach. A pleasant shopping street of pastel buildings has been built near by. *The Riu Taino* is the most affordable of the Riu hotels. It includes 90 small villas with four rooms each. **The Riu Naiboa** offers modern and comfortable rooms located in a large, uninspiring multi-story building. **The Riu Melaohas** 244 very pretty rooms set in quaint villas. **Bambi** also possesses rooms of an irreproachable comfort. **The Riu Palace Macao** is one the prettiest hotels in the region. The rooms, set in one large building, are splendid. The lobby, with its rich wooden accents, the restaurants and the bars are magnificent.

The Fiesta Bavaro
$200, all-inclusive
Playa Bavaro
☎ 221-8149
The elegantly decorated rooms at the Fiesta Bavaro are set up inside small pastel-coloured buildings, surrounded by a magnificent, well-groomed garden that opens out onto a picturesque beach. As with the other hotels along the coast, swimming and other sports activities are offered as a means of enjoying the ocean's turquoise waters.

The Allegro Resort Bavaro
$200, all-inclusive
ℜ, ≈, ℝ, =
Playa Bavaro
☎ 687-5747
≈ 687-1381
The Allegro Resort Bavaro is a huge hotel complex with more than 500 rooms in nine buildings surrounded by gardens. The entrance leads to the sunny hall with a palm-thatched roof and a skylight in the middle. The rooms in each building are charmingly decorated with rattan furniture and salmon-coloured walls. The gardens give way to a long white-sand beach where all kinds of activities take place.

Barceló Bavaro Resort
=, ≈, ℜ, ♠, ○, ☉
☎ 686-5797
≈ 682-2169
Barceló Bavaro Resort consists of five hotels (**The Beach, Garden, Golf, Casino and Palace Hotels**) that together can accommodate up to 3000 people any, making this complex larger than some Dominican towns. The enormous resort is bordered by a heavenly, 2-km-long beach, and huge fountains can be found on the grounds, as well as a pretty church by the lake. Basically, everything has been done here to make your stay a memorable one. The rooms are immaculate and beautiful; they are even more luxurious in the Palace. There are tons of activities, such as deep-sea fishing and scuba diving. And there

couldn't be a better place for golf: the course is one of the most beautiful in the country. Finally, you'll never be at a loss for food or fun with the restaurants, bars, night-clubs and pool all on the premises. Reservations are recommended; otherwise, you'll have to deal a long time with the guard at the entrance.

The Hodelpa Bavaro Hotel
=, ≈, ℜ
☎ 683-1000
≈ 683-2303
The Hodelpa Bavaro Hotel has no less than 380 rooms in pastel-coloured buildings surrounded by beautiful gardens. The quality of the rooms are typical of this type of establishment. Vacationers have everything at their disposal: a fine, white-sand beach with endless ocean, as well as organized activities including kayaking, sailing, windsurfing, and scuba diving.

Catalonia Bavaro
$190, all inclusive
≈, =, ⊗, ℜ
Playa Bavaro
☎ 412-0000
≈ 412-5036
At Catalonia Bavaro you can stay in one of the lovely blue villas surrounded by a palm grove. The rooms in each villa are painted blue and bright yellow resembling the sea and sky, and are furnished with handsome rattan furniture. The rooms also come equipped

with hair dryers, refrigerators, private terraces with hammocks, and other little minute details to ensure total comfort. Paths, benches, and a pool can be found in the carefully tended gardens that surround the hotel. And yes, the beach runs along the premises.

Natura Park
$160 all-inclusive
=, ≈, ℜ
☎ 221-2626
≈ 221-6060
Natura Park is in a category of its own. Everthing has been done here to create a pleasant stay without spoiling the environment. Not only has this concept worked, but Natura Park has also won an award for preserving the natural surroundings.

The minute you arrive you'll notice how wonderfully the place is set up: the lobby is covered by an enormous wooden roof that opens up to a magnificent palm grove surrounding the park. The buildings were constructed out of natural materials such as wood, terracotta and stone, reflecting the environmental theme. The rooms have beautiful wooden ceilings, large bay windows and wicker furniture. The garden is something to see with its pools of fish and turtles, as well as its several kilometres of trails where you can see other animals. Finally, a magnificent white-sand beach runs along the premises.

The Iberostar Hotel
$280, all-inclusive
ℜ, ≈, ℝ, ≡
Punta Cana
The Iberostar Hotel is a magnificent 750-room complex located on a vast property shaded by coconut trees and offering direct access to the superb Macao beach. The rooms are tastefully decorated, and each one has either a balcony or terrace. Horses can be rented here as well.

The Club Med
$260, all-inclusive
≡, ≈, ℜ
Punta Cana
☎ 687-2767
≈ 687-2896
The Club Med is equipped with comf rooms in several three-floor buildings facing either the sea or a coconut grove. The key to Club Med's success is in the extensive choice of activities available from morning to night. As far as sports go, guests can try snorkelling, scuba diving, windsurfing, sailing, tennis and archery. Children are in for a special treat as well, since the Miniclub features a variety of facilities that cater to their special interests and needs.

In the evening, you can take in live entertainment and dance at an open-air disco. The huge buffet meals prepared nightly by the chefs of the main

restaurant are delicious. A second, quieter restaurant by the beach specializes in seafood. Though it is possible to stay for only one day, one- or two-week packages are a better value.

The Punta Cana Beach Resort
$160, 1/2p
ℜ, ⊗, ≡, ≈
Punta Cana
☎ 541-2714
≈ 547-2200
The Punta Cana Beach Resort is a little village unto itself spread out along the magnificent Punta Cana beach. The property is well laid out, with lots of flowers, plants and trees lending the place the feel of a tropical paradise. The rooms are large, prettily decorated and brightly painted. They are set in numerous pavilions and a few large multi-storied buildings. The package deal includes two meals per day and access to all the activities offered on site. In the evening, there is fine dining at the La Cana restaurant.

chicken (*pollo* in Spanish) and has a nice terrace facing the street. Playa Bavaro

Pica Pollo
$
There are several small restaurants at Plaza Bavaro, including a Pica Pollo, which serves cheap chicken.

Capitaine Cook
$$$
at the Bavaro Hotel
Capitaine Cook is a must for its fish and seafood dishes, which you can enjoy with an ocean view. The tables all have parasols made out of palm leaves and are set up by the beach. One of the best restaurants around these parts.

The Húracan Café
$$-$$$
Playa Bavaro
☎ 710-4094
The Húracan Café is reputed for being one of the best restaurants in the region. It serves some wonderful international cuisine, mostly Italian specialties.

Restaurants

Higüey

Pollo Victoria
$

Right next to the El Naranjo Hotel, Pollo Victoria serves cheap

Entertainment

Playa Bavaro

The best nightclub in town is supposedly the one at the **Barcelo Bavaro Resort** (*$6 cover, free for guests of the hotel*). Each night around 11pm, the club fills up with both Dominicans and tourists, who come to drink and dance the night away to the mostly American but sometimes Caribbean music.

Tropicalissimo (*$16, free for guests of the hotel*) at the Bavaro hotel presents big musical shows with flashy dancers. Admission includes a glass of rum and coke served at your table.

If you're feeling lucky, then **The Bavaro Casino** is the place to try it out.

Shopping

Right next to the Melia Bavaro hotel is **Plaza Punta Cana**, a small shopping centre which is really a series of outdoor stalls.

Among the items on display, the handicrafts Those whose shopping frenzy has not made them drop should browse through **Plaza Bavaro**, where there are more shops and restaurants.

The Southwest

The Southwest region of the Dominican Republic includes the area along the Caribbean Sea between Santo Domingo and Barahona, as well as the point of land at the western extremity of the country, where Lago Enriquillo, the Bahoruco Valley and the Bahoruco mountain range are located.

This region of the country is astonishing because of the tremendous variety of its flora ranging from subtropical forest to desert. The section of highway between Baní and Barahona is over 100 kilometres long and crosses beautiful and often desolate countryside. The drier climate brings a gradual change in the vegetation; it becomes sparser and less verdant as scrub growth replaces luxuriant palm trees.

Beyond Azua, huge stretches of dry earth and sandy hills dominate the landscape. The Neiba Mountain Range begins in this region, and the road becomes steeper. Before long, you wil start to spot cacti, which are plentiful in this area.

The region between Azua and Barahona is even more arid and consequently less populated. Villages along this virtually uninhabited road become increasingly far apart.

The barren land produces so little that this is one of the poorest regions in the Dominican Republic. The contrast between the rest of the country and these modest villages, with their small huts of bleached dry wood and scraggy vegetation, is striking.

A startling and unexpected spectacle unfolds as you weave your way through the bare hills. In fact, the road merits exploration simply for the beauty of the terrain through which it passes.

The Bahoruco Valley is characterized by incredibly lush, green fields. Coffee, sugar cane, grapes and bananas are all grown here in large quantities. The steep Caribbean coastline, with little coves nestled here and there, adds to the beauty of the region.

The tourism infrastructure is less developed in the South West than it is elsewhere in the country. Cerrtain towns - like Barahona for example - are beginning to promote their tourism industry, leaving some important developments to be anticipated in the future. As yet, there are no bustling resort towns like those that can found elsewhere on the island, and so far the number of deluxe hotels can be counted on the fingers of one hand.

The Southwest would appeal to those who would like to visit a region that is at once spectacular, different and picturesque.

Finding Your Way Around

A fairly good highway links Santo Domingo and Barahona; it goes through San Cristóbal, Baní and Azua. Though there are only a few villages along the road, traffic is fairly heavy. There are gas stations in all the larger towns. Buses also make stops throughout the region.

San Cristóbal

To reach San Cristóbal from Santo Domingo, stay on the road that follows the water (*Avenida George Washington*). You will eventually end up on the highway that runs along the southern coast of the island and through San Cristóbal.

Bus Station: buses heading west and elsewhere on the island stop on the way out of San Cristóbal.

Baní and Azua

The highway goes through both these towns.

Bus station (Baní): at the western edge of town, next to the market.

Bus station (Azua): buses heading east-west stop in front of the central park (*Calles Emilio Prodan and Colón*).

Barahona

The highway splits in two a few kilometres beyond Azua; to get to Barahona, keep left.

The highway from Santo Domingo becomes Calle Jaime Mota in Barahona. It crosses the whole town all the way to Calle Enriquillo along the sea, where all the hotels are located. This road provides access to the southern part of the peninsula.

Bus station: at the corner of Calles Padre Bellini and 30 de Marzo, a few steps from the central park.

Caribe Tours:
☎ 524-2313

Parque Nacional Jaragua

Parque Nacional Jaragua is the largest national park in the country, but still has the least facilities for visitors and getting to it remains difficult. The eastern part is accessible via Oviedo, a town near the Laguna de Oviedo. Before entering the park, however, you must get a permit from the warden's office: find out about this in the town. The west coast of

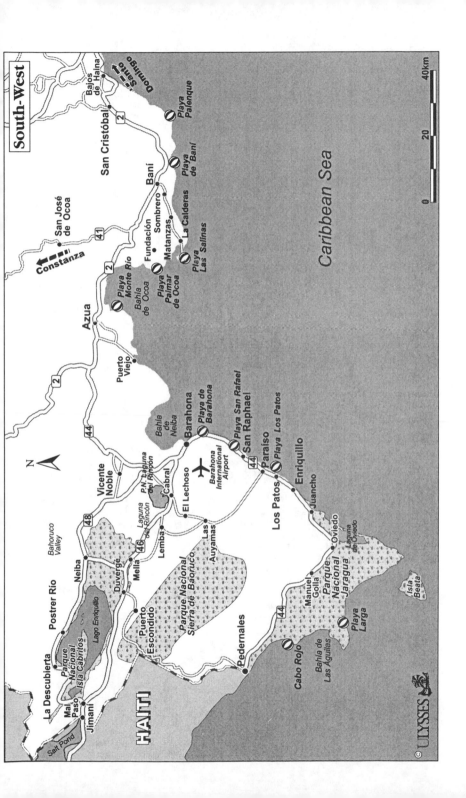

the park is accessible via the road that crosses Cabo Rojo south of Pedernales.

Parque Nacional Isla Cabritos

If you go beyond Azua, where the highway splits in two, and follow the road to the right (*when coming from Santo Domingo*), you will end up in the Parque Nacional Isla Cabritos, at the centre of Lago Enriquillo. To get there, head towards the northern shore of the lake. Take the turn-off after the village of Mella. Follow this road to Neiba and then head west. The entrance to the park is in the town of La Descubierta.

Parque Nacional Sierra de Bahoruco

To get to the park from Barahona, follow the road to Duverge. From there, take the small road that leads to the village of Puerto Escondido and then take the path to the park. The path can be difficult to find, so don't hesitate to ask the locals for help. When you get to the entrance of the park, you must buy a permit from the warden's station.

Haiti

To reach Haiti, take the highway to Jimaní, the main border crossing between the two countries.

Practical Information

San Cristóbal

The road from Santo Domingo goes through the centre of San Cristóbal.

The *Codetel* is at *14 Calle Palo Hincado.*

Baní

The highway leads directly to the downtown area, centred around Calles Padre Bellini and Mella. There are many shops and restaurants here. At the western edge of town, you'll find a market.

The *Codetel* is at *3 Calle Padre Bellini.*

Azua

The highway passes through downtown Azua, which is bordered by Avenidas Emilio Prodan and Colón, around the park. There are a few

banks and shops on Avenida Emilio Prodan, and some small restaurants near the park.

The *Codetel* is at *118 Calle 19 de Marzo.*

Barahona

The downtown area is centred around the central park, on Calles Jaime Mota and Padre Bellini. There are several little shops and restaurants here. Most of the banks are on Calle Jaime Mota.

The *Codetel* is *next to the central park at 36 Calle Nuestra Senora del Rosario.*

Neiba

The road from Barahona leads directly to the centre of town.

The *Codetel* is on *Calle Cambronal, at the corner of Calle Felipe Gonzales.*

Exploring

San Cristóbal

The history of San Cristóbal began in 1575 with arrival of colonists attracted by the discovery of gold in the Río Haina. The city was named after a fort that had been built in the region under the orders of Christopher Columbus. The city prospered and even played a part in Dominican history, as the site of the signing of the country's first constitution (November 6th, 1844). It is better known, however, as the birthplace of **Trujillo**, the Dominican Republic's terrible dictator (1891-1961). San Cristóbal is far from a haven of tranquillity, rather, it is a bustling urban centre with 140,000 inhabitants. It is therefore preferable to visit the city on day trips from Santo Domingo, which lies only about thirty kilometres away and has much more in the way of accommodations.

Some magnificent buildings were erected in San Cristóbal in the first half of the 20th century, several of which belonged to President Trujillo. These buildings, now in ruins, reflect a tiny fraction of the wealth the dictator accumulated during his reign.

Built in the 19th century, the **Iglesia de San Cristóbal**, facing the town's central park, houses Trujillo's tomb. The interior is attractive; the religious scenes painted in the choir are particularly striking.

On a hillside just outside the city is the **Castillo del Cerro**, formerly owned by President Trujillo — though he didn't like it and never lived here. This magnificent 1920s residence had six living rooms, each decorated in a different style. As the house is presently under renovation, it is difficult to get a true sense of its original beauty and opulence.

The **Casa Caoba**, or "mahogany house", located on the outskirts of town, was Trujillo's country house. It too sits atop a hill overlooking the city. The house has been abandoned and is in even worse shape than Castillo del Cerro. There are plans to restore it, but the work could take many years.

Baní

Baní is the main city in the province of Peravia, a prosperous agricultural region primarily devoted to the production of coffee, bananas and sugar cane.

Located in the centre of the city, the park is a pleasant verdant place to rest, as well as the hub of most of the local activity. Though its authenticity is appealing, the city has little to offer visitors. You can, however, see the **Casa de Máximo Gómez** (*Calle Máximo Gómez*). **Máximo Gómez** (1836 - 1905) was born and spent his childhood in this house before going to Cuba to become a hero in this country for leading it to independence at the end of the last century. It is also possible to visit the municipal museum located close by.

South of Baní, beautiful wild beaches await those who prefer their independence. There are three noteworthy beaches in the area: Palenque, Baní and Las Salinas (see p 106). Only about 60 kilometres from Santo Domingo, but far from the frenzy of tourist development, Baní is a charming place to pull off the road heading west.

From Baní, there are two options. Either continue west on the highway toward Azua, or take the little road to Las Salinas, which crosses the villages of Sombrero, Matanzas and Las Calderas.

Las Salinas

The town of Las Salinas developed on a long reef that projects into the Caribbean Sea. The location was propitious for a salt-works (hence the name of the town), and the ocean hid a million treasures. This certainly explains the size of the town, which is relatively large for this arid region of the country.Very authentic with its charming, brightly coloured cabins, Las Salinas is mainly known today for its long, grey-sand

The Southwest

beach, which is the pleasure of the many Dominicans who come to swim at it on Sundays.

Azua

Azua was founded in 1504 by Diego Velásquez on the shores of the Caribbean Sea. The town soon enjoyed a period of prosperity as a port city before being completely destroyed by an earthquake in 1751.

Azua was rebuilt five kilometres away on its present site at the foot of the Ocoa mountains. The town's location, halfway between Santo Domingo and the border with Haiti, has been a source of trouble; several times in the 19th century, Azua was set on fire by Haitian invaders. The main attractions, both testaments to this bygone era, are the **Puerto Viejo**, or old port, and the **ruins** of the old city.

Azua is the second biggest city on the road through the southwestern Dominican Republic. It is located in a rich agricultural area where sugar cane, rice, coffee and fruit are the main cash crops. The economy of the region is also boosted by mining (minerals and precious stones) and lumbering. This busy city is not particularly charming or relaxing. You can plan on stopping here awhile since

there are some boutiques and restaurants that you may find of interest.

There are two wild beaches nearby, **Monte Río** and **Blanca** (see p145).

The Southwestern Peninsula

Barahona is essentially the gateway to the peninsula; a large city, it serves as a departure point for travellers wishing to explore the western extremity of the Dominican Republic. Two roads leaving from Barahona provide access to the southwestern peninsula. The first one runs along the Caribbean, then heads over to Pedernales, on the Haitian border. The second crosses the northern part of the peninsula, passing Lago Enriquillo and going all the way to Jimaní, main gateway to Haiti.

Because of fluctuations in rainfall throughout the territory, there is a wide variety of plant life, and the landscape undergoes several transformations, ranging from desert zones around Lago Enriquillo to sub-tropical forests which cover part of the mountain chain. There are few historic relics or luxurious tourist developments on this peninsula, whose appeal lies instead in its varied and unique landscape.

Before arriving in Barahona, you will notice many fields of sugar cane. During Trujillo's years as president, thousands of hectares of land around the city were seized for the cultivation of sugar cane. This culture was as difficult for the locals as it was profitable for the *generalissimo*.

Fishing is another important economic activity in this coastal region, and a relatively lucrative one as well. The waters around this point of the island are teeming with fish and shellfish, due to the shallow marine platform along the peninsula, which is ideal for the development of many species. You will no doubt have a chance to visit one of the charming fishing villages along the coast, with a scattering of colourful little boats bobbing on the waves in the distance.

Barahona

Located on Bahía de Neiba, Barahona has a population of some 50,000, making it the largest urban centre in this arid landscape. It is nevertheless pleasant due to its enviable location on the Caribbean Sea, hemmed in on one side by a pretty bay and on the other by impressive cliffs.

In fact, as with most towns in the country, the downtown area of Barahona developed around a central park, where strollers can sit and take a break before continuing their exploration of the Creole cottages, little shops and restaurants that line the streets.

There are no major attractions here and the town is typically Dominican. For a picturesque example of what this means, visit the lively public market near the central park. Barahona also has a busy port that serves all the small neighbouring communities and therefore plays a central role in the region's economy. Follow Avenida Enriquillo if you want to check it out.

Barahona does not yet resemble one of the Dominican Republic's huge resort towns, like those on the northern coast, or to the east of Santo Domingo. Several modest hotels have been built to cater to visitors and the area's first major hotel complex was recently completed. The local tourism industry is likely to take off in the coming years, especially because an airport capable of receiving large carriers has just been built here.

If you exit the city by Avenida Enriquillo, you will follow the southern coast of the peninsula and pass by several beautiful

sandy beaches, including **Barahona, Los Patos** *and* **San Rafael.**

La Reserva Cientifica Laguna Radonda y Limón

This scientific reserve is situated about 20 kilometres east of Miches, on the Atlantic Ocean. It protects two of the largest fresh-water lagoons in the country, the Redonda and Limón lagoons. The reserve contains a mangrove swamp sheltering many different kinds of birds, as well as beaches providing nesting grounds for several species of sea turtles.

The Barahona - Pedernales Route

Leaving Barahona, the road heads south, passing through some of the most beautiful scenery in the Dominican Republic. A section of the road is flanked by the Bahoruco mountain range on one side and the Caribbean on the other. The ocean views along much of the road are stunning. In some places, the play of sunlight on vast stretches of open water creates distant mirages of shifting blue islands. Waves crash into steep cliffs that occasionally

give way to little coves where waves wash up on golden sandy beaches perfect for swimming. Here and there, quaint villages spring up by the side of the road, reminding us that people live here. This region is less arid, with lush verdant vegetation.

Continuing south, the road follows the shoreline to Enriquillo, the last seaside village. It then heads inland towards Pedernales, eventually following the Bahoruco mountains. Running along a hillside, the route is still charming, though the scenery is less impressive. The southernmost point of the route has been protected by the creation of the Parque Nacional Jaragua, the largest park in the country.

San Rafael

The hamlet of San Rafael, directly on the sea, has a marvelous pebble beach as it principal attraction. This beach, which cannot be seen from the highway, is indicated only by a small sign and is thus easy to miss. To get there from the highway, take the dirt road that abruptly zigzags among the fishermens' cabins on its way towards the sea. The beach, covered with pebbles, opens out onto a magnificent bay that is surrounded by steep cliffs.

A creek that goes through the beach forms a superb natural pool. There is no touristic infrastructure here; just a small restaurant that has expanded over the years can be found on the shore. During holidays and weekends though, the tranquility of the spot is often disrupted by Dominican vacationers.

Los Patos

Another tiny village on the coast, Los Patos is blessed with an incredibly beautiful pebble beach. This spot has charm and authenticity. A natural pool of soft water has formed on this beach, much like the one in San Rafael.

Paraíso

The little village of Paraíso lies next to the beautiful Bahoruco beach. The village has little to offer besides its Caribbean charm. The beach, on the other hand, is a stunning ribbon of sand washed by refreshing and limpid waters.

Pedernales

The road across the peninsula ends at Pedernales, a little port city at the western extremity of the Dominican Republic, on the Haitian border. Permission from the Dominican Repub-

lic is needed in order to enter Haiti. The only official border crossing in the region is in Jimani, more to the North. There are some nice beaches in the area, including **Cabo Rojo**.

Parque Nacional Jaragua

Parque Nacional Jaragua, which encompasses the southern extremity of the southwest peninsula, is the largest national park in the Dominican Republic. It includes all the land on this part of the peninsula, some of the ocean floor along the coast, and two islands, **Beata** and **Alto Velo**.

This rocky point, formed around 50 million years ago, is composed of marine limestone which is rich in

Green Heron

ferric oxide and gives the cliffs their beautiful red colour. Today, this sparsely populated

region attracts flocks of birds and hoards of other animals. However, to date, no outfitters offer excursions that would allow visitors to discover the the beauty of this vast, arid stretch of land covered with scraggly vegetation. The government plans to look into developing the region, but for the time being you will have to settle for visiting the edge of the park. It is virtually impossible to make your way into the heart of this gigantic wild garden, as there are no marked trails leading through it. A **trail** on the west side of the peninsula, past **Cabo Rojo**, makes it possible to visit a tiny part of the park, including one of the loveliest beaches in the country, **Bahía de las Águilas ★★**, where you can admire scores of tropical birds from afar. Among the most fascinating birds that can be seen in the park are **flamingos** (particularly near the Oviedo Lagoon), **green herons**, **frigate birds**, **white egrets** and **pink spoon-bills**. **Ricord** and **rhinoceros iguanas** can be found in the sunnier parts of the park, and the coastline attracts four species of **sea turtles:** the **leatherback**, **green**, **hawksbill** and **loggerhead turtle**. Remnants of Taino culture – the original inhabitants of this area – can also be found here: there are caves with drawings on their walls as well as a few **petroglyphs**. These

Pre-Colombian sites are not easy to reach, however.

Parque Nacional Sierra de Bahoruco

The park was created to protect the **Bahoruco Mountain Chain** that runs along the Barahona Peninsula to the border of Haiti. This part of the country receives little rain, except for the park where it is abundant. Precipitation in the park varies according to the altitude and ranges between 1,000 mm and 2,500 mm. The vegetation also varies according to altitude: at the foot of the mountains, a dry tropical forest grows, which is then replaced with rising elevation by a wet tropical forest.

Orchids

This park is renowned for its exceptional variety of **orchids**, with no less than 166 species or 55% of all the orchids grown in the country. **Pine trees**, **wild cherry trees** and **Hispaniolan mahoganies** also grow here. Many different kinds of birds such as **doves**, **Hispaniolan parrots** and **hummingbirds** can be seen here as well.

It goes without saying that the park has exceptional vegetation, but, unfortunately, not enough facilities have been set up for visitors to discover it. There are trails that run through the park, but they are for four-wheel drive vehicles only.

★

Around Lago Enriquillo

Another road runs through the peninsula, from Barahona to Jimaní; it then heads back south of Lago Enriquillo, thus skirting around this stunning lake.

A few modest, peaceful hamlets have sprouted up here and there, cut off from the frantic pace of life in the big, modern urban centres.

The centrepiece of the trip, however, is Lago Enriquillo, an amazing stretch of salt water visible in the distance for a good part of the ride. Before setting out, take note that careful driving is a must the entire length of this

Enriquillo

In 1532, the Sierra de Bahoruco was the scene of a conflict between the Spanish and the Tainos, led by their *cacique*, Enriquillo, known by his people as Guarocuya.

Enriquillo managed to hold out against the Spanish and created a small independent area on top of the mountains. For this he is considered a hero, and Lago Enriquillo as well as several streets in the region were named in his honour.

little-used road, as many animals make their way across it, and parts of it are in poor condition.

Neiba

Located in a region with particularly scraggly vegetation, Neiba is a small, dusty town made up mainly of modest little wooden

The Southwest

houses. Life seems to move at a completely different tempo here than in the big cities: there are only a few stores in the centre of town, the main streets are lively in a more subdued way, and the residents go calmly about their business. The place offers quite a change of scenery, especially compared to the bustling villages elsewhere on the island, but that lends it a certain charm.

Postrer Río

You will also pass through Postrer Río, another simple little hamlet that seems untouched by time. Few visitors come here, and the place is not really equipped to welcome travellers; some residents even seem hostile.

Parque Nacional Isla Cabritos

Lago Enriquillo, the largest lake in the Caribbean, is definitely one of the most impressive natural attractions in the region. It is located some 35 metres below sea level, and the concentration of salt in its waters is three times higher than that of the Caribbean. As there is little precipitation in this region, the shores of the lake are desert-like, especially to the west,

where nothing but cacti and a few dwarf plants grow.

Lago Enriquillo was formed about a million years ago. Until then, the Bay of Neiba in the Dominican Republic and the Bay of Port-au-Prince in Haiti were linked by a channel of water. Constant ground movement and the accumulation of sediment transported by the Yaque del Sur River dried up part of this channel, creating Lago Enriquillo.

There are three islands in the centre of the lake, **Barbarita, Islita** and **Cabritos**.

Isla Cabritos is one of three islands in Lago Enriquillo, and the only one where the rich flora and fauna have been protected by the creation of a park.

To reach the island, you must cross amazing Lago Enriquillo, the largest saltwater lake in the Caribbean and home to a number of fascinating wildlife species: **American crocodiles** up to two metres long, **pink flamingoes**, **iguanas** and **rhinoceros**.

Excursions are organized to provide visitors with an opportunity to observe these fascinating animals that are otherwise very difficult to see.

In fact the chances of seeing a crocodile are quite slim as they usu-

ally spend the day hidden under water lilies. The best time to spot them is early in the morning or as the sun sets. A visit is nevertheless quite something. If such an excursion doesn't interest you, at least go to the lakeshore where tropical birds, including **pink flamingoes**, **green herons** and **bananaquits** - *Amazons Hispanolia* can be seen.

A few kilometres before the village of La Descubierta, a rusted sign by the side of the road announces the entrance of Parque Isla Cabritos. The only building is a rundown wooden shack. **Excursions** to Parque Isla Cabritos start here, but you'll find the person who organizes them at the **Brahamas Restaurant**, in the village of **La Descubierta**.

It generally costs a minimum of *400 pesos to rent a boat (up to 10 people can share the cost), 50 pesos per person for a permit to enter the park and 80 pesos to get from the village to the starting point of the tour.* If you get on well with the person in charge (at the restaurant), you shouldn't have to pay for anything else, but the price of the excursion should be determined before setting out and paid upon return. It is possible to camp on the island, but you have to get a government permit issued by the Santo Domingo Parks Office.

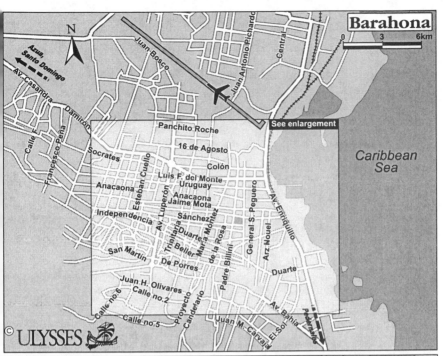

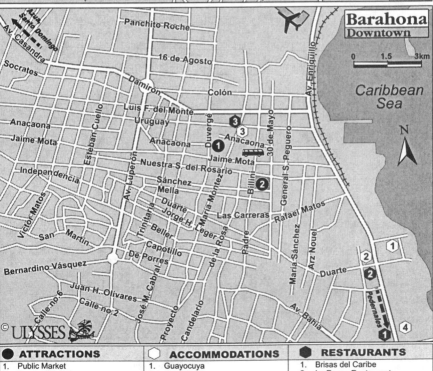

● ATTRACTIONS	○ ACCOMMODATIONS	● RESTAURANTS
1. Public Market	1. Guayocuya	1. Brisas del Caribe
2. Parque Central	2. Hotel Caribe	2. La Rocca Restaurant
	3. Las Magnolias	3. Melo's Café
	4. Riviera Beach (R)	
	(R): Property with restaurant (see description)	

La Descubierta

Made up of small, wooden houses, the village of La Descubierta will delight visitors in search of picturesque spots that make them feel far from home, though there is nothing enchanting about the place itself. It is a sizeable village (the largest in the region), but has managed to retain a peaceful, rural atmosphere. La Descubierta has all the resources necessary to welcome visitors who stop here mainly because the town is the starting point for excursions to the Isla Cabritos National Park.

Trips to the Parque Isla Cabritos do not start in downtown La Descubierta, but rather at a small station a few kilometres east of the village, where boats set out to conquer Lago Enriquillo and its fascinating animal life. The only sign showing how to get there from the road is rusted and easy to miss. You will notice a sulfur water spring not far from the parking lot at the station.

Jimaní

Jimaní, located close to the Haitian border, is the last Dominican town on the highway leading westward to Port-au-Prince, the capital of the neighbouring country. Strolling down the main street on market days, it would be hard to ignore the Haitian presence in the air, as the fruit and vegetable stalls contain scores of handcrafted items from across the border.

Mal Paso

The village of Mal Paso is set right on the Haitian border. In fact it looks more like an enormous market that a border-crossing because such numbers of Haitian craftspeople come here to sell, often at discount prices, their most beautiful pieces. This spot is worth visiting both for its ambiance and for the thousands of finds that one can walk away with.

Duvergé

The road that runs along the south shore of the lake leads back to Barahona. It is in excellent condition and offers a chance to contemplate more lovely, arid landscapes, with the perpetually calm waters of the lake off in the distance. It leads through several modest towns whose sole interest lies in their authenticity. The only food you'll be able to find here are fruits and vegetables displayed in a few forlorn stalls. Duvergé is the largest hamlet on this route, though it has no particular attractions.

The road leads eastward to Barahona.

Outdoor Activities

Swimming

Baní

There are a several pretty beaches along the shore south of Baní, including **Palenque, Baní, Las Salinas and Palmar de Ocoa**. The Las Salinas beach is located about 20 kilometres south of Baní, beside the village of the same name. It runs along the west side of a strip of land that stretches out into the Caribbean, forming a small cove with calm waters that are perfect for swimming. Lined with shrubs, it boasts a pretty setting.

Some people might be put off by the grey sand, which is nonetheless just as soft and clean as the golden sand of the other beaches in the country. If you are among them, or the lively atmosphere here does not appeal to you (on Sunday, the beach is overrun by fun-loving Dominicans) and you have an all-terrain vehicle, you can head to the more beautiful, unspoiled **Palmar de Ocoa Beach**. *To do so, follow the little road from*

the hamlet of Fundación.
The ride is hardly relaxing, but the beach is worth it.

Azua

Around Azua, you will have no trouble finding a few strips of golden sand where you can relax and soak up the sun. One of the more noteworthy of these is the **Monte Río** beach. To get there, take the dirt road on the way into town (*2-3 kilometres*); keep your eyes peeled, though, as the beach is only indicated by a small sign. You might also opt for the decidedly prettier **Playa Blanca**, located west of town.

The Southwestern Peninsula

In **Barahona**, there is only one beach, itself of limited appeal; the poor quality of the water (due to the proximity of the port) and the resident jellyfishes detract considerably from its charm. On the way out of town, on the grounds of the Hotel Riviera, another part of the beach has lovely golden sand and is just fine as far as cleanliness is concerned. Still, the beaches south of Barahona have more to offer.

On the road to Pedernales, you will pass several magnificent coves well suited to swimming or lounging about. You could

start with the **San Rafael** ★ beach, whose presence is indicated by a single, modest sign.

Continuing southward, there is another lovely, untouched beach, the **Los Patos** ★ beach, which is also covered with pebbles. A real little paradise for those who love solitude, the beach attracts very few visitors aside from the children from the neighbouring village, who come here to play.

Scuba Diving

Off the shores of **Barahona** and along the coast, there is a wealth of marine animal life, creating natural scenes of remarkable beauty. You can explore these outstanding underwater landscapes by taking part in a scuba diving or snorkelling expedition organized by the diving centre on the beach of the Riviera hotel in Barahona.

Bird and Crocodile Watching

Lago Enriquillo is the largest nature reserve for that most formidable of reptiles, the American crocodile. If you would like to observe this ferocious

animal in its natural habitat, take an excursion to the centre of the lake, where they can be seen in the early morning and late afternoon. This region is also wonderful for bird-watching, as the shores of the lake are home to scores of tropical birds, including flamingoes.

Parque Jaragua, which covers the entire southern portion of the southwest peninsula of the Dominican Republic, is another unparalleled refuge for all sorts of birds, and though it isn't really possible to make your way into the heart of this wild garden, avian species can be spotted all along the shore (if you take the trail south of Pedernales).

Accommodations

San Cristóbal

San Cristóbal is not a very touristy town and thus has very few hotels. Most people that visit San Cristóbal make it part of a day-trip from Santo Domingo or stop for a few minutes on their way to Barahona. You will, however, find some small, modest hotels downtown.

The American Crocodile
(*Crocodylus acutus*)

The American Crocodile lives in several parts of Central America, Colombia, Florida and on some of the Caribbean islands. One crocodile population that is receiving some well-needed attention is that of Lago Enriquillo, on Isla Cabritos, in the Dominican Republic. Long hunted, this crocodile owes its survival to conservation efforts. One program has involved breeding crocodiles in captivity and re-introducing the young to their habitat, which has increased the lake's dwindling crocodile population to about 200.

Measuring up to six metres in length with a 66- to 68-tooth jaw, this reptile is both fascinating and feared. It is, however, very rare that an American crocodile attack a human being; it feeds rather on birds, fish and crustaceans and can live for several decades.

Oviparous, the female lays her eggs (from 30 to 60 on average) in a nest near water. The eggs hatch after about 90 days. The females are so protective that some even help their babies come out of the eggs, while others keep watch from a distance. The young can measure up to 25 cm and leave the nest shortly after birth. Few of them ever grow to maturity.

The American Crocodile

Baní

Located on the highway to Barahona, Baní has the necessary facilities to feed travellers, but the town just isn't interesting enough to spend more than a couple of hours here. Those who do choose to spend the night, however, will find some comfortable hotels.

The Hotel Alba
$18
at the corner of Calles Padre Bellini and Mella
☎522-3590
The Hotel Alba, in a quiet part of the city near the central park, offers satisfactory rooms with simple furnishings.

Las Salinas

The Salinas High Wind Center Hotel
$35; ≡, ≈, ℜ;
☎ 223-7144
An ochre-coloured building on the way into Las Salinas, this is the only hotel worth mentioning in this region. Though its name might lead you to think otherwise, it is a modest little hotel with a few decent rooms and a pool. It has the advantage of being

built at the edge of a small beach.

Azua

Like Baní, Azua is not the paradise you may be looking for, and has little to offer in the way of accommodation — deluxe hotels, and only a few modest bed and breakfasts. You can nevertheless stay inexpensively close to the central park, where various low-budget hotels are located.

Barahona

Barahona has the best selection of comfortable hotels. Budget travellers will also find simple but adequate rooms in one of the small hotels in the centre of town. There are a good number of hotels that have been constructed on Avenida Enriquillo, facing the sea.

The Hotel Las Magnolias
$16; ⊗, ≡
Calle Anacaona, corner of Maria Montez
☎ 524-2244
Conveniently located near the bus station, the rooms are well

kept, and some have air conditioning. The service is courteous, and the rooms are simply decorated but comfortable enough for the price.

The Guayocuya
$20; ⊗
Avenida Enriquillo
The Guayocuya hotel is a pink building attractively located by the sea. Set back from the road, it offers a peaceful atmosphere. The rooms are clean, sparsely furnished and functional.

The Hotel Caribe
$20; ⊗, ℜ
Avenida Enriquillo
The Hotel Caribe is a modern white building located at the edge of town. It has spacious and comfortable but otherwise unspectacular rooms, each with a clean private bathroom. Good value.

🐟 The Riviera Beach
$50 to $80 rooms, all-inclusive.; ≡, ≈, ℜ
Calle Enriquillo
☎ 524-5111
Without question the loveliest and most comfortable hotel in town. Its two elegant white stucco buildings stand in the centre of a large piece of property giving onto the sea. Guests thus get to enjoy the most peaceful setting imaginable, a pretty beach and a lovely garden full of flowers, the perfect place to relax. Everything has been designed to ensure that

your stay is a pleasant one: the pool is large, the restaurant serves delicious food and the spacious, airy rooms are attractively decorated with curtains in tropical hues and have a large balcony and big windows opening onto the garden.

South of Barahona

Club Hotel El Quemaito
$52; ≡, ≈, ℜ
10 km south of Barahona, on the highway
☎ *545-1496*
To relax in complete peace and quiet, go to the Club Hotel El Quemaito, located about 10 kilometres south of Barahona, atop a cliff that offers a splendid view of the shimmering water stretching to the horizon. Besides its magnificent site, it has some spacious, well-kept rooms, an inviting garden and a small restaurant (*$$*) with a varied menu.

Baoruco Beach Resort
$120, *1/2p*, ℜ, ≡
☎ *696-0215*
✉ *223-0548*
The most luxurious hotel in the region is found in the small community of Baoruco, approximately 17km south of Barahona. This property, also called the Casa Bonita, was constructed on a promontory high above the Caribbean Sea.

La Descubierta

Those wishing to take an excursion on Lago Enriquillo can stay in Barahona and set out early in the morning (in order to arrive early enough to see the crocodiles) or spend the night in La Descubierta. The latter has a few small inns that could hardly be called charming, but offer a basic level of comfort that is fine for one night.

Hostal del Lago
$10; ⊗
This small wooden house has reasonably well-kept rooms.

Restaurants

Baní

Pollo Rey
$
Calle Bellini
It's hard to miss Pollo Rey, since there are signs for it along the highway for at least five kilometres before the city. This busy fast-food restaurant serves decent breaded chicken for a few pesos. Since buses often stop here, mealtimes can bring long line-ups. There is another **Pollo Rey** in the centre of town, on a quieter street. Its dining

room is a little more comfortable.

There are many little restaurants near the central park. As well, you can buy fresh fruits and vegetables from the **market** at the western edge of the city.

Barahona

Restaurants and food stalls line **Calle Enriquillo**, which runs along the sea. These places are easy to find, and usually have nice terraces.

Melo's Café
$
Calle Anacaona
A friendly spot facing the Las Magnolias hotel. Just a few tables make up the decor. Delicious breakfasts are served, as well as snacks during the day. The service is friendly.

La Rocca Restaurant
$$
adjacent to the Hotel Caribe
La Rocca Restaurant is a long wooden building that opens onto the street. Beneath a roof made of palm fronds, you can enjoy delicious local fish and seafood dishes in a peaceful, friendly atmosphere.

The Brisas del Caribe
$$-$$$
Avenida Enriquillo
The Brisas del Caribe has a large terrace that looks out onto Avenida Enriquillo and is decorated with wooden

furniture, a very pleasant place to have dinner. This restaurant is sure to appeal to visitors who like lots of choice, as the menu is extremely varied, ranging from Chinese food to pizza, and including meat, chicken, fish and seafood dishes. The only letdown is that the meat is not always top quality.

Hotel Riviera
$$-$$$
Calle Enriquillo
☎ *524-5111*
The restaurant in the Hotel Riviera has one big advantage: it is air conditioned. You can thus spend a cool, comfortable evening in a lovely dining room, without having to battle any mosquitoes (there are a lot of them in this area). The menu, which changes daily, is short, but the food is always good and served in generous portions.

La Descubierta

Brahamas
$
in the centre of town
Excursions to Isla Cabritos park start at the Brahamas restaurant where you can also grab a bite to eat. The menu includes *pica pollo* dishes.

Coffee Plant

The Mountains

M ost visitors who stay in seaside resorts cannot imagine that this country, primarily known for the splendour of its beaches, also conceals a mountainous landscape of exceptional beauty.

There can be no doubt that the mountains of the Cordillera Centrale are one of the most eloquent testimonies to the stunning geographical diversity that is the Dominican Republic.

Starting from the vast plains of the Cibao Valley or the southwestern part of the country, winding roads climb up to this wild region where high, verdant summits succeed one another, stretching out as far as the eye can see. With the exception of a few rare agglomerations nestled in the hollows of valleys or along narrow plateaus, the biggest of these being Jarabacoa and

Constanza, the Cordillera Centrale is huge, virgin territory. These "Dominican Alps", as the Cordillera Centrale is often referred to, form the most impressive chain of mountains in the Caribbean. Indeed, lost among the clouds, its highest peak, the Pico Duarte (3,175 metres), surpasses all other summits in the country as well as those of the West Indies.

For several years now, the Cordillera Centrale has been a popular holiday resort, though it was once known only to Dominicans themselves who came mostly during the summer months to take advantage of its cool temperatures, play golf or go horseback riding. The growing infatuation with outdoor activities now attracts an increasing number of foreign visitors to the region; leaving from large coastal tourism complexes, excursions are now organized on a regular basis, as the cordillera's main cities have improved their facilities remarkably.

Finding Your Way Around

Travellers can reach this region from the Southwestern part of the country (The Barahona Region) or from the Cibao Valley.

The Southwest

The road between San José de Ocoa and Constanza can seem very attractive, as it shortens the trip by several dozen kilometres and allows travellers to avoid Santo Domingo. However, this rocky trail, which runs for approximately 80 kilometres, is in very bad condition and if travelling by car, chances of experiencing mechanical breakdowns are considerable; there are no mechanics between the two cities, of course. Four-wheel drive vehicles generally make it through alright. The average driving speed on this road is about 30 kph. Travellers take note: some recent maps show a road between Padre Las Casas and Constanza. In reality, this is nothing more than a path that can only be travelled on horseback.

The Cibao Valley

From the highway that links Santo Domingo to Santiago, excellent roads run to Constanza (*the road begins between Bonao and La Vega*) and to Jarabacoa (*the road begins just north of La Vega*). The road to San José de Las Matas is in good condition; it starts from Santiago's western periphery.

San José de Ocoa

An excellent road breaks off from the highway about 20 kilometres west of Baní, allowing travellers to reach San José de Ocoa. For those who decide to continue on to Constanza, San José's service station is the last one on the road.

Jarabacoa

Approximately 10 kilometres north of La Vega, a road heads west to Jarabacoa, passing several hotel complexes on the outskirts of the city. It is also possible to reach Jarabacoa from Constanza. The road is unpaved half the way, but it is passable by car.

San José de Las Matas

From downtown Santiago, take the new

bridge over the Río Yaque del Norte. Shortly thereafter, turn left onto the well-maintained but winding road to San José de Las Matas (pay attention, there are very few signs).

Practical Information

Constanza

Tourist Information
18 Calle Matilde Vijas
☎ *539-2900*

Exploring

San José de Ocoa

A thriving little village, San José de Ocoa draws its principal sources of income from market gardening and trade. It is built across small valleys at the foot of the magnificent **Cordillera Centrale** and constitutes the point of departure of the magnificent mountain road to Constanza. There are restaurants and a few modest hotels here as well. For over 20 years now, **Father King**, of Canadian origin, has been one of San José de Ocoa's most respected figures. Since his arrival, Father King has become deeply

involved in improving the financial condition of the community. Through his efforts, San José de Ocoa quite frequently hosts aid workers or Canadian students.

Constanza

Situated at an altitude of more than 1,000 metres, Constanza is a charming valley town surrounded by the high peaks of the Cordillera Centrale and lies at the heart of a horticultural region. About 70% of the country's cultivated flowers (mainly roses, chrysanthemums, gladiola and birds of paradise) are produced here, mostly for export. Fruit not found elsewhere in the country such as raspberries, strawberries, peaches, pears, apples and grapes also grow in the Costanza region. Because of its high altitude, Constanza is cooler than the rest of the country; the temperatures can even drop below freezing in winter. A more "nordic" vegetation, mainly of coniferous trees, grows in the surrounding mountains.

Constanza was founded at the end of the 19th century. Today its population is culturally diverse, which is very

surprising for a town of this size. There are large Lebanese, Spanish, Hungarian and Japanese neighbouhoods in Costanza. The Japanese neighbourhood, for instance, is located on the way out of town towards San José de Ocoa and is indicated by a sign. Also on the way out of town is the Hotel Nueva Suiza which has a good view of the city. This hotel, now closed, was built during the dictatorship of Tujillo.

The Salto de Aguas Blancas ★★ is a waterfall about 20 km from Constanza. To get there, take the road to San José de Ocoa for about ten kilometres until the tiny hamlet of La Curva, where there is a fork in the road. If you continue straight, you will

Grapes

reach the falls, which are visible from the road. If you turn right, you will end up in San José de Ocoa. The road is in very bad condition. This superb waterfall, about 30 m high, is the highest waterfall above sea

level (more that 1,600 m) in the Caribbean and one of the most spectacular in the country. From the road, it takes only a few minutes on a small path to reach the bottom of the falls.

Reserva Cientifica Nacional Valle Nueva

Just south of Constanza and traversed by the road to San José de Ocoa, is the **Reserva Nacional Científica de Valle Nuevo** ★★, which covers 657 km² of mostly alpine plateau situated at an altitude of some 2,640 m. Pine forest predominates, but there are at least 249 other kinds of plants and trees. Dominican magnolias grow in the western part of the reserve and are endemic to the island. Unfortunately, about a third of the reserve was destroyed by a forest fire in 1983, and traces of this natural disaster are still visible. The temperature in the Valle Nuevo varies from -5 °C to 20°C, and the annual average rainfall is 2,500 mm. From a hydrological point of view, the Valle Nuevo is very important because it is the source of two of the country's main rivers: the Yuna and the Nizao rivers.

The Mountain Routes

San José de Ocoa to Constanza

Exceptionally beautiful mountain scenery unfolds all along the road between San José de Ocoa and Constanza. Lush coffee plantations hugging the slopes of verdant mountains quickly give way to narrow valleys cut by raging rivers. In this region known locally as the Dominican Alps, the spectacular panoramas encountered on this mountain pass are unequalled anywhere else in the country (or the Caribbean for that matter). In some completely uninhabited regions, the vegetation changes, consisting solely of coniferous trees. The only problem with this dirt road is its pitiable condition.

Seasoned drivers can venture here by car, but will rarely be able to go faster than 30 kph. Expect this extraordinary and memorable drive to take at least five hours, and remember to fill up with gas, because there is no station between San José de Ocoa and Constanza. Also, the road is very poorly marked, so avoid driving it after dark. Despite all of this, the singular wild beauty of this mountainous and isolated region is worth the adventure.

Constanza to Jarabacoa

Jarabacoa may be reached by crossing the mountainous landscape of Cordillera Centrale. Drive about 20 kilometres from Constanza towards La Vega, until you see a road branching off to the left, in the direction of Jarabacoa. This dirt road continues for another 30 kilometres to Jarabacoa, affording stunning panoramas along the way. Although not in very good shape, it is passable for cars, except in the days following heavy rains.

Santiago to San José de Las Matas

The road between Santiago and San José de Las Matas is in excellent condition, but tortuous and very steep in some places, both uphill and downhill. It offers a chance to admire a superb mountain landscape dominated by coffee plantations.

TheMountains

Jarabacoa

Located in the mountains of the Cordillera Centrale, at an altitude of more than 500 metres, Jarabacoa is blessed with pleasant temperatures all year long. Many wealthy Dominicans have their second home here, and the attractive houses that line the streets give the city an affluent look. The lively downtown area features an attractive little park, beside which stands an elegant colonial-style church.

While the city has its appeal, visitors and artists are more often attracted to the rolling countryside surrounding it. The region is also renowned for horse breeding, and equestrian sports are very popular here. Golf, swimming at the foot of waterfalls and in *balnearios*, as well as a host of other sports activities visitors can practise in the region, make Jarabacoa an increasingly popular holiday resort.
Rancho Baiguate, now a well known company, organizes several sports activities in the region such as river rafting.

El Salto de Jimenoa ★★ (*$1; 10 km from Jarabacoa on the way to La Vega, near the Alpes Dominicanos hotel, a road about 5 km long leads to the entrance to*

the site, from there it is a 5 min walk) is one of the most beautiful waterfalls in the country. The water cascades down about 30 metres into a natural pool, perfect for swimming. The setting is idyllic. Footbridges lead up the river to the falls, and there is a little café that sells refreshments.

El Salto de Bayagate ★ (*free admission; heading to Constanza, take the third road to the right after the Pinar Dorada Hotel, after a few kilometres, you'll see a parking lot; from there it's a 10-min walk*) is not as spectacular a waterfall as the former, but is nonetheless very pretty. It, too, is about 30 metres high, with a natural pool at its base. The area, however, is less developed than Salto de Jimenoa.

The Balneario de la Confluencia (*at the end of Calle Norberto Tiburcio*), at the confluence of the Jimenoa and Yaque del Norte rivers, is a tumultuous whirlpool where you can go swimming. There is a small park beside the balneario.

The Balneario de la Guazaras (*take Calle Norberto Tiburcio, then turn left on the third road after the fork*), near the centre of Jarabacoa, is a waterfall and a popular swimming spot with the city's younger population.

Parques Nacionals Armando Bermudez and José del Carmen Ramirez

In order to protect the flora and fauna of the central mountain range, the Dominican government created the **Parque Nacional Armando Bermudez** in 1956 (*766 km²*) and the **Parque Nacional José del Carmen Ramirez** (*764 km²*) two years later. Located side by side, these two national parks form the largest protected are in the country.

Uninhabited and very mountainous, these two parks are home to the highest peaks in the Caribbean: **Pico Duarte** (*about 3,090 m*), **La Pelonna** (*about 3,070 m*), **La Rusillia** (*3,035 m*) and **Pico Yaque** (*about 2,760 m*). These parks are also the source of some of the longest rivers in the country such as the **Yaque del Sur**, the **Río San Juan** and the **Río Mijo**. **Pre-Columbian petroglyphs** can also be seen in the **Telero Valley**, in the middle of the **Parque Nacional José del Carmen Ramirez**.

These parks are mainly covered by two kinds of forests: tropical and subtropical. Depending on the altitude, different kinds of trees grow including the cherry laurel, the sierra palm, the West Indian pine and the sorrel tree.

These parks are the natural habitat of birds such as the **Hispaniola amazon**, the **Hispaniola woodpecker**, the **red-tailed buzzard** and the dove. You can also see **wild pigs** and **hutias** as well as nearly 50 kinds of amphibians and reptiles.

The average temperature varies from 12 to 21°C, except during December and January when it can drop to -8°C at night. Depending on the area of the park, the average rainfall varies from 1,000 mm to 4,000 mm a year.

These parks can be visited only on foot or by mule because there are no roads. To visit the park, even for a day, you must have a permit (*about $3*) and be accompanied by a guide. Permits can be bought at the game-keepers' stations at any of the five following entrances to the parks: **La Cienaga, Mata Grande, Sabanneta, Las Lagunas** and **Constanza**. The gamekeepers can also find you a guide.

San José de las Matas

San José de las Matas is a peaceful little town nestled among pine-covered mountains. It is a popular resort area with wealthy Dominicans. Throughout the year, the temperature is slightly cooler here than it is in Santiago or on the coast. San José is a charming and visibly prosperous town. Though there isn't much to do, the beautiful road that leads here makes the excursion worthwhile.

The Salto de Agua Blanca
★★(*approximately 20 kilometres in the direction of San José de Ocoa, in Valle Nuevo's national reserve*) is a magnificent waterfall, about 30 metres high. Not easily accessible, the area is much less developed than the falls of the Jarabacoa region.

Outdoor Activities

Hiking

No vehicles are allowed in **Armando Bermudes** and **José del Carmen Ramirez National Parks**. In the last ten years, the government of the Dominican Republic has created numerous hiking trails throughout these parks. Most hikers come here to scale the summit of the **Pico Duarte** (*3090 m*), the highest peak in the Caribbean. This feat takes more than a day, so make sure to bring along adequate gear.

There are only five entrances to the parks, at **La Cienaga, Sabaneta, Mata Grande, Las Lagunas**, and **Constanza**. Each of these towns has a park warden from whom you must obtain a mandatory permit (*about $4*) to access the parks. This permit is required even if you are only visiting for a day. You will also need a guide to hike up the mountain (one guide is required for every three people). Guides cost about $32 a day and the park warden can recommend some good ones. Hiring more than one guide is indispensable for large groups: for example, if you are in a group that includes both fast and slow hikers, there should be one guide leading and another trailing behind to prevent anyone from getting lost en route.

Because many of the excursions last more than a day, you will have to stay overnight in the park. Accommodations are in *cabañas*, which provide rudimentary comfort and are sometimes not well maintained, or on free camping grounds that have been set up along the main trails.

The parks contain nothing but wilderness and do not provide any

The Mountains

services other than the *cabañas* and camping grounds. Therefore, every hiker is responsible for bringing along necessary gear for an excursion: a tent, sleeping bag, cooking supplies, utensils, food, and water. There are a few rivers and streams along the trails, but the water is not safe for drinking, unless it is boiled. Furthermore, the hike can be physically challenging, so it's a good idea to bring good hiking shoes, warm clothing (for evenings), a raincoat, a hat (for sun protection), and a first-aid kit.

It is highly recommended that each person rent a mule to carry all the equipment, or just in case someone gets hurt or tired. Mules can be rented at the park entrances for about *$22* a day.

The Main Trails

La Cienaga to Pico Duarte
The most popular trail starts at the small town of La Cienaga and runs 23 km one-way to Pico Duarte. The hike takes two to three days there and back. You can get to La Cienaga from Jarabacoa.

Mata Grande to Pico Duarte
The trail from Mata Grande to Pico Duarte is 45 km long one way. The return trip takes three to four days. You can get to Mata Grande from San José de Las Matas.

Sabaneta to Pico Duarte
Even longer than the previous two, the trail from Sabaneta to Pico Duarte is 48 km long. It is designated for hikers in good physical shape, because the return trip can take three to four days to complete. Sabaneta can be reached from San Juan de la Maguana.

Las Lagunas to Valle del Tetero
This 36-kilometre trail runs from Las Lagunas to the Valle del Tetero. It takes three to four days to hike there and back. You can get to Las Lagunas from Padre de las Casas.

Constanza to Valle de Tetero
You can also hike from Constanza to the Valle de Tetero. This trail is slightly longer (*43 km*) and takes three to four to complete.

Guided Tours

Rancho Baiguate
☎ *574-6890*
⇆ *574-4940*
In Jarabacoa The Rancho Baiguate arranges organizes hikes to the summit of Pico Duarte. English-speaking guides lead the hikes and provide the proper gear including food and water. The La Cienaga-Pico Duarte trail is one of the most popular hikes offered by Rancho Baiguate. You can also plan your own hike according to your level and convenience.

Horseback Riding

Horseback riding is the most popular sport in Jarabacoa. Horses can be rented in **Parque La Confluencia**, near the Salto de Bayagete, or at

The Rancho Baiguate
1 km past the Hotel Pinar Dorado
☎ *696-0318*
☎ *563-8005*
☎ *574-4840*
⇆ *574-4940*

Rafting

River rafting has just recently become a very popular sport in the Jarabacoa region. Aboard a rubber dinghy large enough to transport a dozen people, the descents generally take place on the Río Yaque del Norte.

The Rancho Baiguate
1 km past the Hotel Pinar Dorado
☎ *696-0318*
☎ *563-8005*
☎ *574-4840*
⇆ *574-4940*
Le Rancho Baiguate is the main company in the region organizing this activity and is affiliated with several tour operators on the coast. However, visitors need not go through the tour operators to participate in these excursions; book di-

rectly with the company for around $60 per person. The price includes transportation from Rancho Baiguate to the river, the necessary equipment and lunch. The company

Get Wet
1 km east of Jarabacoa
☎ *586-1170*
≈ *586-1655*
also organizes similar excursions.

Other Activities

Rancho Baiguate
First road on the left after the Pinar Dorado hotel
For the last few years, the Ranco Baiguate has been specializing in organizing a host of outdoor activities: besides horseback riding, hikes and river rafting, visitors can practise such sports as mountain biking, rock climbing and hang-gliding.

The Rancho Baiguate is affiliated with several tour operators on the Atlantic Coast. However, you do not have to go through these tour operators to take part in these various activities. For the past several years, the company:

Get Wet
1 km east of Jarabacoa
☎ *586-1170*
≈ *586-1655*

has also been organizing these kinds of activities.

Accommodations

San José de Ocoa

Hotel Marien
$16; ≡, ℜ
Calle Pimentel
☎ *558-3800*
This hotel has few well-kept rooms and a small restaurant.

Constanza

The El Gran Hotel
$10, ⊗
on the way into the city
Despite its somewhat unappealing

appearance, The El Gran Hotel, has perfectly decent rooms on the second floor and quiet, wooded and relaxing surroundings.

The Mi Casa
$10, ⊗
Calle Sanchez
☎ *539-2764*
Located on a quiet street, The Mi Casa is a friendly, family-run

establishment. The guestrooms are not very big, but are nevertheless clean and pleasant. Offers excellent value for the price. There is a restaurant on the ground floor.

The Mi Cabana Resort
$25, K, ≈, ⊗
1 km from downtown
☎ *539-2930*
≈ *539-2929*
This is a small residential complex that rents and sells small two-storey accommodations with a lovely view of Constanza. Each pavilion has two guestrooms with slightly deteriorated furnishings. The place can seem isolated, especially since the complex is virtually unoccupied most of the time. To get there, take the road towards San José de Ocoa for about one kilometre.

Right next door, the **Nueva Suiza Hotel** should open for business soon, after many years of renovation. Perched on a hillside, it offers a striking view of Constanza.

Hotel California
$20, ⊗, ℜ
77 Calle Luperon
☎ *539-2498*
Its one room is large and well kept, but a little dark. It has a large bathroom. Unfortunately, it faces the street and can be noisy at times.

The Altocerro
$30,
Colonia Kennedy
☎ *686-0202*
Close to Constanza, The Altocerro includes about 20 villas equipped with one, two or three bedrooms, in addition to guestrooms. The rooms are not luxurious, but they are comfortable. There are also camping lots and rental bikes available on site.

Jarabacoa

Jarabacoa has the greatest number of hotel rooms in the region. The least expensive are in the *cabañas* located at the city's entrance.

Hotel Holly Day
$13, ⊗
1 km in the direction of Constanza
☎ *574-2778*
Hotel Holly Day rents small, clean and basically comfortable rooms. They are situated in a two storey renovated building on the road to Constanza.

The Hotel Hogar
$20, ⊗, ℜ,
Calle Melia
This hotel offers rooms with very basic furnishings. The interior courtyard, however, is peaceful and charming. This is the perfect place to meet locals or young Dominicans on vacation.

Pinar Dorado
$36, ⊗, ≈, *tv,* ℜ
just outside of town on the way to Constanza
☎ *574-2820*
Located in a gracious landscaped area on the outskirts of town, the Pinar Dorado is a congenial hotel with spacious, air-conditioned rooms. This is a comfortable hotel although the furniture and the bathrooms are somewhat dilapidated. Some of the rooms have been repainted.

The Alpes Dominicanos
$45, ⊗, ≈, ℜ
on the highway, a few kilometres before Jarabacoa
☎ *581-1462*
≈ *689-3703*
This is a large complex surrounded by forest situated about a

dozen kilometres from Jarabacoa.

Although this complex is made up mostly of beautiful private homes, you can spend the night here. The rooms are large and

clean, but a little worse for wear.

The Rancho Baiguate
$80, fb, ℜ, ⊗;; ≈
first road on the left after the Pinar Dorado Hotel
☎ *696-0318*
☎ *563-8005*
☎ *574-4840*
≈ *574-4940*
The Rancho Baiguate is mainly known for the great outdoor activities it offers in the Jarabacoa region such as river rafting on the Río Yaque and climbing the Pico Duarte. The hotel itself is pretty but small and has about 20 basic but charming rooms located in several buildings on a large area of land bordering the river. The owners of Rancho Baiguate have made commendable efforts to preserve the local environment, the most ingenious of them, perhaps, being an efficient waste-water system. There are also plans to create a small botanical garden.

San José de las Matas

Until recently, there was a very beautiful resort in San José de las Matas called **La Mancion**, which is now closed. However, the town still has a few inexpensive hotels.

The good life on the beach at Punta Cana.
- *B. Perousse*

Tobacco drying sheds like this one are seen all over the Dominican Republic.
- *Claude Hervé-Bazin*

The Dominican Republic is the largest cigar exporter, after Cuba. There are many cigar factories in the country, like this one in Santiago.
- *L. Pierson*

"Take the time
to take the
time".
- *T. Philiptchenko*

A symphony
of colours and
aromas on the
streets of
Puerto Plata.
T. Philiptchenko

Playa Cabarete, one of the mos[t] popular beache[s] in the country.
- *T. Philiptchenk[o]*

The boutiques of Puerto Plata, where jewellery, souvenirs and a variety of other objects are found side by side.
- *T. Philiptchenko*

The Oasis
$11; ℜ, ⊗
facing the Parque Central
Downtown, you'll find
the Oasis, whose
rooms are pretty basic.

The Hotel Las Samanás
$11, ℜ, ⊗
Avenida Santiago
☎ 578-8316
You might also opt for
The Hotel Las Samanás,
in the same category,
located on the way into
town. This small hotel
has reasonably priced
and a good restaurant.

Restaurants

Constanza

As in all small Domi-
nican towns, the streets
of Constanza are lined
with cafes and restau-
rants that serve varied
and inexpensive food.

Lorenzo
$$
Calle Luperon
For a more elaborate
meal, try the Lorenzo.
Its decor and four
television screens are
sure to please sports
fans. As for the food,
the creolla steak is
particularly good. The
restaurant is air-condi-
tioned and serves less
expensive meals during
the day.

California
$-$$
Calle Luperon
☎ 539-2498
This is one of the best
restaurants in
Constanza. There is
something for everyone
on the elaborate menu
which lists meat, fish
and pasta dishes as
well as pizzas and light
meals.

Jarabacoa

The Don Luis
$$
next to Parque Duarte
The Don Luis is well-
located right in
theheart of town, near
Parque Duarte. It is a
pleasant spot, but can
get noisy. The menu
consists mainly of steak
and chicken prepared
in a variety of ways.
Great ice cream is
available next door.

El Sotanno
$-$$
Calle Duarte opposite Parque
Duarte
El Sotanno is another
pleasant place to eat in
Jarabacoa. Its menu is
varied but mainly
composed of meat,
chicken and pasta
dishes, as well as pizza.
You can either eat
inside the restaurant or
on the pretty terrace
overlooking Jarabacoa's
main square.

San José de las Matas

La Caoba
$-$$
Fernando Valerio
☎ 578-8141
A pleasant restaurant,
La Caoba serves a
variety of local dishes,
including good grilled
chicken. The host of
this small, quiet spot
makes every effort to
provide service worthy
of the best restaurants
in Santo Domingo.

The Cibao Valley

This vast region of the Dominican Republic encompasses the Cibao valley and the Cordillera Septentrionale mountain range, which isolates it from the Atlantic coast.

The one common denominator is the quality of the arable land. An astonishing variety of agricultural products grow in these remarkably fertile lands, which also provide pasture for nearly all of the Dominican Republic's livestock. The fact that the Dominican Republic is one of the only islands that can produce most of its foodstuffs locally is above all due to the formidable agricultural potential of this region.

The natural riches of the central region have been coveted for many years. Christopher Columbus wrote enthusiastically in his logbook about the area's enormous potential. From the start of colonization, the Spaniards set out to tap its resources, cultivating the Cibao valley, though many were initially attracted here by the rich gold deposits discovered there. Some of the first European settlements in the New World began as fortifications built to protect gold mining operations. A number of these have grown into the most prosperous and important cities in the country. The Cibao valley is the most densely populated part of the Dominican Republic after the Santo Domingo region. The valley is home to the city of Santiago de los Caballeros, the second largest city in the Dominican Republic.

Finding Your Way Around

The highway that links Santo Domingo to Santiago de los Caballeros is the main trunk road crossing the Cibao valley. In the course of the last few years, major government funding has allowed for this arterial road to be widened. The highway now has two lanes in each direction the length of the journey. Traffic, therefore, moves along much faster now, and the risk of accidents has been greatly reduced. This highway transects the cities of Bonao, La Vega and Santiago. Another major road allows drivers to quickly reach the Samaná peninsula from Santo Domingo. This road leaves the Santo Domingo-Santiago highway in Piedra Blanca, a small town approximately 60 kilometres north of Santo Domingo. It then goes through the city of Cotui, leading to Nagua on the Atlantic coast. Drivers can also easily reach the mountainous region, notably in Constanza and Jarabacoa, from the Cibao valley.

Santiago de Los Caballeros

If you are coming from La Vega and want to avoid the downtown area, turn right at the traffic circle in front of the Monumento. Several downtown arteries are one-way, including Calle del Sol, which goes from Parque Duarte towards the Monumento, and Calle Las Cabreras, which runs in the opposite direction.

The city's airport is less than two kilometres from downtown, near the highway leading to Monte Cristi.

Several car rental companies have offices in Santiago, including:

Budget
☎ *575-9230.*

Moca

Several well-maintained roads lead to Moca from the highway that links Santiago to Santo Domingo. It is also possible to reach Moca from the tiny town of Sabaneta, just a few kilometres east of Cabarete on the Atlantic Coast.

Cotui

From Santo Domingo, drivers can travel north on the highway leading to Santiago until reaching the small town of Piedra Blanca. From there, a road heading east leads straight to Cotui.

San Francisco de Macorís

From Cotui, continuing toward the northwestern part of the country, drivers can reach San Francisco by taking a left at the turn-off that suddenly appears a little after the small town of Pimentel. Conversely, the road on the right leads to Nagua, then to the Samaná peninsula. In other respects, for travellers coming from Santiago, San Francisco is a necessary crossing point on the way to the peninsula.

Practical Information

Santiago de Los Caballeros

The downtown area extends around Parque Duarte and onto Calle del Sol, which is lined with a series of shops, banks and restaurants.

Metro
At the corner of Avenidas Duarte and Maimón
☎ *582-9111*
☎ *587-3837*

Tourism Agency
Caribe Tours
Avenida 27 de Febrero
☎ *576-0790*

La Vega

The downtown area of La Vega is on the west side of the Duarte Highway.

Metro
Duarte Highway km 1
☎ *573-7099*

A **Codetel** can be found at *21 Avenida Circunvalación.*

Moca

Metro
At the corner of Morillo and Salcedo
☎ *578-2541*
or 577-6566

The **Codetel** is located on Nuestra Señora del Rosario, at the corner of Calle Duvergé.

San Francisco de Macorís

The downtown area and its numerous shops are concentrated the central park (*Avenida Castillo*).

The **Codetel** is located at *54 Avenida 27 de Febrero*.

Metro
Avenida de Los Martires, km 1
☎ *588-8080*

Exploring

Bonao

Once a fort erected on Admiral Christopher Columbus' orders, in 1493, Bonao was one of the country's very first settlements. Today, it is a peaceful little town in the hollow of the Cibao valley. Though lacking any particular charm, it affords a view of the lovely landscape of mountains in its vicinity.

Bonao draws its prosperity from agriculture, but also, to a great extent, from the mining of rich nickel deposits found in the region. The Dominican Republic is the seventh largest producer of nickel in the world and the second in the Americas. Bonao's nickel deposits are mined by Falconbridge, a Canadian multinational corporation.

La Vega

The history of La Vega began in the 15th century when Christopher Columbus ordered a fort built here to protect the region's bountiful gold mines. Within a few years, La Vega had become one of the most important cities on the island, as well as the summer residence of Viceroy Diego Columbus, his father's successor. However, this prosperity came to an abrupt end in 1562, when the city was completely destroyed by an earthquake. La Vega was rebuilt the next year on the banks of the Río Camu, its present location, but did not regain its former economic and political stature until it was linked to the coast by rail during the 19th century.

It is now a rather noisy, crowded city of moderate size, whose economy is closely linked to the fertile agricultural land surrounding it. La Vega is known primarily for its carnival masks (depicting devils). The carnival takes place at the end of February.

La Vega has a pretty central park next to the stunning **Cathedrale Concepcion de la Vega** *Av. Independencia*

To get to Santo Cerro from La Vega, take the highway heading north for a short distance until you reach a turn-off on the right. After approximately four kilometres along this narrow road, a rocky trail will appear on the left, climbing up to the convent.

Santo Cerro ★ (*about 5 km northeast of the city*) is a small hill topped by a church built in the 1880s, which houses a portrait of La Virgen de las Mercedes (Our Lady of Mercy).

Christopher Columbus ordered the construction of a large wooden cross at the summit of **Santo Cerro**, or *holy hill*, in 1495 (the first crucifix erected in the New World), after the Virgin Mary was said to have appeared there and helped the Spanish win a decisive victory over the natives. In one of the naves of the **Iglesia Las Mercedes** (*open after 2pm*), you can see the **Santo Hoyo**, the exact place where The Cross was raised. Also, at the entrance to the church is a beautiful big tree which may have been born from the tree whose wood was used to construct The Cross. The site offers an excellent view of the Cibao valley which is also called The La Vega Real Valley.

To reach the ruins of La Vega Vieja, continue along the same road for about two kilometres.

The archaeological site of the ruins of **La Vega Vieja** (*2 km farther on the same road*) is one of the largest in the country. Visitors can see vestiges of a Franciscan monastery (1512) and a fortress (1495). Built around the time of Christopher Columbus, this town was completely destroyed by an earthquake in 1562.

Santiago de Los Caballeros

To get to Parque Duarte (downtown), take the road skirting the Monumento on the right (Las Cabreras), then turn left onto Calle 30 de Marzo.

In 1494, Christopher Columbus ordered a fort built on the banks of the Río Yaque del Norte river, once again to protect gold mining operations in the region. Some years later, in 1503, one of the first waves of Spanish agricultural workers chose to settle in this village.

As the group was made up of about thirty *caballeros* (gentlemen) belonging to the Order of St-James (El Orden de Santiago), the new colony was called Santiago de Los Caballeros.

Destroyed in 1562 by a strong earthquake, the city was rebuilt the next year on its present site, a few kilometres from the former location. Later, its strategic position in the centre of the rich Cibao valley allowed it to prosper and to play an important role in the history of the country. As shown by the many monuments throughout the city, it played a crucial role during the War of Independence (1844) and the Restoration of the Republic (1865). Santiago is also the proud birthplace of several of the country's presidents.

With a population of over 500,000, Santiago is the second largest city in the country after Santo Domingo. It is generally quieter than the capital, though downtown traffic is heavy and **Calle del Sol** is one of the liveliest commercial streets in the country. Like its rum and tobacco production, the *merengue*, which supposedly originated here, has earned local residents a reputation for their vitality.

The best time to visit Santiago is during **Carnival**, which takes place in February. This tradition originated in the last century, and is marked by colourful parades and celebrations and by a competition between residents of the Los Pepines and La Joya neighbourhoods, who are easily identifiable by the shape of their respective carnival masks.

El Monumento de los Héroes de la Restauración de la República ★ (*free admission; on the road from Santo Domingo*) was erected in the 1940s under the dictator Trujillo and served as a monument to himself; it was originally known as the Trujillo peace monument. The 67-metre-high marble structure, visible throughout the city, has since been dedicated to the heroes of the Restoration. It presently houses a museum displaying works by Spanish painter Vela Zannetti. There is an excellent view of Santiago and the Cibao valley from its top.

The **Parque Duarte** (*at the corner of Calle del Sol and Calle 30 de Marzo*) is an oasis of peace in the heart of the bustling city centre. It encloses an elegant Victorian-style pavilion and a monument to the heroes of the Restoration. Carriage drivers wait near the park, offering tours of the city (*$8 US*). Nearby **Calle del Sol** is one of the most vibrant commercial streets in the country.

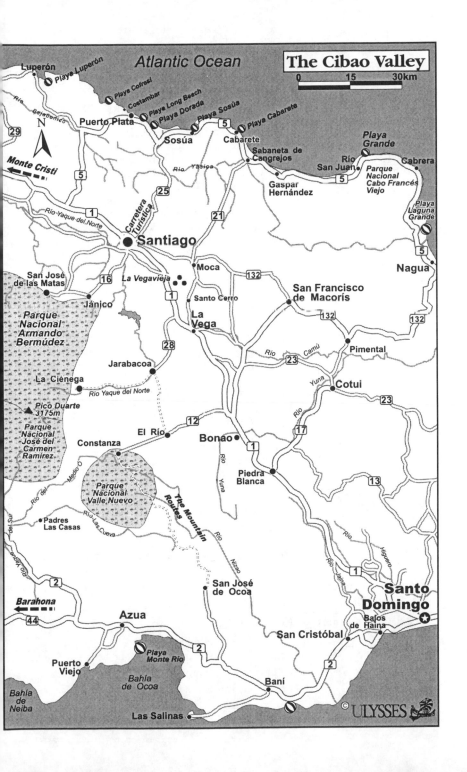

A few streets from the park on Calle del Sol is the *Mercado Modelo*, Santiago's small traditional market.

The **Catedral de Santiago Apostol** (*free admission; facing Parque Duarte*), built between 1868 and 1895, has neoclassic and republican architectural features. It contains the tombs of the dictator Ulysses Heureaux and several Restoration heroes. The beautiful stained-glass windows are the work of the Dominican artist Rincón Mora.

The **Palacio Consistorial** (*free admission; facing Parque Duarte*) was the city hall for a good part of the 19th century. It now houses the **Santiago Museum**, which exhibits old and recent works by local artists.

Situated right beside the Palacio, **Edificio del Centro de Recreo** (*opposite Parque Duarte*) houses one of the oldest private clubs in the country, reserved almost exclusively to members.

Santiago is the main cigar-producing centre in the Dominican Republic. Many factories have been set up in the free zone and elsewhere in the city. If you like cigars, the **Leon Jimenes** factory organizes **guided tours** ★ (*free admission; from 9am to 5pm*) of the facilities. It is most

Dominican Tobacco and Cigars

Although the cigar-making industry in the Dominican Republic is not as old or as large as Cuba's, it produces some of the finest cigars in the world by such famous brand-names as Davidoff, Juan Clemente, and Arturo Fuente. Dominican cigars are much appreciated by aficionados.

The cigar was invented in Seville in 1676 and was made entirely of tobacco. In the next few centuries, many cigar factories were established throughout Europe, but the quality of the cigars was limited, because it took a long time to ship the tobacco leaves from Caribbean plantations.

Finally, in the late 19th century, some producers in Cuba began to open factories near their plantations, significantly improving the quality of the cigars. This is how Cuban cigars came to be famous all over the world. When Fidel Castro nationalized the cigar industry, some producers decided to move their factories to the neighbouring Dominican Republic, mostly around Santiago. So for the last 10 years, Davidoff cigars, one of the most renowned brands in the world, have been made exclusively in the tiny republic.

Some well-recommended Dominican cigars:

Double R and Special T by Davidoff

Churchill, Obelisco and Rothschild by Juan Clemente

No 9 by Avo

Rothschild by Canaria d'Oro

Gran Corono by Montesino

Pythagoras and Magnificat by Credo

Briva Fina and Briva Conserva by Henry Clay.

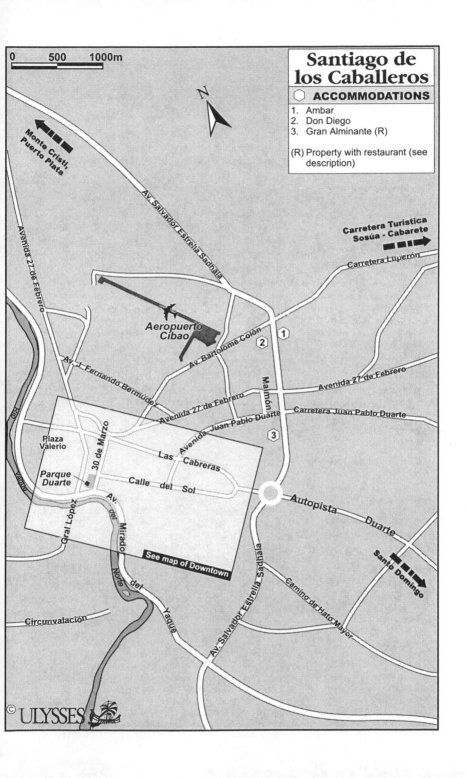

0 500 1000m

Santiago de los Caballeros

⬡ **ACCOMMODATIONS**

1. Ambar
2. Don Diego
3. Gran Alminante (R)

(R) Property with restaurant (see description)

N

Monte Cristi,
Puerto Plata

Av. Salvador Estrella Sadhalá

Avenida 27 de Febrero

Carretera Turística
Sosúa - Cabarete

Carretera Luperón

Aeropuerto
Cibao

Av. Bartolomé Colón

Av. J. Fernando Bermúdez

Avenida 27 de Febrero

Avenida 27 de Febrero

Malmón

Carretera Juan Pablo Duarte

Avenida Juan Pablo Duarte

Plaza
Valerio

30 de Marzo

Las   Cabreras

Parque
Duarte

Calle   del   Sol

Río Yaque

Gral. López

Av. del Mirador

See map of Downtown

Autopista

Duarte

Santo Domingo

Norte   del

Circunvalación

Yaque

Av. Salvador Estrella Sadhalá

Camino de Hato Mayor

© ULYSSES

interesting to watch the workers make the cigars by hand, delicately rolling the tobacco leaves. This factory produces Leon Jimenes and Aurora cigars, which are sold on the spot.

The **Museo del Tabaco** (*free admission; facing Parque Duarte*) houses an exhibit on the history of the tobacco industry and its importance to Santiago's and the country's economies. The exhibit may not be spectacular, but it is nonetheless interesting. The museum's staff can tell you which cigar manufacturers in Santiago allow visits. One that offers impromptu tours is just a few streets from the museum.

The **Centro de la Cultura** (*free admission; 100 m north of the park on Calle del Sol*) regularly puts on interesting exhibits of works by Dominican painters.

The **Thomas Morel Folkloric Museum** (*free admission; Mon to Fri 8:30am to 1:30pm; Calle Restauración*) houses a private collection of popular art pieces as well as articles related to Santiago's carnival. The exhibition is interesting.

A pretty road runs through the northern mountain range, from Moca to the Atlantic coast.

The Valley Routes

The Carratera Turística: Santiago to Sosúa

The Carratera Turística provides a quick link between the Atlantic coast and Santiago, through the majestic landscape of the Cordillera Septentrionale in the centre of the country. The road is in excellent condition, and traffic moves quite fast, since weight limits are enforced. It takes about an hour to reach Santiago from the Atlantic coast. The road starts on the coast between Sosúa and Puerto Plata.

Moca to the Atlantic Coast

The road from Moca to the Atlantic coast has recently been repaved. It, too, runs through mountainous landscapes of the Cordillera Septentrionale, offering magnificent views of the Cibao valley. This road begins on the Atlantic coast in the village of Sabaneta, near Sosúa.

Moca

Located in the mountains of the Cordillera Septentrionale range, the town of Moca is the hub of a major coffee growing region. Plantations abound on the slopes of the nearby mountains, lending a touch of green to the surrounding landscape. The town itself is peaceful and appealing. At its centre stands a monument to Ramón Caceres, who assassinated the terrible dictator Ulysses Heureaux on July 25, 1899. Its main streets are lined with buildings, including the beautiful **Iglesia del Sagrado Corazón de Jesús** and the **Iglesia del Rosado**. The town also has a small **zoo**, whose interest lies mostly in its luxuriant gardens.

Cotui

Passing through the city of Cotui is necessary for those who wish to get to Santo Domingo in the Samaná Peninsula.

Cotui is a peaceful, charming little town that, like many of the Cibao valley's agglomerations, was estab-

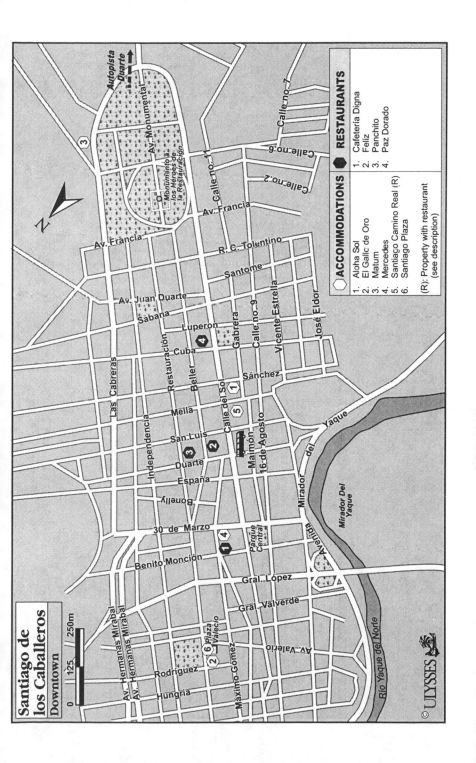

Santiago de los Caballeros
Downtown

0 125 250m

N

Autopista Duarte

Av. Monumental

Monumento a los Héroes de la Restauración

Calle no. 7

Calle no. 6

Calle no. 2

Av. Francia

Av. Francia

R. C. Tolentino

Santome

Av. Juan Duarte

Sábana

Luperón

Cuba

Gabrera

Calle no. 9

Vicente Estrella

José Eldor

Las Cabreras

Restauración

Beller

Mella

Sánchez

Calle del Sol

Independencia

San Luis

Duarte

Maimón

Yaque

Mirador del

España

16-de-Agosto

Bonelly

30 - de - Marzo

Parque Central

Mirador Del Yaque

Benito Monción

Gral. López

Avenida

Gral. Valverde

Av. Valerio

Río Yaque del Norte

Av. Hermanas Mirabal

Av. Hermanas Mirabal

Plaza Valecio

Rodríguez

Máximo-Gómez

Hungría

© ULYSSES

ACCOMMODATIONS
1. Aloha Sol
2. El Gallo de Oro
3. Matum
4. Mercedes
5. Santiago Camino Real (R)
6. Santiago Plaza

(R): Property with restaurant
(see description)

RESTAURANTS
1. Cafetería Digna
2. Feliz
3. Panchito
4. Paz Dorado

lished at the very on-set of colonization on Christopher Columbus' orders. Today, a central park, some restaurants and a few rather modest hotels can be found here. Known for its major agricultural production, the Cotui re gion can also be counted among the country's large mining centres.

San Francisco de Macorís

Covering an area of several square kilometres at the foot of the Cordillera Septentrionale, San Francisco de Macorís is one of the largest urban areas in the country.

The fertile land nearby, used primarily for grazing and growing rice, contributes significantly to the economy of the city. This town has also prospered because of the many wealthy families that came here from the United States. These "York Dominicans", as they are called here, like to display their wealth. It is even said that there are more Mercedes Benz in San Francisco than in any other city in the Dominican Republic.

San Francisco de Macorís has few attractions to speak of, except its **Parque Central**, located on

The Carnival

Twice a year, in February and August, the carnival descends upon the Dominican Republic. The days leading up to and following this popular festival are animated with parades, large gatherings and dancing. The highlight of these wild festivities is unquestionably the carnival characters, dressed in brightlycoloured costumes and masks, which are often endowed with huge horns. Whether *diablos cojuelos* from Santo Domingo or La Vega, *lechones* from Santiago, *toros y civiles* from Monte Cristi, *papeluses* from San Francisco or buyolas from San Pedro de Macorís,

these amusing devils roam the streets in search of sinners. Some of the masks are on display in the Museo del Hombre Dominicano in Santo Domingo (see p78).

The carnival's origins are obscure, but celebrations such as these take place in a good number of Latin countries. They may be derived from a pagan ritual that once honoured the coming of spring and the rejuvenation of nature, or perhaps even from an ancient Roman festival. The fact remains that this celebration has come down through the ages and has adapted to each country's customs and traditions.

Avenida Castillo and flanked by two imposing churches, a university building and several restaurants and small businesses. For most travellers, San Francisco de Macorís is just a stop along the way between Santo Domingo and the Samaná Peninsula.

Accommodations

La Vega

A few hotels along the highway to the north offer adequate, but very basic and noisy rooms. Warning: if you are looking for accommodation that is even the least bit comfortable and quaint, then avoid La Vega.

The San Pedro Hotel
$10 ⊗
87 Avenida De Carceres
☎ 573-2814
On a calm street in the heart of town, the San Pedro Hotel has quiet, simply furnished rooms. Some are supplied with air conditioners but are more expensive ($22).

The Astral Hotel
$20 US ⊗
78 Avenida De Carceres
☎ 573-3535
This property is right across the street, and offers rooms only of a similar standard to those at the San Pedro.

Santiago de Los Caballeros

Santiago Plaza
$10 ⊗
Plaza Valerio
Most of the inexpensive hotels are clustered around the Plaza Valerio. Among these, the Santiago Plaza offers basic rooms. The

El Gallo de Oro
$10 ⊗
Plaza Valerio
El Gallo de Oro in the same area, has several clean but rather Spartan rooms.

The Mercedes Hotel
$17 ⊗
18 Calle 30 de Marzo
☎ 583-1171
This is a charming old building, and part of the city's architectural heritage. A pleasant, traditional atmosphere prevails here, though the rooms are simple, noisy and not always well kept. The hotel is located right at the heart of the downtown area.

The Ambar Hotel
$30, tv, ≡, ℜ
Avenida Estrella Sadhala, outside the downtown area
☎ 575-4811
The Ambar Hotel offers plainly decorated but clean rooms. It is quite far from the city centre in an uninteresting area, near the airport which explains its very affordable rates.

The Matum
$42, ≡, ℜ
facing the Monumento
☎ 581-3107
⇆ 581-8415
The Matum has a stately air about it, but it has clearly seen better days. Although not very luxurious, the rooms are large and clean. This charming establishment is well-located near downtown Santiago and may soon be renovated.

The Don Diego Hotel
$40, ≡, ≈, ℜ,
Avenida Estrella Sadhala, outside the city centre
☎ 575-4186
The Don Diego Hotel has 40 decent, comfortable rooms. It is a bit far from downtown, but the price is reasonable for what you get. Like the Ambar, the Don Diego is next to the highway heading to the northern part of the island.

Santiago Camino Real
$66, tv, ≡, ℜ
at the corner of Calle del Sol and Calle Mella
☎ 581-7000
⇆ 582-4566
This hotel is centrally located on the liveliest street in the city, close to the main sights. Modern and comfortable, this hotel has a piano bar, a disco and a restaurant with a good reputation. The Camino Real is one of Santiago's institutions; it has recently undergone some renovations. It offers good quality accommodation.

The Aloha Sol Hotel
$66, ≡, ℜ
Calle del Sol
☎ 583-0090
or 581-9203
⇆ 583-0950
Since its recent opening, this beautiful hotel with comfortable rooms has given the Camino Real, located right nearby, some stiff competition. Like the Camino Real, it has suites (*$90*) as well.

The Cibao Valley

The Gran Almirante
$75, =, ℛ, ≈, ♠
Avenida Estrella Sadhala, on the periphery of the downtown area
☎ *580-1992*
≈ *241-1492*
This is Santiago's most luxurious hotel. Gran Almirante has spacious, well-kept and comfortably furnished rooms. Popular with business people, this establishment has a casino as well as excellent restaurants. The property is currently being expanded and the work is scheduled to be completed sometime at the beginning of the year 2000.

Restaurants

La Vega

The Vega Vieja Cafe
$
Calle Independencia opposite the cathedral
A perfect place for a light snack at noon. Its menu includes sandwiches, cakes and juice. The location is pleasant because it is quiet and overlooks the attractive square in front of the cathedral.

Santiago de Los Caballeros

A good choice of restaurants with outside terraces can be found on the streets around the Monumento de los Héroes de la Restauración de la República. The atmosphere in this part of town, like downtown Santiago, especially along Calle del Sol, is often very lively in the evening.

Caldero Feliz
$ *lunch only*
Located at the corner of Calles San Luiz and Beller this is a cafeteria which prepares inexpensive, copious servings of Dominican family cooking. Workers in the area meet here at noon to enjoy a quick meal in a friendly atmosphere, and you should join them!

Panchito
$
at the corner of Calles Restauración and Duarte
This is fast-food Dominican-style! Sandwiches, ice cream and pizza are among the very inexpensive offerings.

Cafeteria Digna
$
at the corner of Calles Maximo Gomez and Benito Manción
A variety of inexpensive sandwiches can be enjoyed in the friendly and laid-back atmosphere of the Cafeteria Digna. Breakfast service begins in the wee hours of the morning. This is something of a meeting place for locals.

The Altav
$$-$$$
Calle del Sol, Camino Real Hotel
☎ *581-4566*
Altav prepares international specialties, as well as a selection of fine Dominican dishes. Diners can enjoy a wonderful view of the city from the terrace on the top floor of the Camino Real.

Paz Dorado
$$
43 Calle de Sol
☎ *582-4051*
Over the years, Paz Dorado has become one of Santiago's finest gourmet restaurants. Both local and international specialities are prepared and presented with flair. The restaurant's classic, elegant decor also adds to the pleasure of dining here.

Don Cristobal
$$$
Hotel Gran Almirante
☎ *589-1792*
One of the best restaurants in Santiago. Comfortably decorated in an old Spanish style, this restaurant serves international gourmet cuisine and is the perfect place for fine dining. The Hotel Gran Almirante also has a less fancy restaurant, Las Tapas, which serves bistro-type food.

Cotui

El Río
$-$$
Facing the parque
central, and opening
onto the street, is the El
Río Restaurant, where
visitors can have a bite
to eat. Sandwiches,
pizza, and several
Dominican fish and
meat dishes are served
here.

San Francisco de Macorís

There are several res-
taurants in the down-
town area, but also on
the way out of town
heading toward
the middle of
the country.

Entertainment and Shopping

Santiago de los Cabelleros

Gran Almirante Casino
Avenida Estrella Sadhala
☎ *580-1992*
Those who wish to
try their luck can
head to The Gran
Almirante Hotel's
Casino, close to
the downtown
area.

Calle del Sol is the
shopping mecca of
Santiago. All kinds of
shops are to be found
here, particularly cloth-
ing stores. Cigars can
be purchased in a num-
ber of grocery stores, at
the tobacco museum as
well as in the city's
various factories.

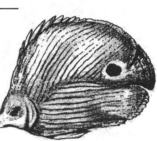

The Cibao Valley

Glorieta - Parque Central, Puerto Plata

Puerto Plata and the Atlantic Coast

T ravelling from Puerto Plata to the Samaná Peninsula, a formidable 150-kilometre-long seafront, takes you through one of the best known regions of the Dominican Republic.

More than anywhere else in the country, the development of tourism has been particularly intense over the last 20 years, and many of the region's towns and villages have become major resort areas. Following Puerto Plata, Sosúa and Cabarete, development of the superb beaches has now moved further east, to the region of Río San Juan and Playa Grande.

However, despite the ever-increasing popularity of this coast, the daily lives of its inhabitants still revolve around the traditional economic activities they always have, that is fishing and farming. With a relatively low population, these vast expanses remain untamed in many spots, and countless splendours await discovery by adventurous travellers.

Finding Your Way Around

Highway 5 links the coastal cities from Puerto Plata to the Samaná Peninsula. Most of the road is in excellent condition.

Several roads branch off of Highway 5 and head across the magnificent Cordillera Septentrionale toward the centre of the country. One of the most picturesque and useful is the **Carretera Turística**, which provides a quick link between Santiago de los Caballeros and the coast. The advantage of this lovely mountain road is that trucks are not allowed on it, so traffic is faster and more pleasant.

The Port of Silver

When Christopher Columbus landed on the northern coast of the island of Hispaniola, he noticed a particular tree, the *grayumo*, whose leaves reflected silver in the sun's rays. It so inspired Columbus that he named the site Puerto Plata, which means "port of silver" in Spanish.

Road Conditions

The roads on the Atlantic coast are generally in good condition and have little traffic. This changes dramatically around Puerto Plata, however, where the road widens to include as many as four lanes. Many of the motorists take advantage of the situation, and accelerate their speed in an attempt to bypass - sometimes in a somewhat reckless way - mopeds and other slower vehicles . Caution is advised, especially during the morning and late-afternoon rush hours, if you would like to avoid getting flustered by a rash vehicle coming out of nowhere to cut you off.

Taxis

Since all of the coastal cities abound with taxis, it's never a problem to find one. In Puerto Plata as much as in Sosúa, Carabete and Río San Juan, there are taxi-stands that openly display price lists (the prices indicated are always one-way).

Guanillo Palm Tree

The cars are not always in great condition, but you're likely to reach your destination in spite of this. If you've hired a taxi and plan on making a return trip, count on paying at the very end of the ride.

Guaguas

In order to get to the different areas of this zone you can engage the services of one of the *guaguas* which are efficient but not very comfortable. They stop frequently to let passengers on and off, and are always packed. This mode of transportation is very economical, offering frequent service and providing an interesting way to meet the locals.

Puerto Plata International Airport

The Puerto Plata International Airport is only 18 kilometres east of the city and 8 kilometres west of Sosúa. It is the point of arrival for most visitors to the Atlantic Coast, and is the second largest airport in the country after Santo Domingo's. The recently enlarged airport is well laid-out, and includes waiting rooms, a few boutiques and a restaurant. The personnel is generally quite efficient.

Taxis

A taxi from the airport costs around *$14 US* to Puerto Plata, *$7 US* to Sosúa and *$20 US* to Cabarete. A considerable number of taxis wait outside the airport.

Buses (*Guaguas*)

There is no regular bus service (*guaguas*) from the airport to the city. However, guaguas and collective taxis stop on

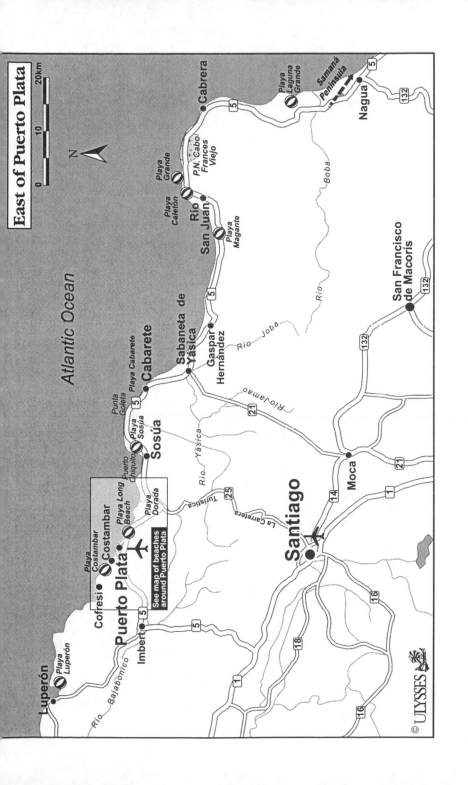

East of Puerto Plata

0 10 20km

N

Atlantic Ocean

© ULYSSES

the highway, which is only about a ten-minute walk from the airport. The bus fare is about *$1 US* to Puerto Plata or Sosúa and *$2 US* to Cabarete.

If the notion of riding onboard a crowded and swaying guagua does not appeal to you, the bus is always a good option. Although a bit pricier, the buses are comfortable and air-conditioned. Addresses of bus terminals located in the major cities of this region, namely Puerto Plata and Sosúa, are listed in this guide.

Renting a Car

The international car rental agencies have offices in Puerto Plata and at the airport. National rental companies occasionally have offices in the other urban areas along the coast. These companies rarely offer better rates, and their vehicles are more likely to be in poor condition. In any case, before renting a car, compare prices and insurance policies carefully, as they can vary greatly from one agency to another, and make sure the car is in good condition.

The following agencies can be contacted by telephone:

Budget
☎ *586-4480*

Hertz
☎ *586-0200*

Thrifty
☎ *586-0242*

Always ask if there are any specials. Budget's rates are often less expensive. It is possible to rent a car in advance by contacting the international reservation service offered by the major rental agencies.

Puerto Plata

There is only one main road into Puerto Plata. It crosses the city from west to east, where it becomes Avenida Circunvalación Sur. Running parallel, Avenida Circunvalación Norte (which becomes Avenida Luperón) follows the ocean from Long Beach to the San Felipe Fortress.

These two main roads are linked to the west by Avenida Colón and to the east by Avenida Mirabal. The four avenues form a rectangle around the city, making it easy to find your way around. Most of the hotels in Puerto Plata are located on the east side of town, facing Long Beach, or along Avenida Mirabal.

If you haven't got a car, it is easy to get around by hailing a motorcycle, locals are used to picking up passengers and will take you from one end of the city to the other for about *$1 US*.

Bus Stops

The following two companies offer inexpensive and direct long-distance bus service aboard air-conditioned vehicles:

Métro
Calle 16 de Agosto corner of Beller
☎ *586-6061*

Caribe Tours
Calle 12 de Julio
☎ *586-4544*

Guagua Stops

Guaguas to and from the western part of the island or Santo Domingo stop on Avenida Imbert (the continuation of Avenida Circonvalación Sur), about 500 metres west of Avenida Colón. For destinations east of Puerto Plata, buses stop in front of the hospital.

Taxi

It is possible to get from Puerto Plata to other resort towns by private taxi. In Puerto Plata, there is a taxi stand next to the central park and another in the hotel zone across from Long Beach.

Sosúa

The bus company Caribe Tours stops at the edge of Los Charamicos, a few hundred metres from the beach.

Public buses (*guaguas*), heading east or west, stop along the main road. Service is frequent in both directions.

Cabarete

To catch a *guagua* heading east or west, just wait along the main street, which is part of the Atlantic coast highway.

Practical Information

Puerto Plata

The Parque Central (*at the corner of Beller and Separacíon*) is right in the heart of town. The *Codetel* and bank are right beside it.

Tourist Information Office
1 Avenida Hermanas Mirabal
Parque Costeroé
☎ *586-3676*

Sosúa

Several shops, a bank and the *Codetel* are all located around Plaza Maxim, on Calle Alejo Martínez.

Tourist Information Office
Autopista
Edificio Erick Houser
2nd floor
☎ *571-3433*

Cabarete

Most of the town is spread out on either side of the highway. You'll find shops, an exchange office and a small bank. The *Codetel* is on the highway, about one kilometre in the direction of Sosúa.

Tourist Information Office
Autopista
Plaza Aloa
☎ *571-0962*

Río San Juan

Downtown Río San Juan is spread out primarily around the Calle Duarte, and comprises a number of shops as well as a bank.

Exploring

Some are drawn here by the magnificent beaches, which are among the most beautiful in the Caribbean and lined with resort villages offering accommodation for every taste and budget; others prefer the splendid mountain scenery and lush vegetation of the Cordillera Septentrionale. Whatever the reason, this region has plenty to please all types of travellers.

Puerto Plata

Puerto Plata was founded in the early days of Spanish colonization (1502) by **Nicolás de Ovando**, in order to give the Spanish fleet a port on the northern coast of the island. Its first years were prosperous, but with the discovery of riches elsewhere in the Americas, the port of Puerto Plata became less important to the Spanish Crown.

To make up for the lack of activity in their city, the residents of Puerto Plata began dealing in contraband

M.K.Pierson

Puerto Plata and the Atlantic Coast

Puerto Plata

Scale: 0 — 500 — 1000m

N

ATTRACTIONS
1. Pico Isabel de Torres

ACCOMMODATIONS
1. Camacho
2. Puerto Plata Beach and Casino Resort (R)
3. Puerto Plata

(R): Property with restaurant (see description)

RESTAURANTS
1. Portofino

Atlantic Ocean

Long Beach

Sea map of Downtown

Fortaleza San Felipe

Santiago, Santo Domingo

Av. Colón
30 de Marzo
C. Eduarto Brito
Pedro Clisante
San Felipe
Calle Separación
C. Duarte
Beller
Mella
12 de Julio
Av. General G. Luperón
Margarita
Maicón
16 de Agosto
Prudhomme
F. Deschamps
John F. Kennedy
José López
Beller
Francisco J. Peinado
Antera Mota
Emilio
C. Villanueva
C. E. J. Kunhart
Av. Isabel de Torres
Av. Virginia Ortega
30 de Mayo
Av. 27 de Febrero
Gregorio del Toro
Av. 27 de Agosto
Av. Luis
Carolina
Av. Circunvalación Norte
Ginebra
Sosúa, Brugal Rum Distillery
Av. Hermanas Mirabal
Av. Circunvalación Sur

© ULYSSES

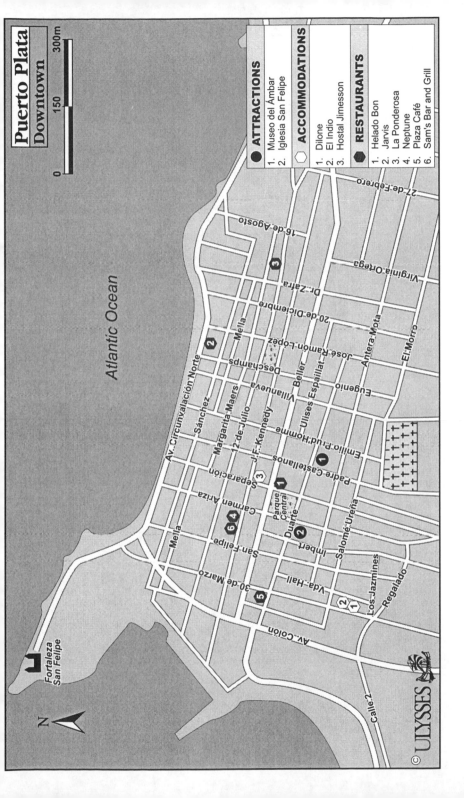

Puerto Plata
Downtown

0   150   300m

Atlantic Ocean

Fortaleza
San Felipe

ATTRACTIONS
1. Museo del Ámbar
2. Iglesia San Felipe

ACCOMMODATIONS
1. Dilone
2. El Indio
3. Hostal Jimesson

RESTAURANTS
1. Helado Bon
2. Jarvis
3. La Ponderosa
4. Neptune
5. Plaza Café
6. Sam's Bar and Grill

© ULYSSES

with the French and English. To reaffirm its power and put a stop to smuggling in the area, the Crown ordered that the city of Puerto Plata be destroyed and abandoned a century after it was founded.

The city was not rebuilt until 1742, when a few Spanish families arrived from the Canary Islands. Once again, the city became an important seaport used for shipping out natural resources and agricultural products from the centre of the country. Today Puerto Plata is a lively, medium-sized urban centre with the busiest seaport on the northern coast.

The city's beautiful location, nestled between the Atlantic Ocean and the Cordillera Septentrionale mountain range, adds to its allure. Despite the constant development in Puerto Plata, its downtown has remained largely unchanged, retaining its

typical Caribbean flavour. A number of Victorian and Republican buildings from the last century still line the avenues near the **Parque Duarte**, where most of the commercial activity takes place.

The main tourist facilities in Puerto Plata are located on the east side of the city, near **Long Beach** and its pleasant promenade. Since Long Beach is not very good for swimming, many visitors head for the beaches just outside Puerto Plata.

The **Fortaleza San Felipe de Puerto Plata ★** (*$1 US; at the western end of the Malecón*) is located on a point of land that juts into the ocean at the western edge of the city. Built in the 16th century to defend the port against pirates, this massive fortress is the only remnant of Puerto Plata's first period of colonization. At several points in its history the fort served not only to defend the city but also as a

penitentiary. Visitors will find a small military museum, as well as the cell that held the great hero of the country's war of independence, **Juan Pablo Duarte**, in 1844.

The site has a good view of the city, the ocean and the mountains. To get there, walk to the end of the **Malecón ★**, the long promenade that runs alongside the ocean for several kilometres. In the evening, the Malecón is a popular meeting place for Dominican families and couples, and countless stalls selling snacks and drinks line the sidewalks.

Parque Central ★ (*at the corner of Calles Beller and Separacíon*) is one of the busiest areas in the city. On the lively neighbouring streets you will find restaurants, market stalls and stores, while the park itself is surrounded by Victorian buildings. The beautiful **Glorieta ★**, whose construction dates back to 1872, stands at the centre. The **Iglesia San Felipe**, , an Art Deco church with a very sober interior, dating from 1934, also stands on the south side of the park. Also minutes from the park is the **Museum of Taïno Art** (*Calle San Felipe, corner of Beller*).

The Museo del Ámbar ★★ *($2.50 US; Mon to Sat 9am to 6pm; at the corner of Calles Prudhomme and Duarte,* ☎ *586-2848)* situated in a neoclassical building that was built in 1918, possesses a small but beautiful collection of amber, the fossilized resin found throughout the Dominican Republic. A succession of little display windows protect some interesting pieces, several enclosing insects – especially beetles - as well as some plants entombed in amber during the early stages of its genesis. One can further cultivate one's knowledge and appreciation of amber by engaging the services of a guide, or by taking a few moments to read the informative panels that trace the origins and the creation of this fascinating resin. The little shop below the museum has a good selection of souvenirs, including jewellery made of amber and larimar, a pretty blue stone also found in the Dominican Republic.

One of the most popular attractions in town for a long time now, the **cable car** up to the summit of **Pico Isabel de Torres** ★★ *($2 US; about 500m out of town to the west, a well-marked 500-m trail leads to the cable car)* was unfortunately undergoing renovations at press time. Be sure to check on the progression of the work before heading

all the way there. Though some taxi drivers are willing to take you all the way up to the summit, be aware that the road leading you there is very steep and dangerous. From its highest point, at 793 metres above sea-level, the Pico Isabel de Torres provides an exceptional view of Puerto Plata and the surrounding beaches, mountains and towns. At the summit there is an impressive statue of Christ the Redeemer and trails leading through the flowering gardens. This mountain is in the centre of the **Reserva Científica Isabel de Torres**. Vegetation such as wild tamarinds and Hispaniola mahoganies grow in the reserve and some 32 kinds of birds can be observed.

If you are curious to know how rum is made, tours are offered at the **Brugal Rum Distillery** *(free guided tours; Mon to Fri 9am to noon and 2pm to 4pm; 500 m outside of town on the east side, buildings are visible from the road).* This small, modern distillery produces about 1,300,000 litres of white and dark rum each year, 95% of which is consumed in the Dominican Republic. The tour of the premises is short, amounting to little more than a look at the bottling process. However, the guides can provide a wealth of information on the rum

industry. There is also a small kiosk that sells souvenirs sporting the Brugal logo, as well as the different varieties of the famous rum at a slight discount.

Baseball fans will be happy to learn that it is almost certain that the next baseball team in the Dominican Republic professional league will be in Puerto Plata. October to January is baseball season in the Dominican Republic. Games are played at Quisqueya Stadium ☎ 565-5565. Games start at 7:30pm on weekdays and 4pm on weekends. Tickets go for anywhere between $1 and $10, and fans will be disappointed because Dominican baseball is professional – even some American players come to practise with Dominican teams off-season, during the winter months. Many Dominicans also make it to the Major Leagues.

Banco de la Plata

Humpback whales also come to the calm waters of the Atlantic Ocean north of Puerto Plata where they are protected by a coral reef. A number of these whales reproduce here. The 3,700-km² Banco de la Plata Reserve was created to protect this area. Because navigating on the coral reefs is dangerous, virtually no whale-watching excursions are offered.

Puerto Plata and the Atlantic Coast

Costambar

Costambar is located three kilometres west of Puerto Plata. From there (there is a sign), a dirt road leads to Costambar after one kilometre.

Costambar lies alongside the first small **beach** west of Puerto Plata. It is a peaceful, fairly undeveloped area with few hotels, but a fair number of villas belonging to foreigners or wealthy Dominicans. A nine-hole golf course is located nearby, while a few restaurants, a motorcycle rental shop and some markets round out the facilities on site. Few vacationers end up staying here, most come for the golf course or the beach.

Playa Cafresi

Still on the main highway, but a few kilometres west of Costambar, a well-marked road branches off and leads directly to Playa Cofresi after about one kilometre.

Making Rum

Sugar cane has been grown in the Dominican Republic for centuries, long requiring hard labour on the part of local men and women, especially at harvest time. The men were responsible for cutting each plant down to the soil, stripping off the leaves (for fodder) and cutting each cane into one-metre-long pieces. The women followed, tying up the pieces into bundles of 10 to 12 pieces. This work required a lot of manpower and was carried out in the hot sun. Although harvesting sugar cane is somewhat easier today thanks to modern instruments, it is still an arduous task.

After being tied into bundles, the sugar cane is taken to the factory so that its juice can be extracted. When pressed the first time, it produces a substantial quantity of juice. To collect the remaining liquid, the cane is moistened with water, and then pressed a second time. The crushed fibres, the bagasse, become fuel for the mill, while the sweet juice is used to make a variety of other products, notably sugar and rum.

The sweet juice (molasses) is fermented to produce a liquid with an alcohol content of 95%, which is then diluted with distilled water in copper barrels. The alcohol is then decanted into another set of copper barrels and sometimes mixed with almonds or caramel to give it its characteristic flavour and colour. This blend is decanted yet again, this time into wooden barrels and aged for one to 25 years. Afterward, it is filtered and sampled, then left to settle for 15 days in copper barrels to make sure there will be no sediment in the finished product. Finally, the rum is bottled, thus becoming the favourite companion in both the joy and sorrow of the Dominican population.

Recent years have seen considerable growth in Playa Cofresi, due mainly to the opening of the large **Hacienda Resorts** Complex, which includes several hotels. The site also includes many private villas, fine restaurants, grocery stores and various other businesses. The main reason for coming here, the pretty little white-sand **beach** ★, remains unchanged.

Playa Dorada

From Costambar or Playa Cofresi you will ve to retrace your steps and go through Puerto Plata to reach Playa Dorada. It is about three kilometres east of Puerto Plata on the main road.

This is neither a village nor a town that became touristy, but rather a few square kilometres of buildings erected solely for tourism. It has about a dozen luxury hotels offering a wide range of services and activities.

The area is very pleasantly landscaped with lovely gardens, hibiscus bushes, a few ponds, a superb 18-hole golf course designed by Robert Trent Jones and a beautiful long white-sand **beach** ★. Visitors can enjoy a wide range

of water sports, set off on excursions and adventures into the surrounding region or simply relax with a drink on one of the many terraces. For many years now, Playa Dorada has been the most popular of the large resort areas. It is perfect for travellers looking for a beautiful, safe seaside resort with luxury hotels and all the modern comforts. Those in search of more of an introduction to the Dominican culture and way of life, however, will be somewhat disappointed. Playa Dorada is accessible from Highway 5, which follows the northern coast.

Puerto Chiquito

Continue along Highway 5 for about 20 kilometres. About 1.5 kilometres before Sosúa, a large colourful sign clearly marks the road to Puerto Chiquito. The village lies less than a kilometre away.

Located a bit more than one kilometre west of Sosúa, Puerto Chiquito lies alongside a pretty little bay surrounded by towering rocky cliffs. The setting is definitely worth a look, especially from the terrace of the Sand Castle hotel, which offers a stunning panoramic view of the ocean. The white-sand **beach**, divided in two by the Río Sosúa, is several hundred metres long. It is

used mostly by guests of the Sand Castle, who enjoy all manner of water sports in the calm waters of the bay. The water here is unfortunately not very clean.

Sosúa

The city of Sosúa consists of the Los Charamicos and El Batey neighbourhoods. These two areas are separated by a long, sandy beach. When coming from Puerto Plata, you will pass by Los Charamicos first, then El Batey, about one kilometre farther along, where most of the hotels are located.

Sosúa was little more than a small banana-growing centre when a group of European Jews took refuge here in the 1940s. The president at the time, the dictator Trujillo, agreed to welcome these refugees in an effort to improve his poor international reputation. The new arrivals were to have a significant impact on the development of Sosúa, especially its economy, by setting up the prosperous dairy and livestock farms for which the region is known. A number of these refugees and their descendants still live in the area.

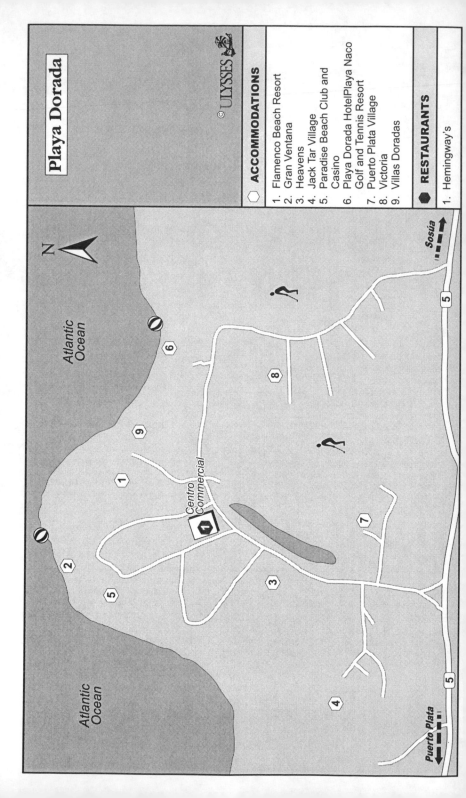

Playa Dorada

© ULYSSES

◇ ACCOMMODATIONS

1. Flamenco Beach Resort
2. Gran Ventana
3. Heavens
4. Jack Tar Village
5. Paradise Beach Club and Casino
6. Playa Dorada HotelPlaya Naco Golf and Tennis Resort
7. Puerto Plata Village
8. Victoria
9. Villas Doradas

● RESTAURANTS

1. Hemingway's

N

Atlantic Ocean

Atlantic Ocean

Centro Commercial

Sosúa

Puerto Plata

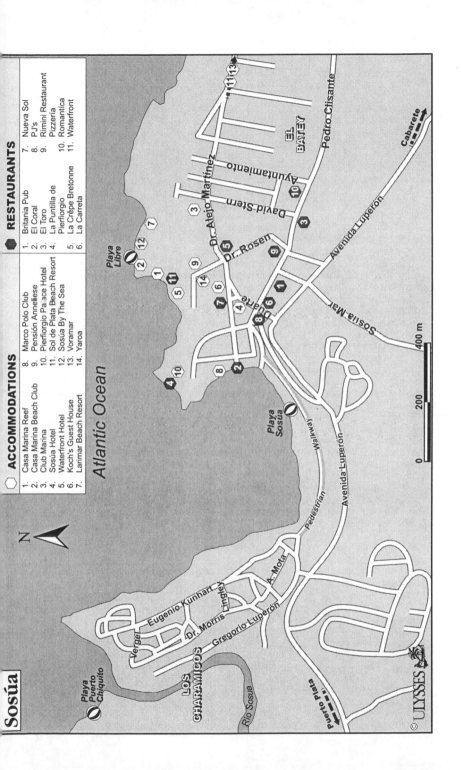

Sosúa

◇ ACCOMMODATIONS

1. Casa Marina Reef
2. Casa Marina Beach Club
3. Club Marina
4. Sosúa Hotel
5. Waterfront Hotel
6. Koch's Guest House
7. Larimar Beach Resort
8. Marco Polo Club
9. Pensión Anneliese
10. Pierfiorgio Palace Hotel
11. Sol de Plata Beach Resort
12. Sosúa By The Sea
13. Voramar
14. Yaroa

◆ RESTAURANTS

1. Britania Pub
2. El Coral
3. El Toro
4. La Puntilla de Pierfiorgio
5. La Crêpe Bretonne
6. La Carreta
7. Nueva Sol
8. PJ's
9. Rimini Restaurant Pizzeria
10. Romantica
11. Waterfront

Atlantic Ocean

Playa Puerto Chiquito

Playa Sosúa

Playa Libre

LOS CHARAMICOS

EL BATEY

N

Río Sosúa

Vega

Eugenio Kunhart

Dr. Morris Linghey

A. Mota

Gregorio Luperón

Pedestrian

Walkway

Avenida Luperón

Puerto Plata

Dr. Alejo Martínez

Ayuntamiento

David Stern

Dr. Rosen

Duarte

Sosúa-Mar

Avenida Luperón

Pedro Clisante

Cabarete

0   200   400 m

© ULYSSES

The city they helped build seems to have escaped them, however, lost to the ever-increasing throngs of tourists. Their synagogue, for example, looks out of place among the restaurants, bars, discotheques and hotels, as if it belonged to another era and another civilization.

In fact, with the exception of Puerto Plata, Sosúa has undergone more tourist development than any other area on the coast, and the general appearance of the city has unfortunately suffered as a result. Little remains of its traditional architecture, and large parts of the city are devoted completely to commerce. The ambience has also changed considerably; vendors of all sorts have become pushier, and prostitution is flourishing (the government intervened in 1996 in an attempt to ban prostitution and return a certain respectability to the city).

Nevertheless, Sosúa can still be a pleasant place to stay, due to its abundance of restaurants, hotels and outdoor diversions. The jagged coastline makes for some beautiful landscapes, and the bay's waters are alwayscrystal-clear.

Sosúa has two beaches: **Playa Sosúa** ★, about one kilometre long and always crowded, and **Playa Libre**, smaller but also much calmer.

The two neighbourhoods located on either side of the bay are separated by Playa Sosúa. Most of the hotels and touristy development is on the east side, in the **El Batey** neighbourhood, which is also home to several beautiful residences. The **Los Charamicos** neighbourhood has remained essentially residential, thus preserving a typical small-town Dominican atmosphere.

Sosúa's **Sinagoga** (*Calle Alejo Martinez*) is a small, modest-looking building still used as a place of worship by the city's Jewish community.

Right next door is the **Museo de Sosúa** (*free admission; 6pm to 11pm; Alejo Martinez*), whose mission is to inform visitors about the city's history. Historical documents and personal objects belonging to Sosúa's first Jewish settlers are on display.

From the outskirts of Sosúa, visitors can enjoy beautiful excursions to the Cordillera Septentrionale on the Carretera Turistica. This highway is closed to big trucks and offers **magnificent views ★** of the mountainous landscape of the Cordillera all the way to Santiago de los Caballeros in the centre of the country. The Carretera Turistica starts along the main road midway between Sosúa and Puerto Plata. The drive to Santiago takes about an hour.

Punta Goleta

To reach Punta Goleta from Sosúa, follow the highway for about ten kilometres.

The pretty, sandy **beach** of Punta Goleta runs along the ocean for a few hundred metres and is an extension of the superb Playa Cabarete. The beach is not particularly crowded, as there are few big hotels nearby. Pretty thatched parasols have been set up on the sand for shade.

Cabarete

Continue east on the highway to get to Cabarete.

Cabarete is considered the windsurfing capital of the country, and with good reason. The conditions for this sport are excellent, especially on windy summer days. Cabarete has actually become somewhat famous; each June windsurfing professionals gather here to take part in an international competition. Windsurfing is not the only reason to go to Cabarete, however. Its **magnificent beach ★★** stretches nearly three kilometres, making it perfect for long walks. Contrary to the beach at Sosúa, for example, Cabarete's beach is large enough that you don't feel hemmed in on all sides by hotels and sunbathers.

Though tourism has become the main-stay of the village's economy, Cabarete has retained a pleasant, casual atmosphere and also offers a good selection of hotels, generally small or medium-sized, as well as several restaurants. Those who choose to stay will also find themselves well situated for excursions along the Atlantic coast.

Behind the village, there is an interesting **lagoon**, where the comings-and-goings of several species of birds, including the pelican, can be observed.

To visit Cabarete's **caves** ★ (*$12 US; take the road near the Codetel, on the west side of Cabarete, for 1 km to the Cabarete Adventure Park*), you must be accompanied by a guide from the Cabarete Adventure Park, the only outfit with the rights to market this place. The three-hour guided tour leads through the countryside and a tropical forest, but unfortunately includes several uninteresting stops along the way. Once at the caves, however, you are allowed to look around and swim in one of the natural

pools. The caves are interesting, but the rest of the tour is uninspiring, and the guides and owner of the place are downright unpleasant.

Gaspar Hernández

An unremarkable but always busy little coastal town, Gaspar Hernández is a little more than 15 kilometres from Cabarete on the road to Río San Juan and Samaná. The town has a few banks and gas stations, a Codetel, and some small, inexpensive hotels of dubious quality.

Playa Magante

About halfway between Gaspar Hernandez and Río San Juan, a sign on the highway points out the direction of Playa Magante. Along this small, sandy beach, which is a great place to swim, you will find some good restaurants.

Rio San Juan

Río San Juan is about 30 kilometres east of Gaspar Hernández. To reach the beach of the Bahía Blanca hotel, follow the lagoon shore to the left

Río San Juan is a

pleasant fishing village in an area known for farming and dairy production, where life still revolves around the sea. Some of the village streets, with their small houses painted in pastel shades, correspond to the romantic images people often have of small Caribbean towns.

Although most visitors come here to visit the famous **Laguna Gri-Gri** ★ and its striking stands of tangled, tropical mangrove trees, Río San Juan has enough to offer to make a longer stay worthwhile. The region is full of enchanting landscapes, and beautiful sandy **beaches** line the shore in front of the friendly little Bahía Blanca hotel. There are several other small beaches, virtually deserted most of the time, around the lagoon. And finally, about two kilometres west of Río San Juan, is **Playa Caletón**, accessible either by boat from the Laguna Gri-Gri, or by foot from the road towards Cabrera.

Laguna Gri-Gri is accessible from the highway by following Calle Duarte, the main road in Río San Juan.

Boats are always available for visits to the **Laguna Gri-Gri** ★★

($26 US per boatload of up to 15 people; departure from the end of Calle Duarte, at the corner of Calle Sanchez).

The tour leads around the lagoon all the way to the ocean, through a magnificent mangrove forest where a variety of tropical bird species can be observed at close range. The excursion continues along the coastline to a small inlet called **La Piscina**, whose crystalline waters are perfect for swimming. You will also stop at Playa Caleton long enough for another swim before returning to the lagoon. Those who would like to spend more time bird-watching around the lagoon can get there on foot by following the Bahía Blanca's road to the end. Early morning is the best time to observe and photograph birds.

El Barrio Acapulco *(near the ocean on the west side of town)* is a working-class neighbourhood where most of the fishermen in Río San Juan live. Those interested in boat-building and fishing will appreciate a visit to this unfortunately very poor area.

Playa Grande

About eight kilometres from Río San Juan is Playa Grande, without a doubt one of the most impressive beaches in the country. This long crescent of white sand extends for some two kilometres between a splendid bay and a string palm trees. The surrounding scenery is lovely, and the hardy waves delight swimmers and surfers alike. The large Caribbean Village Hotel Complex opened near the beach in 1994; fortunately, it has not marred the beautiful setting. Most beach-goers here are either guests at this hotel, or part of organized tours from Playa Dorada, Sosúa, Cabarete or elsewhere. Nevertheless, Playa Grande is still the least crowded beach of this calibre in the western part of the country.

Cabrera

A few kilometres further along, the highway passes along the outskirts of Cabrera.

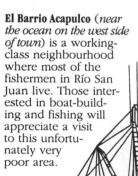

To reach Cabrera from the highway, you must follow a small road on the left side. Watch carefully because it is poorly marked and located in a curve in the road.

Cabrera is a typical Dominican coastal town pleasantly located on a small cape. While it has no major attractions, the view of the ocean and the cliffs nearby is spectacular. A good spot to take in this beautiful seaside panorama is **Parque Nacional Cabo Frances Viejo** *(2 km before Cabrera)* is a small, protected area along the coast. It is a quiet, virtually deserted spot, where you can observe the waves crashing into the surrounding cliffs. This is a good place for a picnic. There are a number of interesting undeveloped beaches close by, but most are hard to get to. You'll need a good map and directions from the locals to find them.

A visit to the brand new **Amazone 2** *($3 ; east of Cabrera)* ecological park offers a chance to take an interesting 20-minute walk in a dense forest, where you can see some of the plants typical of this region and learn about certain aspects of the local geology. Before setting out, you will be given a small map indicating the various points of interest in the park (marsh plant zone, fern valley, bat cave, etc.). Visitors will also find a gigantic canvas aviary containing a variety of birds, and another, smaller one sheltering scores of pretty butterflies.

The Palm Tree Route

For more than ten kilometres the road between Cabrera and Nagua runs alongside the ocean through a striking palm grove. After cutting across the palm grove to the shore, you'll find some superb wild beaches. If you decide to swim, be very careful because the current and undertow can be very strong here.

Nagua

Highway 5 passes through the town of Nagua. The road forks here, with one side (to the left) heading to the Samaná Peninsula, and the other (to the right) to San Francisco de Macorís.

Nagua is a medium-sized town at the intersection of the roads from Puerto Plata and San Francisco de Macorís, and anyone on their way to the magnificent Samaná Peninsula must inevitably pass through here. It has a number of commercial streets, gas stations, and a **Parque Central** (*Calle Duarte*), where several

restaurants can be found. As the town is of little

interest, few visitors passing through decide to stay. There are, however, a few lovely, undeveloped beaches farther south, between Nagua and the Samaná Peninsula, with a few small hotels nearby.

Outdoor Activities

Nothing has been overlooked in making the Atlantic Coastal Region an important centre for outdoor activities. In fact, this is one of the great qualities of this part of the country, because most water sports are available as are many other sports such as golf, horseback riding, cycling, tennis, etc.

Swimming

Long Beach extends over several kilometres, lining Puerto Plata's seascape. Unfortunately, this sandy beach is poorly maintained and located much too close to the road to make it a very enjoyable place to swim.

One of the first beaches you'll encounter west of Puerto Plata is **Costambar Beach**, which has the benefit of being relatively uncrowded on weekdays. It is a totally different story on the weekends, when city dwellers descend upon the beach in hordes, vying with each other for a piece of this narrow band of sand that will give them access to the rejuvenating effects of the sea.

Surrounded by the large complex of Hacienda Resorts, the **Playa Cofresi ★** is predominately frequented by tourists staying at these hotels. They benefit from a beautiful stretch of fine, white sand, comfortable facilities, and a welcoming stretch of sea.

Playa Dorada ★ consists of a long stretch of blond sand speckled with palm trees, chairs and parasols, thus making it ideal for a pleasant swim. Most of the beach is lined with the large hotels of this popular resort area, so a comfortable terrace for a drink or quick bite is never far away. The beach can get very crowded in winter, when most of the hotel rooms are rented. The prettiest section of the beach is to the west, in front of Jack Tar Village. The waves are also rougher here.

Playa Puerto Chiquito, near Sosúa, presents itself as a long ribbon of white sand divided in half by the Río Sosúa. The bay's waters are calm, and the surrounding scenery is very pretty, as the beach is flanked on both sides by small cliffs. Unfortunately, the waters of the bay are not always that clean and this sometimes detracts from the allure of swimming.

There are two beaches in Sosúa: **Playa Sosúa** and **Playa Libre**. Playa Sosúa, a beautiful fine-sand beach about one kilometre long, opens out onto the crystal-clear waters of the bay. The setting is beautiful, but hardly relaxing as the beach is always overrun with tourists and vendors. Restaurants, bars and souvenir stands have been built all along it. It is a noisy place, and the vendors can be very pushy. This is a shame, because the beach is one of the best on the coast. Playa Libre (El Batey neighbourhood)

is another option for swimming. This small beach, lined with quality hotels, is quieter and the vendors are less conspicuous here. Less than one kilometre to the east are a few small stretches of sand where you can swim.

A few kilometres before Cabarete, a sign on the left indicates the way to **Playa Punta Goleta**. This splendid beach of delicate sand, rarely frequented and bordered by only a few hotels, will delight aficionados of the more tranquil spots.

Devotees of the longer beaches with a stronger surf are bound to find fulfilment at **Playa Carabete ★★**. Although tourists from the village next door often crowd into the chairs and parasols left at their disposal, it is possible to find a quiet spot in the sand. Carabete spans 3km – perfect for long romantic strolls. The waves can be quite high especially in the afternoon, and windsurfing is very popular here.There e are restaurants and terraces close by, and vendors wander about selling

their wares.

The seashore of **Río San Juan** includes a few beaches. Those near the Bahía Blanca hotel are pretty and have showers. Small stretches of wild, deserted beach can also be found near the Laguna Gri-Gri. Furthermore, about two kilometres east of Río San Juan, there is a sign for Playa Caleton, which is about a 10-minute walk from the small parking lot by the side of the road. It is also accessible by boat from the Laguna Gri-Gri. This pretty little beach is washed by calm turquoise waters. A few vendors walk about selling food and drinks.

Among the most spectacular beaches in the country, the Playa Grande is remarkable for the sheer length and width of its ribbon of fine sand. Lined with coconut palms from one end to the other for some two kilometres, **Playa Grande★★★** is an excellent place to go swimming, despite the occasionally heavy surf. The Caribbean Village hotel complex sits nearby on the west

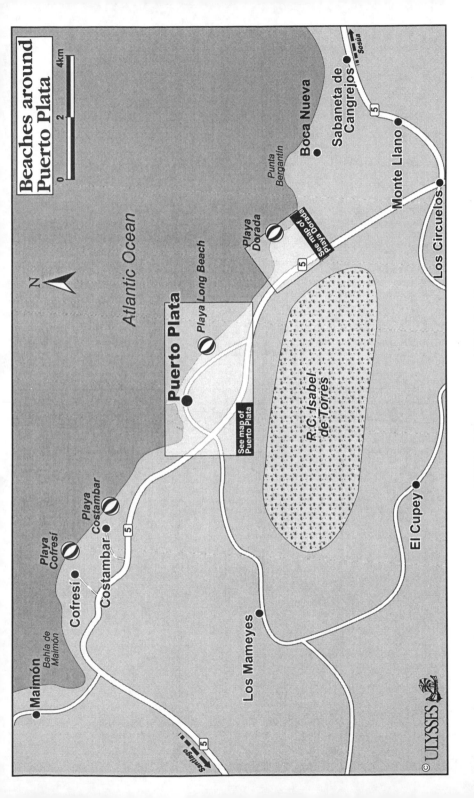

Beaches around Puerto Plata

Atlantic Ocean

0   2   4km

N

Maimón
Bahía de Maimón
Cofresí
Playa Cofresí
Costambar
Playa Costambar
5
Puerto Plata
Playa Long Beach
See map of Puerto Plata
Playa Dorada
See map of Playa Dorada
Punta Bergantín
Boca Nueva
Sabaneta de Cangrejos
Sosúa
Monte Llano
5
Los Circuelos
R.C. Isabel de Torres
Los Mameyes
El Cupey
5
Santiago

© ULYSSES

ern side. Its architects had the good sense not to construct the hotel right on the beach, thereby preserving the harmony of the landscape. There is, however, a small pub on the beach reserved for guests of the Caribbean Village. For those who are not staying at the hotel, vendors rent beach chairs and sell refreshments.

Wild beaches dot the coastline between **Cabrera** and **Nagua**. You can swim here but be careful, the undertow can be very strong and just may carry you out to sea.

Navigation

Playa Dorada

Most of the hotel complexes on Playa Dorada offer guests the opportunity to rent small windsurfing boards and catamarans to take them gliding out into the bay.

Excursions, departing from Playa Dorada to Sosua, are organised daily abord a 35-passenger catamaran christened the **Freestyle**. These outings last the whole day and include meals and drinks as well as the prospect of a delightful dip in the ocean or a snorkelling escapade. On certain days, it is even possible

to catch a glimpse of a dolphin.

Sosúa

Comfortably settled aboard the **Glass Bottom Boat** (*departures from the beach at 9am and 5pm*), you can explore the depths of the ocean without having to learn the A-B-Cs of deep sea diving. This sea outing, which is 45 minutes in duration, unveils the myriad of fish and coral life that live along the Playa Sosúa.

Cabarete

The necessary equipment can be rented on site at Cabarete at two specialized shops. If the hotel where you are staying does not put windsurfing boards at your disposal, the Carib Bic Center will allow you to take off on the waves, accompanied by an instructor, aboard a catamaran.

Carib Bic Center
$50/hour
☎ *571-0640*

If you prefer, kayaks can be rented from:

Vela
$8/hour
☎ *571-0805*

Windsurfing

Cabarete

Although it is possible to go windsurfing in many places along the coast, Cabarete is without a doubt the best spot. Cabarete is not called the "windsurfing

capital" for nothing. Its strong winds and protected bay make it one of the top ten places in the world for this sport. The majority of the hotels along the coast ensure that windsurfing boards are available for their clientele.

Carib Bic Center
☎ *571-0640*
↩ *571-0649*
www.caribwind.com

Windsurfing boards can be rented at a cost of *$45 for half a day*, but there are also hourly and weekly rates available for those who need them. Courses are also available.

La Vela
☎ *571-0805*
↩ *571-0856*

One can also rent windsurfing boards here by the hour (*$20*), the half-day (*$40*), or even the week (*$250*). Course are also offered to wind-surfers of all levels.

Scuba Diving

Playa Dorada, Sosúa, Cabarete and Río San Juan are the principal places along the northern coast that offer diving excursions. Deep-sea dives are available at each place, as are courses for beginners. Scuba diving can be a dangerous sport, so be sure to check that the diving centre you sign up with follows all safety guidelines (see p 62).

No matter which diving centre you choose to disembark from, chances are you will be doing it offshore from the Playa Sosúa, which encompasses some of the most intriguing spots. Depending on your level of expertise, you can plunge down into the depths of the water to observe coral reefs, sponge barriers, rock formations, or - better yet - to explore an underwater cave.

Playa Dorada

All of the major hotels organize scuba-diving tours, opening the door to the possibility of exploring the underwa-

ter marvels of the Playa Dorada.

Sosúa

Northern Coast Diving
8 Pedro Clisante
☎ *571-1028*
⌕ *571-3883*
If the urge to plunge beneath the water is nipping at your heels, Northern Coast Diving is a fine centre from which to disembark. Whether it be your first time diving - or should you wish to obtain your *PADI* scuba-diving certificate - or perhaps you would like to give night-diving a try - this centre will respond to your wishes. You can count on paying about *$55* for an introductory dive, which includes a gear set-up and swimming pool practice, followed by an escorted dive in the afternoon.

Cabarete

Caribbean Divers
Cabarete
☎ *571-0218*
Carabete also runs its own diving centre, Caribbean Divers. The courses offered here cover all kinds of diving, and included among them are some which lead to *PADI* certification. An introductory dive costs around *$55*.

Río San Juan

Gri-Gri Divers
☎ *589-2671*
Whether you're a beginner or a seasoned

pro, the instructors at Gri-Gri Divers are equipped with the necessary expertise to ensure that your dive is safe and well mapped out. Count on paying roughly *$50* for an introductory dive. Expeditions are operated off-shore from the Río San Juan.

Snorkelling

Snorkelling equipment can be rented at all the resorts along the coast, either from hotels or specialized shops. In many cases, excursions out on the high seas are offered. Sosúa is the most popular place along the coast for this activity.

One can rent gear or sign up for a sea expedition at one of the following diving centres:

Sosúa

Northern Coast Diving
8 Pedro Clisante
☎ *571-1028*

Cabarete
Caribbean Divers
☎ *571-0218*

Deep-Sea Fishing

Deep-sea fishing excursions are not offered in all tourist centres.

Sosúa and Playa Dorada are usually the departure points for these outings.

Río San Juan

Two agencies in Río San Juan organize deep sea fishing expeditions:

Magante Fishing
Calle Duarte
☎ *589-2677*
☞ *589-2600*
The cost is approximately $80.

Campo Tours
☎ *589-2550*
Costs range from $70 to $95.

Water Sports

Next to the road between Sosúa and Cabarete, a water park has been built that is guaranteed to please the young and young at heart.

The Colombus Aqua Parque
$10 for adults, $6 for children
☎ *571-2642*

Golf

Golf enthusiasts vacationing on the North Coast will be truly spoiled, as there are several excellent courses , several of which are among country's most beautiful.

Playa Cofresi

The Hacienda Golf Course, an 18-hole course bordering the impressive Hacienda Hotel Complex, should be open and running by the end of 1999.

The Hacienda Golf Course
☎ *970-7434*

Playa Dorada

Playa Dorada's 18-hole golf course, designed by Robert Trent Jones, has what it takes to lure even the most discriminating of golfers. Extending out over part of the beach, it is situated at a prime spot close to the major hotels, some lush gardens, and, of course, the ocean.

Playa Dorada
☎ *320-3803*

Playa Grande

While the greens at Playa Dorada have earned the acclaim of countless golf enthusiasts, a new 18-hole course on the Playa Grande is posing a serious challenge to its ranking as the golfing mecca of the North Coast. Nothing has been overlooked in the design of the striking 18-hole grounds of the Playa Grande; inlayed on the summit of some steep cliffs overlooking the ocean, the site is nothing short of exceptional, providing the golfer with the double advantage of a chal-lenging golf course and an alluring panorama of the coast.

Playa Grande
☎ *248-5313*

Horse-Back Riding

The Atlantic Coast is an ideal place for excursions on horseback. There is the Cordillera Septentrionale to explore, as well as the coast and countryside. Most of the big hotels offer either half-day or full-day rides.

Río San Juan

It is also possible to embark on an all-day excursion (which includes breakfast) or to simply partake in a one-hour stroll at the:

Rancho de la Esperanza
3-11 Magante
☎ *223-0059*

Birdwatching

Numerous species of birds can be seen along the Atlantic coast, be it on the beaches, in the forests or in the countryside: cattle egrets, hummingbirds, turtledoves and especially pelicans.

Rio San Juan

One spot guaranteed to have some winged activity is the **Laguna Gri-Gri**, at the Río San Juan, the nesting grounds of many species, most notably the hummingbird. Most can be observed during a boat tour of the lagoon, or during a walk to the lagoon (*easy access from the end of the Bahía Blanca Hotel road*).

Accommodations

Puerto Plata

Puerto Plata has a fairly large network of accommodations. However, visitors wishing to stay near a beautiful beach often choose hotels outside of town, in Playa Dorada or in one of the many other resorts in the area. Keep in mind, though, that the big hotels in Puerto Plata often offer lower rates than those in Playa Dorada, and also provide efficient transportation to the best beaches in the region.

Several hotels downtown and near Long Beach offer accommodation suitable for those on a tight budget. Even so, Puerto Plata is not the best place on the northern coast for inexpensive lodging; Sosúa and Cabarete

have a much better selection of hotels in this category.

The Hotel Dilone
$8, ⊗
96 Calle 30 de Marzo
If you decide to stay in Puerto Plata anyway, the Hotel Dilone has rooms that are adequately comfortable.

The El Indio
$20, ⊗, ℜ
94 Calle 30 de Marzo
☎ *586-1201*
The El Indio Hotel has a few rooms that are well-kept. It is located on a quiet street in the heart of the town, and has a pleasant tropical garden. With no pool or beach nearby and no beach shuttle, this hotel is best suited to travellers with their own means of transportation. You can try negotiating the price of your room with the German-born owner.

Hostal Jimesson
$20, ⊗
Calle John F. Kennedy, corner of Separación
☎ *586-5131*
Many historic houses still line the streets of Puerto Plata's old city, losing none of their charm to the passage of time. One of these enchanting dwellings is the Hostal Jimesson. Upon entering the main floor of this building, one's gaze is naturally drawn to the many antiques that adorn each hall. As for the rooms, though lacking in beautiful period furniture, they are inviting and very well kept.

The Camacho Hotel
$20, ≈, ≡, ℜ
on the Malecón
☎ *586-6348*
For those with small budgets, The Camacho Hotel, facing the ocean on the Malecón, is a good place to stay. Rooms are sparsely furnished, but clean and spacious.

The Puerto Plata
$ 35, ℜ, ≈, ≡, ⊗
on the Malecón
☎ *586-2588*
☞ *586-8646*
The Puerto Plata is a new hotel on the Malecón. At first sight, this little place is hardly charming, but its attractive secluded garden, makes it a pleasant place to stay.

The Puerto Plata Beach and Casino Resort
$180, all-inclusive
≡, ≈, *tv*, ℜ, ⊛, ♠
Malecón
☎ *320-4243*
The Puerto Plata Beach and Casino Resort is by far the most luxurious hotel complex in the city. Its excellent restaurants, beautiful gardens, casino, swimming pools and host of activities make it a wonderful place for a vacation. The nicely decorated rooms are clustered in small, pastel-coloured buildings, and they all have balconies. Shows are presented in the evenings, and everyday there is a shuttle to and from the main beaches of the area. It is best to reserve ahead of time during the winter months.

Playa Cofresi

🚢The Hacienda Resorts
all-inclusive
☎ *320-8303*
⇆ *320-0222*
One of the newest of the Dominican Republic's big hotel complexes stands at the edge of Playa Cofresi, just west of Puerto Plata. A veritable tourist village, the Hacienda Resorts are a cluster of no fewer than five hotels, each with its own distinctive features, designed to satisfy the widest possible range of expectations.

The Garden Club
ℜ, ⊗
The Garden Club is made up of pretty buildings that are more like simple, comfortable little cottages than modern hotel rooms, lending this part of the complex an intimate atmosphere.

The Elizabeth
≈, ⊗, ≡, ℜ
The Elizabeth, for its part, will appeal to visitors looking to stay in a lovely hotel that is small but still offers a high level of comfort and has a large, attractive garden. It is distinguished by its vaguely Spanish-style building, which has only 18 rooms and is quite charming.

Andrea
≈, ⊗, ≡, ℜ
The more modern-looking Andrea has two beautiful pools.

The Tropical
≈, ⊗, ≡, ℜ
The choicest of the five hotels, The Tropical, stands next to the beach. In addition to its splendid rooms and outstanding swimming pool, it boasts a lovely garden that opens onto Playa Cofresi.

The Villas de Luxe
≈, ⊗, ≡, *K*
This is not really a hotel, but rather a heavenly little village with magnificent houses scattered across a vast, rolling stretch of land. The developers truly outdid themselves; the place has been designed so that each little house is isolated enough to ensure its occupants' privacy.

As the villas have only a few rooms each, a family can rent an entire one for themselves. Each has its own terrace with a magnificent view, a kitchenette and a private pool. A great deal of care has been taken with another important aspect of these all-inclusive hotels: the restaurants, which always serve a buffet with a good selection of delicious dishes. One last plus: all guests have access to the lovely Playa Cofresi.

Playa Dorada

All the hotels in Playa Dorada meet international standards. All have comfortable air-conditioned rooms, at least one pool, restaurants and dining rooms, bars and nightclubs, shops and sometimes a casino. Prices do not vary much from one hotel to the next, the most affordable being the **Heavens**, and the most expensive, the **Jack Tar Village**. Many hotels offer all-inclusive packages, which include three meals a day, all local beverages (Dominican beer, rum, etc.), taxes and service charges. If you arrive in Playa Dorada without a reservation, expect to pay an average of *$110 US* per night (a bit less in the low season), or even more if you want to stay in a studio or deluxe apartment.

For stays of one week or longer, it is often much more economical to make reservations from home through a travel agent, as they often have discounts. Finally, remember that during the winter season there is always a risk that all of the hotels will be full.

The Flamenco Beach Resort
all-inclusive
≡, ≈, ⊗, ℜ
☎ *320-6319*
⇆ *320-6319*
The Flamenco Beach Resort is a large complex whose architec-

ture has a certain Spanish feel to it. Guests stay in a series of white villas, with large balconies. The service is attentive and the fine woodwork in the lobby, bar, restaurant and elsewhere creates a warm, welcoming atmosphere. Guests have access to the beach.

The Heavens
all-inclusive
≡, ≈, ℜ, ⊗
☎ 562-7475
⇆ 566-2436
⇆ 566-2354
The Heavens Hotel Complex consists of two groups of buildings evidently built at different times. This is a pleasant place, even though some of the buildings are bunched together. The complex is near the golf course, and at a reasonable distance from the beach, which is accessible by way of a small path.

The Jack Tar Village
all-inclusive
≡, ≈, ℜ, ⊗
☎ 320-3800
☎1-800-999-9182
⇆ 320-4161
The Jack Tar Village occupies a large, well-maintained property. The rooms are set in charming villas arranged, like the name suggests, into a little village. The Jack Tar is especially popular with tennis players, as it has a large number of courts; it is also close to a golf course and the beach. Many consider this the most luxurious

hotel complex in Playa Dorada.

The Paradise Beach Club and Casino
all-inclusive
≡, ≈, ℜ, ⊗, ♠
☎ 1-800-752-9236
⇆ 586-4858
The Paradise Beach Club and Casino has a total of 436 units in several buildings decorated with attractive woodwork. The hotel's designers went to great lengths to make it visually pleasing; the impressive grounds feature luxurious gardens, waterfalls, ponds and swimming pools in interesting shapes. This unique and friendly resort offers comfortable rooms and lies right on the beach.

The Playa Dorada Hotel
all-inclusive
≡, ≈, ℜ, ⊗, ♠
☎ 320-3988
☎1-800-423-6902
⇆ 320-1190
The Playa Dorada Hotel has 254 pleasantly decorated rooms, some with a clear view of the ocean. The nondescript older buildings of the hotel are located right on the beach. Guests will also find a casino, restaurants, a pleasant café and a piano-bar.

The Playa Naco Golf and Tennis Resort
all-inclusive
≡, ≈, ℜ, ⊗
☎ 320-6226
⇆ 320-6225
The Playa Naco Golf and Tennis Resort is graced with an imposing colonnaded façade and a monumental

lobby overlooking a very large pool. The comfortable rooms are located in the building that surrounds the pool, where all the action takes place, and in various other structures scattered throughout the vast property. The Naco has several tennis courts, among other things.

The Puerto Plata Village
all-inclusive
≡, ≈, ℜ, ⊗
☎ 320-4012
⇆ 320-5113
The Puerto Plata Village is made up of charming little houses, some painted in pastel colours, others in bright colours, and all equipped with balconies or terraces. The complex is pleasantly located in a large and airy garden, near the golf course and not too far from the beach. The service is excellent.

The Villas Doradas
all-inclusive
≡, ≈, ℜ, ⊗
☎ 320-3000
⇆ 320-4790
The Villas Doradas consists of a grouping of several-story buildings, each housing a few rooms with a balcony overlooking a large tropical garden. The lobby includes a relaxing open-air space with rattan chairs. A trail leads through a thicket, past a pond and on to the beach.

Puerto Plata and
the Atlantic Coast

🦞The Gran Ventana
all-inclusive
≈, ≡, ℜ
☎ 412-2525
📠 412-2526

The newest hotel in Playa Dorada, The Gran Ventana is a grand hotel complex whose buildings, all in warm hues, stand on a large piece of property by the sea. In the centre of this little village lies a huge swimming pool, the focal point of most of the day's activities. Great care has been taken with the decor, so all the rooms are spacious, have big picture windows and are adorned with lovely tropical colours. The restaurants of Gran Ventura are known for the quality of their fare.

🦞The Victoria
all-inclusive
≈, ≡, ℜ
☎ 320-1200
📠 320-4862

If you have no desire to spend your vacation in a place with a perpetually lively atmosphere, opt for The Victoria. This hotel cannot boast a seaside location, but offers a peaceful setting alongside a golf course. The building itself is sober-looking, as if to emphasize the establishment's desire to provide a tranquil atmosphere. Finally, many people claim that the food served here is among the best of any hotel in Playa Dorada.

Sosúa

Sosúa, which lives and breathes by tourism, offers accommodation for all budgets and tastes. Most of the hotels in the city are located in the El Batey neighbourhood, east of Playa Sosúa. None of these have direct access to Playa Sosúa, but they are all within walking distance.

Some hotels, however, face right onto smaller Playa Libre. Lodging is also available on the outskirts of Sosúa, in a few large complexes to the east and west of the city, along the ocean. During the summer, which is the off-season, when none of the hotels are filled to capacity, do not hesitate to negotiate for a better rate.

Koch's Guest House
$25, ≡, K
close to Calle
Martinez, El Batey
☎ 571-2284

Koch's Guest House rents out clean cabañas, each with a kitchenette. The *cabañas* are scattered throughout a narrow well-maintained property, which ends at the ocean. The place may not be very luxurious, but it does offer reasonable rates and lots of peace and quiet, despite being located a few steps from the city's busiest streets. The owner can be a bit surly at times.

🦞The Pension Anneliese
$40, ⊗, ℝ, ≈,
Calle Dr. Rosen, El Batey
☎ 571-2208

The Pension Anneliese is a good, inexpensive little place with ten spotless rooms, each with a balcony and a refrigerator. The rooms at the front boast a pretty view of the ocean, which is just a few metres away. The location is quiet, even though it's close to the heart of Sosúa. There is a pleasant pool in the little garden out back. Hearty and tasty breakfasts are served each morning *(starting at $3 US)*. The Pension Anneliese is run by a German couple who has lived in Sosúa for over 15 years.

The Voramar
$35, ℜ, ≈, ⊗, ≡
at the east end of Sosúa
☎ 571-3910
📠 571-3076

Outside the centre of town, about 500 metres from the last buildings along Playa Libre, there are several inexpensive, well-kept and quiet hotels. One of these is The Voramar which has large, comfortable rooms, each with a balcony. A few hotels in the same category are located near by, as are some narrow, sandy beaches. The Sosúa beach is just a few minutes' drive away.

The Waterfront Hotel

$50, ⊗, ≈, ℜ, ℝ
1 Calle Dr. Rosen, El Batey
☎ 571-2670
⚏ 571-3586
The Waterfront Hotel
also known as *Charlie's
Cabañas*, rents out
small white stucco cot-
tages set in a garden by
the ocean. Without
being
luxurious, this place is
quaint and comfortable,
and features a pleasant
restaurant, a bar and a
small pool. It is located
right next to the Pen-
sion Anneliese and
enjoys the same quiet
atmosphere.

The Sosúa Hotel

*$45, bkfst incl,
≡, ≈, ℝ, ℜ, tv*
Alejo Martinez
☎ 571-2683
☎ 571-3530
⚏ 571-2180
The Sosúa Hotel
is in a
modern
building
located
on a
relatively
hectic
street in
the cen-
tre of Sosúa.
The rooms are pleasant
and are equipped with
a balcony or terrace.

The Yaroa

$35, ≡, ≈, ℜ
Calle Dr. Rosen
☎ 571-2651
⚏ 571-3814
Situated on a quiet
street, The Yaroa has
the benefit of a tranquil
location, though the
decor of the rooms is
somewhat timeworn.

The Pierfiorgio Palace Hotel

≈, ≡, ℜ
☎ 571-2215
⚏ 571-2786
www.pierfiorgio.com
Already reputed for the
excellent setting of its
restaurant, The
Pierfiorgio is now ac-
quiring a name for its
recently erected
Pierfiorgio Palace Hotel
The rooms in this
splendid, colonial-style
edifice are spread out
over two levels and all
benefit from the long,
stylish balconies that
look out onto the sea.
Rattan furniture and
Haitian paintings em-
bellish the ample and
impeccable rooms -
which are also en-
dowed with spacious
bathrooms. Enclosing
the hotel is a lovely
garden
dotted
with
some
whirl-
pools in
addition
to a
pool.

The Sosúa by the Sea

$125, ½ p, ≡, ≈, ℜ, tv
Playa Libre, El Batey
☎ 571-3222
⚏ 571-3020
The Sosúa by the Sea is
a comfortable, attrac-
tively decorated hotel
complex overlooking a
classic tropical garden,
a pool and a restaurant
with a beautiful view of
the ocean. A wooden
staircase leads down to
the pretty Playa Libre,
which is often much
more relaxing than
Playa Sosúa. The centre

of Sosúa is only a few
minutes away by foot.

The Club Marina, The
Casa Marina Beach Club
and The Casa Marina Reef
Hotel are all run by the
same proprietor. Thus,
lodging at any one of
the these three hotels
will include access to
the beach and the facil-
ities of The Casa Marina
Beach Club.

The Club Marina

$120, all-inclusive
≡, ≈, ℜ, tv
Alejo Martinez
☎ 571-3939
⚏ 571-3110
The Club Marina is a
pretty hotel with thirty
comfortable, modern
rooms and a swimming
pool. This quiet place
lies right next to Playa
Libre, and just a few
minutes' walk from
Playa Sosúa.

The Casa Marina Beach Club

$130, all-inclusive
≡, ≈, ℜ
Playa Libre, El Batey
☎ 571-3690
☎ 571-3691
☎ 571-3692
⚏ 571-3110
Among the most com-
fortable establishments
in Sosúa, The Casa
Marina Beach Club
offers direct access to
Playa Libre as well as
well-maintained rooms,
several of which boast
ocean views. These are
spread throughout a
large complex consist-
ing of several pastel-
coloured buildings. The
service is particularly
attentive and profes-
sional. The Casa Marina
is often booked solid in

the winter; during the rest of the year, however, it is possible to negotiate the room rates.

The Casa Marina Reef
$120, ≡, ≈, ℜ
☎ *571-3690*
⇆ *571-3110*
A new addition to Sosúa, The Casa Marina Reef was erected next to the other two Marina properties. It perches on top of some cliffs and offers a stunning view of the ocean below. Even from this height the beach is nearby since there is a short path that can take one there in no time. The architects' use of concrete is rather heavy-handed; but the rooms provide exemplary comfort and a tasteful decor.

The Marco Polo Club
$ 80
ℜ, ≈, ⊗, ≡, K, ⊛
at the end of Calle Alejo Martinez
☎ *571-3128*
⇆ *571-3233*
The Marco Polo Club which enjoys an unimpeded view of Sosúa Bay, is a lovely little hotel built on a well laid-out piece of property on the side of a cliff. Though located almost right in the centre of town, it feels far from all the movement.

The Larimar Beach Resort
$90, bkfst, ≡, ≈, ℜ, pb, tv
Playa Libre, El Batey
☎ *571-2868*
⇆ *571-3381*
Also with direct access to the Playa Libre, The Larimar Beach Resort is

a comfortable, modern hotel complex offering a range of services. Its several tall buildings are surrounded by a large garden of tropical plants and trees. Most rooms have a balcony or terrace.

The Sol de Plata Beach Resort
$140, all-inclusive
≡, ≈, ℜ, tv,
east of Sosúa
☎ *571-3600*
⇆ *571-3380*
A few kilometres east of Sosúa, The Sol de Plata Beach Resort is an immense hotel complex where you can rent a room, a suite or a villa. The modern buildings face onto a private beach. A wide range of sports activities is organized here as well as evening shows, and a shuttle that takes guests to Sosúa and Cabarete.

The Playa de Oro Hotel
$60, ≡, ≈, ℜ, tv
☎ *571-0880*
⇆ *571-0871*
This hotel offers accommodation in comfortable, more than adequate rooms. It stands on the beautiful white-sand beach between Cabarete and Sosúa.

The Bella Vista
$90, all-inclusive
≈, ℜ, ≡
on the way to Cabarete
☎ *571-1878*
⇆ *571-0767*
Right next to the Playa de Oro and in the same category, the Bella Vista, offers all-inclusive packages. The

rooms, each equipped with a balcony, are located inside two rows of rather simple-looking buildings. The back of the hotel looks right out onto the white-sand beach.

The Punta Goleta Beach Resort
$180, all-inclusive
≡, ≈, ℜ
☎ *571-0700*
⇆ *571-0707*
The Punta Goleta Beach Resort is a large, somewhat isolated hotel complex on the road between Sosúa and Cabarete. It offers all of the services one would expect from a luxury hotel — multiple restaurants and bars, a pool, sports and activities, shows, etc. In order to offset the inconvenience of its isolation, a small bridge has been constructed which crosses the road.

Cabarete

Due to its growing popularity, Cabarete now offers a good selection of accommodation. Most of the hotels are of good quality, some offering greater luxury than others. If you visit Cabarete during the summer months, don't hesitate to look at several hotels and negotiate for the best price before making your choice.

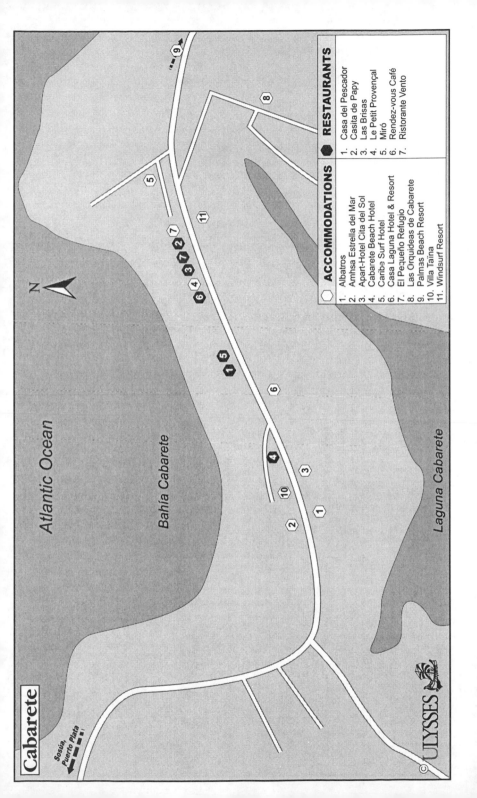

Cabarete

Atlantic Ocean

Bahía Cabarete

Laguna Cabarete

Sosúa, Puerto Plata

N

© ULYSSES

ACCOMMODATIONS

1. Albatros
2. Amhsa Estrella del Mar
3. Apart-Hotel Cita del Sol
4. Cabarete Beach Hotel
5. Caribe Surf Hotel
6. Casa Laguna Hotel & Resort
7. El Pequeño Refugio
8. Las Orquídeas de Cabarete
9. Palmas Beach Resort
10. Villa Taína
11. Windsurf Resort

RESTAURANTS

1. Casa del Pescador
2. Casita de Papy
3. Las Brisas
4. Le Petit Provençal
5. Miró
6. Rendez-vous Café
7. Ristorante Vento

The Caribe Surf Hotel
$36, ≈, ⊗, ℜ
☎ *571-0788*
⇌ *571-3346*
The Caribe Surf Hotel is built right on the beach, but at the east end of town, in the heart of a small residential neighbourhood removed from all the tourist activity. This is not a big, luxurious hotel complex, but rather a pleasant little inn with a great holiday-by-the-sea atmosphere. The rooms are very simply decorated but well kept and perfectly comfortable.

Villa Taïna
$65, ≡
☎ *571-0722*
⇌ *571-0883*
Though the Villa Taïna, a charming little hotel of 16 rooms, is not directly on the oceanfront, it is, nevertheless a short walk away. What distinguishes this hotel is the quality of its rooms, which are stylishly decorated - in addition to being spacious and extremely well-maintained.

The Windsurf Resort
$70, ⊗, ≈, ℜ, ℝ, K
in the centre of town
☎ *571-0718*
⇌ *571-0710*
The Windsurf Resort rents out fully-equipped apartments. All of the rooms have been recently renovated. Weekly rates are available. The grounds include a pool, where all sorts of activities are organized.

The Cabarete Beach Hotel
$70, ≡, ⊗
☎ *571-0755*
⇌ *571-0831*
In the heart of town and directly on the water's edge is The Cabarete Beach Hotel, a handsome hotel of reliable comfort. Admittedly, at certain times of the day, it is at the centre of activity, but the mindful arrangement of the premises succeeds in making one forget this. Other assets of this property include 24 commodious and well-maintained rooms sporting fairly attractive interiors and easy accessibility to the beach are some other assets of this property.

El Pequeño Refugio
$79, bkfst, ≡, ℜ, ⊗
☎/⇌ *571-0770*
The El Pequeño Refugio is another congenial hotel to note if you are prepared to abide downtown. Again you need not fear the central location, for the buildings have been arranged so as to insulate guests as much as possible from the clamour of the street. It is for this reason that the rooms open onto the ocean, assuring a restful ambience and a superb view. All rooms are well-maintained and give access to a long, common balcony that also looks out onto the beach. A small garden provides the final touch to this already inviting environment.

The Albatros
$50, ≡, ≈, K
on the way into town from the west
☎ *571-0841*
One of the first establishments on the way into Cabarete, The Albatros is a pretty hotel with a lovely tropical garden, in the middle of which lies a well-maintained pool. The rooms are well equipped, and complemented by natural lighting and a balcony or terrace. The Albatros was built quite recently.

The Apart Hotel Cita del Sol
$60 ≈, K, ⊗
in the centre of town
☎ *571-0720*
⇌ *571-0795*
The Apart Hotel Cita del Sol rents out clean but rather nondescript apartments which are spacious enough for families.

Las Orquideas de Cabarete
$80, all-inclusive
⊗, ≈, ℜ
east of Cabarete
☎ *571-0787*
⇌ *571-0853*
Las Orquideas de Cabarete offers reasonably priced, perfectly adequate accommodation in clean and comfortable rooms. Hidden behind is a beautiful tropical garden filled with lush vegetation and encircling a swimming pool. Though the beach is only a short walk away, the setting is surprisingly quiet and will please those in search of tranquil surroundings. To get there

follow the little street a few hundred metres beyond the east end of the city. Suites with kitchenettes are also available.

The Casa Laguna Hotel & Resort
$165, all-inclusive
≡, ≈, ℜ
in the centre of town
☎ 571-0725
≈ 571-0704
The Casa Laguna Hotel & Resort offers very comfortable modern studios, each complemented by a balcony or terrace. It is one of the more luxurious places in Cabarete, and despite its central location, boasts a lovely natural ambience. Reserving in advance, especially in winter, is strongly recommended.

Las Palmas Beach Resort
$170, ≈, ⊗, ℝ
☎ 571-0780
≈ 571-0781
It goes without saying that downtown Carabete is fairly animated at times, but that is not to suggest that it is disagreeable. Still, some may prefer to lodge out-of-town in order to be assured of a higher quality of repose away from the bustle of Carabete. A good alternative is Las Palmas Beach Resort located about 1km east of the city. Situated directly on the beach, this resort consists of a dozen modern, two-storey buildings - all endowed with gardens. It houses rooms that are modestly decorated, but perfectly

capable of satisfying a weary traveller's need for relaxation. Caution should be exercised when swimming along this part of the coast as the undertow is particularly strong here.

The Amhsa Estrella del Mar Hotel
$170, ≡, ≈, ℜ
☎ 571-0808
≈ 571-0904
The tourism development that Carabete has known over the last several years has favoured the emergence of hotel complexes that offer an all-inclusive format. The latest addition to this line of establishments is The Amhsa Estrella del Mar Hotel composed of a collection of several prominent buildings spread out in a vast garden that extends into a fine beach of white sand. Comprised of 164 ample rooms that are modestly furnished and equipped with small balconies, this new member of the Amhsa chain has the blessing of a restful setting in the heart of downtown Cabarete.

Río San Juan

The Apart-Hotel San José
$14, ⊗
facing the lagoon
The cheapest place to stay in Río San Juan is the Apart-Hotel San José whose rooms are very basic.

The Río San Juan Hotel
$30, ≡, ≈, ℜ
Calle Duarte
☎ 589-2379
☎ 589-2211
≈ 589-2534
The Río San Juan Hotel stands on a large property right in the heart of town. The use of woodwork in the hotel's decor creates a warm atmosphere, and the gardens and the restaurant in the rear are lovely. The rooms, while clean, are a bit stark. The Río San Juan has seen better days.

The Bahía Blanca
$35, ⊗, ℜ
Calle G.F. Deligne
☎ 589-2563
≈ 589-2528
The Bahía Blanca is a veritable tropical paradise, and the choicest spot for a peaceful stay in Río San Juan. It is located on a quiet street just outside the centre of town, next to several small beaches. The beautiful design of the Bahía Blanca allows for exceptional views of the ocean from the lobby, the restaurant and the terraces. Rooms are perfectly adequate. Because this is a small hotel, it is very peaceful and a convivial atmosphere prevails. Upon request, the hotel's staff can organize all sorts of excursions, like horseback riding, to help guests explore the region. It is also possible to rent out smaller rooms (*$25*).

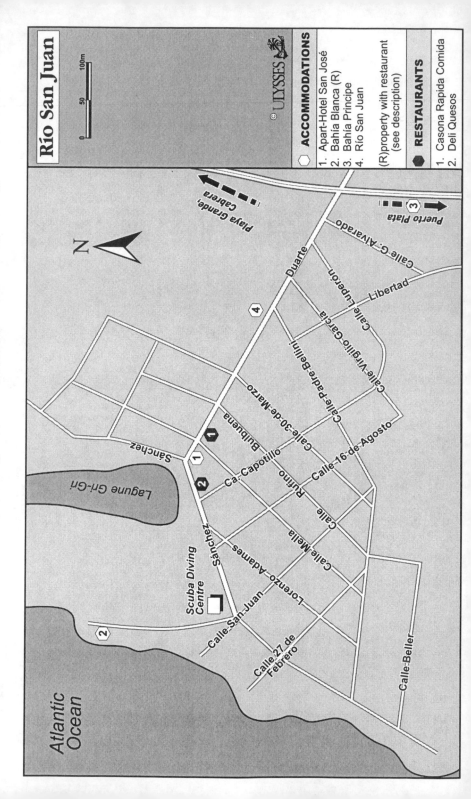

Río San Juan

© ULYSSES

0 50 100m

ACCOMMODATIONS

1. Apart-Hotel San José
2. Bahía Blanca (R)
3. Bahía Príncipe
4. Río San Juan

(R) property with restaurant (see description)

RESTAURANTS

1. Casona Rapida Comida
2. Deli Quesos

N

Atlantic Ocean

Laguna Gri-Grí

Scuba Diving Centre

Calle 27 de Febrero

Calle-San-Juan

Lorenzo-Adames

Sánchez

Calle-Mella

Calle-Beller

Calle Rufino

Ca. Capotillo

Bulbuena

Calle-30-de-Marzo

Calle-Padre-Bellini

Calle-16-de-Agosto

Calle-Virgilio-García

Calle-Luperón

Libertad

Duarte

Calle G. Alvarado

Playa Grande, Cabrera

Puerto Plata

The Bahía Principe
$180, all-inclusive
ℜ, ≈, ≡, ⊗
☎ 226-1590
≈ 226-1994

The Bahía Principe stands at the edge of a magnificent, golden, sandy beach, which it has all to itself. Particular care has been taken with the layout, so not only do the rooms have all the comforts, but the setting is magnificent as well, making this a real little Caribbean paradise. The buildings are well maintained, the tropical garden is abloom with hundreds of flowers and guests receive a warm welcome. Even the little shopping gallery displays a remarkable attention to detail, with each shop set up inside a charming, brightly coloured little Creole cottage. The place is truly gorgeous.

Playa Grande

The Caribbean Village
$190, all-inclusive
≈, ≡, ℜ
☎ 582-1170
≈ 582-6094

The Caribbean Village is a large hotel complex located near the superb Playa Grande, one of the most idyllic beaches in the country. Several large buildings house the comfortable, modern and spacious rooms, each of which has a balcony. Those at the back boast a magnificent view of the ocean. The Caribbean has tennis courts, a lovely pool, restaurants, bars and a discotheque, and guests can enjoy a variety of sports activities, excursions and evening shows. A stairway leads from the complex to the beach, where a pleasant bar-restaurant has been built. The all-inclusive package offered by the Caribbean Village includes three meals and all local drinks.

La Catalina
$60, K, ⊗, ℜ, ≈
towards Cabrera
☎ 589-7700
≈ 589-7550

Set back a bit from the road to Cabrera, on a hillside with a far-off view of the ocean, is La Catalina, a wonderful inn surrounded by magnificent tropical gardens. Beautiful vistas and a refreshing breeze create an enchanting ambience on the terrace of the dining room, which serves first-class cuisine. This elegant little complex offers well-maintained and beautifully furnished rooms, as well as one- and two-bedroom apartments. Guest can reach the neighbouring beaches and villages by taxi.

Nagua

The Hotel Carib Caban
$25, ⊗, ℜ
less than 10 km from Nagua on the way to Samaná
☎ 543-6420
≈ 584-3145

Nagua has a limited choice of accommodations, so if you decide to spend more than a day in the region, it is better to stay on the outskirts of town, on the road towards the Samaná Peninsula. The Hotel Carib Caban has small, fairly well-kept rooms and villas overlooking a quiet, undeveloped beach.

Restaurants

Puerto Plata

Puerto Plata has a wide selection of restaurants to suit all budgets and all palates. The best ones are found mainly in the hotel zone. There are, however, a host of small restaurants in the downtown area that serve simple, inexpensive food. In the evening, the promenade along the ocean is lined with food stalls selling light meals and sweets.

Puerto Plata and the Atlantic Coast

Helado Bon
$
at the corner of Calles
Separación and Beller

For a refreshing break
while strolling through
the streets of Puerto
Plata, ice cream is just
the thing, and Helado
Bon located right in
front of Parque Duarte,
is just the place to get
it. This neighbourhood
also has several other
little restaurants.

Plaza Cafe
$
on Calle 30 de Marzo near Calle
Beller

A small restaurant with
a pleasant atmosphere,
the Plaza Cafe, speciali-
zes in pica pollo and
fish. It has an open-air
terrace alongside a
quiet street.

The Portofino
$$
Avenida Mirabal

The Portofino, located
in the hotel zone, is an
attractive restaurant
ensconced in greenery.
The menu consists es-
sentially of pizzas and
other well-prepared
Italian dishes. There is
an outdoor terrace
looking onto the street,
as well as an indoor
dining room.

The Neptune
$$$
inside the Puerto Plata Beach
and Casino Resort Hotel Complex

The Neptune is the
most popular restaurant
in Puerto Plata for fish
and seafood. The atmo-

sphere is relaxed and
cosy, and the service,
excellent.

The Jarvis
$-$$
Malecón, corner of José R. López
☎ 320-7265
Benefiting from a privi-
leged position on the
Malecón, The Jarvis is
an ideal spot for those
looking for a light
meal: sandwiches and
pizzas are prominent
on the menu. Meals are
served on a terrace
covered with a canopy
of local palm leaves in
a peaceful spot nestled
away from the noise of
the street.

Polanco
$$
25 John F. Kennedy
☎ 586-9174
Polanco, an intimate
and congenial restau-
rant, has carved its
reputation from the
quality of the seafood
plates that it manages
to offer at unbelievably
affordable prices (of
particular note is the
rock lobster). A palm-
roofed patio and a sal-
utary service top the
bargain off with a cer-
tain charm.

La Ponderosa
$$-$$$
156 Calle 12 de Julio
☎ 586-1597
Noted for the quality of
its Dominican special-
ties as well as for its
delectable fish and
seafood dishes, La Pon-
derosa is bound to
awaken your appetite.
Considered one of
Puerto Plata's gems,
this little bistro, en-
hanced with a cute

outside patio, exudes a
contagiously casual
spirit.

Playa Dorada

The vast majority of
restaurants in Playa
Dorada are located in
the hotels. A wide
variety of international
cuisine is available, as
well as excellent local
dishes. Make sure to try
the Dominican cuisine,
which is generally
delicious and only
mildly spicy. Light,
inexpensive dishes can
be found at the Playa
Dorada Plaza, and at
the snack bars in most
hotels.

Hemingway's Café
$-$$
Plaza Dorada
☎ 320-2230
For burgers, steaks,
fajitas, pasta, salads and
other simple fare, head
to Hemingway's Café,
which has a young,
convivial atmosphere.
On weekends, in the
evening, you can dine
to the sounds of live
pop music.

Sosúa

Over the years, Sosúa
has seen the opening
of a plethora of restau-
rants for all tastes and
budgets. If you want a
quick bite to eat,
countless stalls up and
down the beach sell
refreshments and fish
and chicken snacks,
plus a variety of other
simple dishes. There
are also several little
restaurants on Calle Dr.

Rosen in the El Batey neighbourhood, which, like those in the hotels, offer mostly affordable international cuisine.

La Crêpe Bretonne
$-$$
Calle Dr. Rosen

La Crêpe Bretonne serves a selection of dinner and dessert crepes. This little place, with about ten tables under a palm-thatched roof, is good for a quick snack or a light evening meal.

PJ's
$-$$

You'll feel more like you are in the United States than the Caribbean at PJ's, but this is still a neat place for an evening drink and a burger or some other American fast food specialty. The atmosphere is friendly, and the decor does have a certain something.

Britania Pub
$$
Pedro Glissante

If you are one of those people who think that there's nothing like a good cold beer after a day in the sun, head to the Britania Pub, where they also serve good steak and shrimp.

The Waterfront
$$
Calle Dr. Rosen in the Waterfront Hotel
The menu at The Waterfront includes both light meals and more

sophisticated local and international specialties. Once a week, there is an inexpensive all-you-can-eat barbecue. This is a pleasant spot with a beautiful ocean view. It becomes a quiet bar towards the end of the evening.

The El Coral
$$
at the end of Calle Alejo Martinez
The menu at the El Coral places special emphasis on Dominican specialties and seafood. Hearty servings of tropical fruit are served for breakfast, and at lunch there is a selection of simple dishes. The terrace, located atop a promontory, offers a striking view of the bay of Sosúa.

La Puntilla de Pierfiorgo
$$-$$$
1 Calle La Puntilla
☎ 571-2215
Every visitor should dine at the La Puntilla at least once. It has been one of the most prestigious establishments in Sosúa for several years, known not only for its excellent Italian cuisine, but also for its splendid location. Its multi-level balconies overhanging the waves offer the most spectacular view in Sosúa. The dishes, mostly Italian and seafood, are all finely-prepared and delicious. To enjoy the breathtaking setting at its best, try to arrive just before sunset.

The Rimini Restaurant Pizzeria
$-$$
Situated on the second floor of a small house with a palm roof, The Rimini Restaurant Pizzeria offers an inexhaustible assortment of pizzas, or, if you prefer, a healthy plate of pasta.

La Carreta
$$
Pedro Clisante
☎ 571-1217
La Carreta is another establishment whose menu is brimming with a variety of plates that, as the name suggests, have an Italian focus. One can count on spending an animated evening here in the dining room that opens out onto one of Sosua's most popular streets, making for an excellent vantage point from which to survey the comings and goings of the city.

The El Toro Restaurant
$$-$$$
David Stern
Even under the hot Caribbean sun one can be overcome with a craving for a tender and juicy steak. If this is something that happens to you, head straight for The El Toro Restaurant where succulent steaks can be savoured in a stylish dining room which opens out onto the thoroughfare. Open in the evenings only.

The Romantica Restaurant
$$
David Stern
☎ *571-2509*
The Romantica Restaurant with its decor of a warm orange hue, its tiled floor, and its enchanting furnishings is bound to please you. The comprehensive menu includes rock lobster, fish, steak, pasta, pizza, in addition to some Italian and German culinary specialties; in short, something for everyone.

Cabarete

Cabarete has a vast array of restaurants in all price ranges. A good number of restaurants on the beach offer inexpensive meals, perhaps because so many young windsurfers come to Cabarete. There are some more elaborate dining possibilities here as well, however.

The Rendez-Vous Café
$
in the centre of town
The Rendez-Vous Café is a friendly place to relax for a drink or a light meal.

Casa del Pescador
$$-$$$
on the main Street
The menu at the Casa del Pescador naturally spotlights fish and seafood. The food is exquisite and the charming beach-side location is propitious to long relaxed meals. Be sure to try the daily special.

The Las Brisas Restaurant
$-$$
on the main street
☎ *571-0708*
A palm-thatched roof, a smattering of tables, and the sea for as far as the eye can see, compose the setting of the Las Brisas Restaurant. Here, the best way to relish one of the savoury dishes, whether it be a seafood, beef brochette, or spaghetti platter, is with one's feet in the sand. The ambience, which is casual and congenial, becomes a little livelier at night when the restaurant is transformed into a bar.

Miró
$-$$

The quintessential charming café, Miró, hides behind the façade of a pretty little hut in which hang painted murals inspired by Juan Miró. It makes for a memorable introduction to this oceanfront café with an unpretentious menu that highlights salads, pizzas, and pasta.

Ristorante Vento
$$-$$$
on the main street
In the heart of the city, Ristorante Vento promises delectable Italian fare, from succulent pasta dishes and salads, all the way to carpaccio. The ambient combination of the waning daylight and comfy seating by the ocean will only heighten the dining experience.

They are only open for dinner.

Le Petit Provençal
$$-$$$
west entrance at Cabarete
Le Petit Provençal provides a welcome change in pace. The proprietor, of French origin, welcomes patrons at the door, and generally oversees the proper running of the restaurant. In the kitchen, the chef creates day after day some of the most beloved delicacies of France. Kidneys in mustard sauce, ribs with roquefort and ceps, fresh fish, and rock lobster might just come your way while you're there. Always delicious, the food is the main star, but the laid-back and hospitable ambience ranks not far behind, assisted by a simple décor of plastic chairs and wooden tables.

Casita de Papy
$$-$$$
Tucked on the first floor of a small cabin, is a restaurant that brings together simplicity and charm. It manages to instill a friendly atmosphere perfect for holiday dining on the beach, with only the help of a few tables, a ceiling fan, and, of course, the view of the beach. The ocean theme carries on to the menu consisting of seafood, rock lobster, and shrimp. Reservations are necessary but you'll need to drop by during the afternoon,

since Papy doesn't have a telephone.

Río San Juan

Most of the restaurants in Río San Juan are on Calle Duarte and along the shores of the lagoon. Generally the cuisine is simple and good. For more sophisticated fare, try the restaurants in the hotels.

The Casona Rapida Comida
$
Calle Duarte, opposite the Brigandina
Located in a pretty little pastel-coloured house, The Casona Rapida Comida serves fastfood, including great empanadas (*less than $1 US*).

The Quesos Deli
$
facing the lagoon
Well-located in front of the lagoon, The Quesos Deli is a small eatery serving sandwiches and other simple dishes that are ideal after a boat trip.

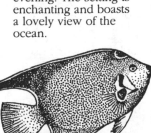 Bahía Blanca
$$
Calle G.F. Deligne
☎ *589-2563*
The dining room in the Hotel Bahía Blanca is an idyllic spot to enjoy a good meal while taking in the sunset from the terrace overlooking the ocean. The menu includes meat, fish and seafood prepared according to local and

international recipes. Professional service.

Río San Juan
$$$
Calle Duarte
☎ *589-2211*
The restaurant in the Río San Juan Hotel enjoys an excellent reputation in the area for its local cuisine. A footbridge leads to the restaurant, which stands on stilts overlooking a garden. Evening shows are presented occasionally.

Cabrera

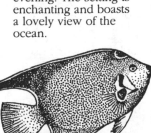 La Catalina
$$-$$$
before Cabrera

Whether you are staying in town or just passing through, be sure to stop for a bite at the restaurant in the La Catalina Inn. Savoury and well-presented light meals are served at lunchtime, while a gourmet French menu is offered in the evening. The setting is enchanting and boasts a lovely view of the ocean.

Entertainment

Playa Dorada

Playa Dorada has an active and varied nightlife centred around the big hotels, almost all of which have at least one bar and often a discotheque and a casino as well. Local performers and groups often perform at the hotels. As the schedules and type of entertainment vary, it's best to check what's on when you arrive.

If the evenings seem a little long to you, you can go to **The Plaza Dorada Cinema**, which shows movies in English every night.

Sosúa

The choice of bars and cafes is never-ending in Sosúa, and includes the pleasant and friendly **Waterfront** (*in the hotel of the same name*), where you can listen to some jazz while imbibing local or imported drinks.

The **Tall Tree**, another pleasant spot is on crowded, noisy Calle Pedro Glissante. Set on the main floor of a small house that opens out onto the street, it is a perfect place to sip a drink while studying the behaviour of the many passers by.

Most of the restaurants in Sosúa become terrace bars as the evening wears on; one of the liveliest is always **PJ's** (*Calle Pedro Glissante*).

If you feel like dancing, most of the discotheques are located at the heart of Sosúa on Calle Pedro Glissante and Dr. Rosen.

Cabarete

Before heading out to dinner, catch a few drinks in the setting sun at one of the many restaurants on the beach.

The place to be for cocktails is none other than **Onno's Bar**, right on the beach,

Amber

Amber is hardened resin from a type of pine tree that has long since disappeared. The oldest pieces date from tens of millions of years ago, and some are so transparent that insects or other animals can be seen trapped inside. For decades, Dominican amber was in high demand on the international markets. At the beginning of the 90s, however, exports plunged due to the brisk competition ensuing from the influx of amber pieces from the mines of the Baltic countries of Latvia, Estonia, and Lithuania. Since then, amber from the Dominican Republic, celebrated for its quality, has known a renaissance, recovering it former position within the global marketplace. Because of the American science fiction film *Jurassic Park*, people the world over now know about this kind of resin. In the film, scientists are able to breed Prehistoric creatures from animal cells preserved in pieces of amber. Since the release of the film, the price of amber has risen considerably, as has attendance at this museum.

from late afternoon to late at night. A smallish house shelters a few tables and a long counter. There are live bands playing on some nights. Río San Juan

The little **Gri-Gri Discotheque** on Calle Sanchez, right near the lagoon, is generally open weekend evenings.
Though slightly more touristy, **Méga Disco** will fulfill those looking for a party, awesome music and dancing.

For a quieter evening, try the **Hotel Río San Juan Piano Bar**, which has regular shows in the evenings.

Shopping

Puerto Plata

In addition to the shops in the large hotels, many places downtown sell souvenirs, jewellery and clothing. The busiest commercial streets are Calles J.F. Kennedy and 12 de Julio, near the central park. One of the best places to buy local crafts and jewellery is the gift shop at the **Museo del Ámbar** (*at the corner of Prudhomme and Duarte*).

Playa Dorada

The **Plaza Dorada** has all sorts of little shops selling rum, cigars, compact discs, jewellery, bathing suits and beachwear.The merchandise is generally of good quality, but the prices are a tad higher than elsewhere in the country. Boutiques can also be found inside many of the hotels.

Sosúa

Stores are certainly not what is missing in Sosúa, both downtown, mostly on Calles Pedro Glissante and Alejo Martinez, and along the beach, which is lined with shops of all kinds. You'll find souvenirs, clothing, local and Haitian paintings, sculptures, etc. Prices are negotiable in many of these places.

There are numerous small shops in the village, some selling jewelry made of silver, shells, amber, or larimar. If your pocket book permits, then head to **Harrison's** (*corner of Clisante and Dr. Rosen*) where you're bound to find some beautiful gold pieces, although at much higher prices.

You can stock up on Dominican cigars of all sizes and all aromas at **Sosúa Cigar Discount** (*in front of the Sosúa-by-the-Sea Hotel*).

The Family Jewel Shop on Pedro Glissante is a good place for jewellery, and also sells pieces of amber at reasonable prices.

Cabarete

If you're in the market for lovely local handicrafts or pretty jewellery, **Atlantis** ☎ *571-2286* is one of the best shops in town.

Harrison's jewelry boutique has also opened its doors in Cabarete, and proudly displays a few of its creations in gold and precious stone. They also carry some magnificient amber and larimar jewelry.

The **Carib Bic Center** not only rents out sailboards, but also has a small shop that carries nice sports clothes as well as some windsurfing equipment.

The Samaná Peninsula

Rich in spellbinding
and picturesque landscapes, this long peninsula covers an area of almost 1,000 square kilometres
and is undeniably one of the most beautiful regions in the Dominican Republic.

The area is crossed from east to west by the Cordillera de Samaná, a chain of mountains whose rounded peaks reach heights of more than 500 metres. At various points, these mountains plunge abruptly into the blue waters of the ocean or the Bahía de Samaná, adding greatly to the charm of the region. Their slopes, furthermore shelter a wonderful variety of lush vegetation.

Mountains give way to magnificent beaches of white sand, extending for kilo-metres in some places along the northern and southern coasts of the peninsula, and on the shores of nearby is-lands. In fact, such a harmonious blend of mountains and beaches, towns and villages is rarely found elsewhere in the coun-try. The Samaná penin-sula is washed to the north by the waters of the Atlantic Ocean, and to the south by those of the Bahía de Samaná. Its main cities are Santa Barbara de Samaná, generally known as Samaná; Sanchez, the gateway to the peninsula, and Las Terrenas, the only one of the three lo-cated on the Atlantic coast of the peninsula.

From the beginning of colonization, the Samaná Peninsula was coveted by the Spanish conquistadors for its strategic location at the extreme northeast end of the island. It was in fact the site of the first battle between Euro-peans and the indige-nous peoples of the Americas, January 12th, 1493.

The conflict unfolded on a beach, since then evocatively named Las Flechas (The Arrows). It was during his first voyage to the New World that Christopher Columbus encountered Caribs on this beach, just a few kilometres from the present site of Santa Barbara de Samaná. The Caribs were much less docile that the Tainos, who lived inland, and it would take several decades before the Spanish were able to "pacify" them and build a series of forts all along the coast to maintain Spanish control of the area.

Even Napoleon Bonaparte, who took over the eastern part of Hispaniola in the early 19th century, acknowledged the strategic position of the peninsula, and chose it as the site of the future colonial capital, a plan that never materialized. A few years later, in the 1820s, African slaves who had fled the United States settled in Samaná. The old Protestant church in Santa Barbara was built by their descendants.

Finding Your Way Around

It takes about two and a half hours to drive the 210 kilometres between Puerto Plata and the town of Santa Barbara de Samaná, the largest urban centre on the peninsula. The road is in generally good condition.

From Santo Domingo, take the excellent road that passes through San Francisco de Macorís and Nagua. This trip takes about four hours by car.

The main roads on the peninsula are in good condition, though they pass regularly through mountainous regions. Some dirt roads can prove difficult for cars, especially after heavy rain.

When travelling by *guagua*, remember to be patient, as service here is less frequent than in more populated parts of the country.

Taxis can be found in front of the big hotels; they travel all over the peninsula and even beyond. The fares to various destinations are clearly posted.

Motorcyclists provide another means of getting around, in exchange for a small fee. Finally, motorbikes and cars can be rented in Las Terrenas and Samaná.

El Portillo Airport

The main airport on the peninsula is in El Portillo, about 10 kilometres east of Las Terrenas. *Air Santo Domingo* (☎ 683-8020) flies twice daily from here to Punta Cana, one once daily to Puerto Plata and Santo Domingo.

Las Terrenas

The road for Las Terrenas starts about one kilometre east of Sanchez (right next to the gas station). It is in good condition, but very narrow and winding. It takes a little less than half an hour to drive the 17 kilometres from Sanchez to Las Terrenas. In Las Terrenas, the road goes through town and ends at the ocean. Turn left and continue about five kilometres to reach Playa Bonita. If you turn right, you'll reach El Portillo after about eight kilometres.

Up until recently, only a small country road linked El Portillo to the village of El Limón. This trail has since been widened, making it easier to travel the distance between the two towns. It is from El Limón that you can embark on a hike that will take you to the El Limón Falls.

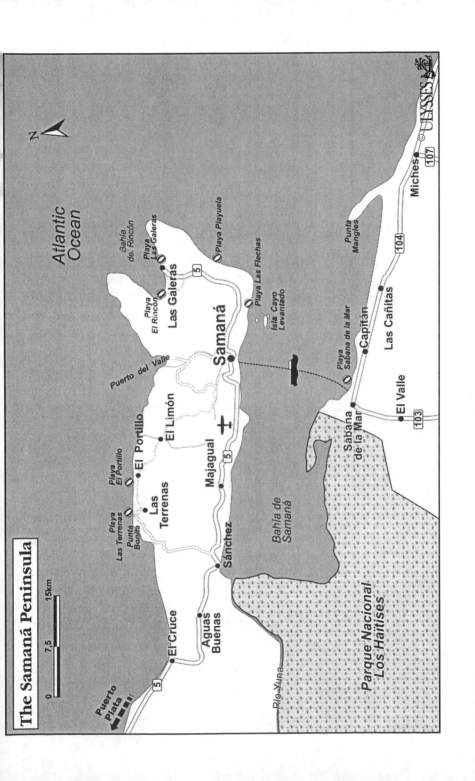

Continuing along the same route will land you in Samana.

Samaná

Highway 5 goes through the city of Sanchez, then continues east toward Samaná.

Samaná has a bus terminal for:

Caribe Tours
and
Metro Bus
on the Malecón
☎ *538-2851*

Cayo Levantado

Small boats traveling back and forth between Samaná and Cayo Levantado leave from the port of Samaná.

There are shuttle boats (*$15 round-trip*) that bring visitors to the island throughout the day. Departures begin at 8 in the morning. It is also possible to rent a private boat (*$30 round-trip*) that can hold up to 10 passengers. The availability of these two options means that the timing of your comings and goings is entirely up to you.

Las Galeras

To get to Las Galeras, travellers should take the road skirting the bay and continue east.

Sabana de la Mar

A ferry (*35 pesos*) runs three times a day between the city of Samaná and Sabaná de la Mar, on the south side of the bay. There are two departures in the morning (*9am and 11am*) and a third toward the middle of the afternoon (*3pm*). Return trips generally leave an hour later. The ferry is only available to pedestrians and motorcyclists, however.

Practical Information

Las Terrenas

The **Codetel** is located at 4 *Calle Duarte*.

The downtown area is concentrated along the main street, where visitors will find a bank, a grocery store and shops.

Tourist Information Office
147 Calle Principal
☎ *240-6363*

Samaná

To exchange American money, go to the bank on Calle Sanchez, next to the traffic circle. Visitors can make phone calls at the **Codetel**, *on the Malecón*.

Exploring

Sanchez

The road from Nagua goes through Sanchez's immediate periphery. Turn right to get downtown or continue straight ahead to reach Samaná. To get to the port of embarkation whence tours of the Parque Nacional Los Haïtises depart, take the first road on the right upon entering Sanchez and continue until you reach the port.

Today, farming and fishing, especially for shrimp, are the bread and butter of Sanchez, a little town beautifully located at the foot of the mountains, facing the Bahía de Samaná. But a stroll through its streets, which are lined with old Victorian residences, offers a glimpse of a much more prosperous past. In fact, from the end of the last century up until only a few decades ago, Sanchez was one of the country's major sea ports. It was linked to La Vega by the only railroad in the Dominican Republic, and so all produce from the fertile Cibao valley destined for exportation had to pass through Sanchez, generating significant financial and economic activity there. Sanchez's port slowed down considerably in the seventies, because trucks had superseded rail transportation and ocean liners were too big to enter the port. Port activity shifted to areas around Samaná, and the port and train station of Sanchez were abandoned.

Sanchez is an excellent departure point for a visit to **Parque Nacional Los Haïtises** (see p222).

Two companies organize excursions to the park:

Amilka Tours
$30, including admission to the park, and a meal; departure at 9am;
Calle Colón 15
☎ *552-7664*
↩ *552-7664*
and
Las Malvinas
$30, including admission to the park, and a meal; departure at 10am from the Las Malvinas Restaurant,
☎ *552-7593*

The visit to this fascinating wild garden lasts about four hours and includes a boat trip alongside a magnificent bird sanctuary and up through a lagoon bordered by mangroves, as well as tours of the park's most interesting caves. The price includes a meal. Excursions up the Río Yuna are also arranged once a week. Rates are similar and it is recommended to reserve the night before.

Las Terrenas

A road cuts through the city, leading right to the ocean. Most hotels are therefore in the immediate vicinity. To get to Playa Bonita, take a left turn approximately one kilometre before reaching the beach (you will see signs).

From Sanchez, you'll have to cross the Cordillera de Samaná to reach Las Terrenas on the Atlantic coast of the peninsula. The 15-kilometre stretch of winding road linking the two towns climbs to an altitude of 450 metres before heading down into Las Terrenas. On the way, it passes through several little hamlets and offers some **magnificent views ★★** of Bahía de Samaná and the region's mountainous landscape.

Until recently, Las Terrenas was a small, hard-to-reach village, somewhat cut off from the rest of the peninsula. Its inhabitants live on farming and fishing, as well as tourism, which is becoming more and more important to the community, for many people view Las Terrenas as a paradise lost. The area boasts several kilometres of magnificent white-sand **beaches ★★** (page?) lined with coconut palms and

perfect for exploring on foot or horseback. Heading west along the water from Las Terrenas, the beach extends for about 10 kilometres, passing by Punta Bonita and running all the way to Cosson.

To the east the long ribbon of sand stretches all the way to the little town of El Portillo, about 8 kilometres away. All of these often untouched beaches are good places to swim, while some of the country's best scuba diving sites lie offshore. Many hotels, inns, restaurants and bars have sprung up along the ocean over the years, but happily they have yet to detract from the tranquil beauty of the setting.

The El Limón Falls ★★ are accessible from Las Terrenas. A dirt road leads from El Portillo to the village of El Limón about 10 kilometres away. From the village, you must continue on foot for about an hour over rough terrain, or you can rent a horse in El Limón or Las Terrenas. Either way, the 50-metre-high spectacle of crashing water is worth the effort, and you can cool off in the natural pool at the base of the falls. The dirt road from El Limón leads to Santa Barbara de Samaná after about 15 kilometres.

Samanà (Santa Bàrbara de Samanà)

After crossing the city of Samaná, the road continues all the way to the promenade skirting the bay. The port is located at the eastern extremity of the promenade.

Samaná has a distinctly more modern and airy feel about it than most Dominican towns and cities. There is a simple reason for this: although its origins date far back, the town was rebuilt after having been completely destroyed by fire in 1946. Today, wide avenues, traffic circles and recently constructed buildings give it a very distinctive look, which is not without its charms. Samaná's location, sheltered by mountains and overlooking the magnificent Bahía de Samaná, with its fishing boats and yachts, adds greatly to the appeal of the town.

Samaná was founded by order of the king of Spain in 1756, as a stronghold against French and English privateers and bandits. Though it is commonly called Samaná, the town was christened Santa Barbara de Samaná in honour of Barbara de Bracance, wife of King Fernando VI. During the French occupation, from 1795 to 1809, the city was to be the capital of the island and was renamed Fort Napoléon; an ambitious urbanization plan was drawn up but never realized (the plans can actually be seen at the Museo del Hombre Dominicano, in Santo Domingo). During the following decades under Haitian control, Samaná became a haven for escaped black slaves from the United States. This influx of people left its mark, perceptible today in the local language, place names and religious practices.

Since Samaná has no nice beach, many visitors skip over it altogether. This lively city does, however, boast a pretty little **port**, one of the most colourful **public markets** in the country, a few hotels of varying quality and several good restaurants.

The structure known as **La Churcha** (*downtown Samaná*) was transported from England in 1820. Originally a Methodist church, it is now the Evangelical Church of Samaná. The little island of **Cayo Vigia** is accessible by a long footbridge just behind the Hotel Cayacoa (if you are not a guest there, be discreet, and nobody will mind if you explore). Though the island is no longer maintained, it bears witness to more prosperous times. The **view ★**, however, is still striking, encompassing Samaná, the port, and the bay. You can swim here, although the little beaches are not very inviting. It takes at least a half-hour to walk to the island and back.

The Parque Nacional Los Haitises

Situated in the extreme southwest of the Samaná peninsula, The Parque Nacional Los Haïtises covers an area of approximately 1200 square kilometres. This fascinating region was formed some 40 million years ago when a mass of limestone, composed mainly of marine deposits such as coral, emerged to the surface when it was propelled by the force of the earth's movements.

With the passage of time, erosion has transformed this rock into a magnificent, rolling countryside composed of small hills that range from 200 to 300 metres in height. Because the rain water is quickly absorbed by the highly porous ground, lakes and rivers have not had the chance to form. In addition, the quality of the soil is very poor. Nonetheless, an abundance of rain has made it possible for a humid, subtropical forest to form where American cedar and Dominican mahogany grow in abundance. The park is also bordered by swamp land which is composed mainly of red and white mangrove trees, making for a zone that favours the development of a varied ecosystem.

The Humpback Whale (Megaptera Novœanglœ)

Every winter, about 2000 humpback whales come to the coast of the Samaná peninsula to reproduce in the warm waters. These huge marine mammals, which measure between 12 and 15 metres long and can live up to 80 years, travel great distances in the Atlantic Ocean, from north to south. In the summer, they journey to Canadian shores, particularly the Gulf of St. Lawrence, because the water is cooler and is rich in plankton. In the winter, they head south to winter in the Caribbean Sea.

The humpback whale has been hunted by whalers for centuries, but has been especially overhunted in the 20th century, significantly reducing their numbers. Today about 10,000 are left in the world. Although the North Atlantic humpback-whale population is probably the largest, this animal is an endangered species.

A humpback whale can be easily spotted in the water from a distance because its very long pectoral fin, which can measure 6 metres in length, sticks out of the water when they dive. The long head of the humpback whale forms more than a third of its body and the underside of its tail ranges in colour from white to black and is a different pattern for each whale. Scientists are generally able to identify individual whales by these unique tail markings.

One can come to this park to marvel at the beauty of its natural geological formations, but catching a glimpse of the incredible variety of birds is another reason that the visit is worthwhile. The most common species are the brown pelican, the frigate, and the tern.

Other treasures are to be found as well, such as the caves where the Amerindians used to live and congregate for various rituals before the arrival of the Europeans. If you have an occasion to visit some of them, you will see walls covered with **Pre-Colombian pictograms and petroglyphs**. This is certainly one of the most interesting and accessible parks in the country.

Excursions to Parque Nacional Los Haïtises (see p222) are organized from the port of Samaná. Trips leave Samaná at around 8am and last about six hours. *The cost is about $40 US per person.* Note that trips also leave from Sanchez, which is closer to the park.

WhalesMarine
about $30
on Avenida le Malecón,
one trip in the morning and one in the afternoon,
☎ *538-2494*
Humpback whale-watching excursions ★★ are arranged from January to March from Samaná (see p226)

Excursions to Sabana de la Mar

You can take a ferry to Sabana de la Mar (*$2 US; departure from port at 9am, 11am and 3pm*), on the other side of the Bahía de Samaná. Although it makes for a pleasant stroll, there is not much to see in the village.

Cayo Levantado

There are daily trips to the magnificent island of Cayo Levantado (*$10 for a seat in the shuttle; you can also rent out a shuttle for $30; daily departures beginning at 8am; departures also from the small village of Las Flechas, about 8 km east of Samaná; arrive early to be able to share a boat*). This island paradise off the shores of Samaná is one of the peninsula's most precious treasures. Luxuriant vegetation, featuring a harmonious blend of beautiful gardens and virgin tropical forest, covers the rolling landscape. Well-maintained trails lead to the southern point of the island, where a promontory offers an excellent view of the bay and the coastline. Cayo Levantado is best known for the magnificent **beaches ★★★** (see p224) that circle the island. The beach on the west coast, tucked inside a bay with turquoise waters and lined with palm trees, is a particularly idyllic spot. From sunrise until around

11am, when the first tourists begin to trickle in, this beach seems like a forgotten paradise. Quality accommodation is available in the one hotels on the island (see p223).

Las Flechas

On January 13, 1493, a beautiful sandy beach about eight kilometres from Samaná was the site of the first battle between Europeans and the indigenous people of the Americas. The beach was named Las Flechas (*The Arrows*) in reference to the hostile greeting that Christopher Columbus and his crew received here during their first voyage to the New World. On this beach one can rent a boat to get to **Cayo Levantado**. A few hundred metres beyond lies the beautiful Gran Bahía Hotel, one of the most luxurious on the island.

El Rincón

To the left of Las Flechas, a dirt road in very poor condition leads to **Playa El Rincón ★★** (page?). This magnificent white-sand beach stretches a full kilometre, and is lined from one end to the other by a palm grove. Hidden along the shores of a calm and beautiful bay, the beach is often empty.

Las Galeras

Las Galeras has managed to retain the quiet charm and atmosphere of a little fishing village despite the push of tourism. Located on the eastern tip of the peninsula, it overlooks a large bay with calm waters perfect for swimming and snorkelling. Facing the village, **wild beaches ★★** (see p 225) stretch several kilometres beckoning to wanderers. Tourism development is recent in Las Galeras, but there are already a few excellent hotels.

Outdoor Activities

Swimming

Las Terrenas

Las Terrenas and its immediate region are adorned with several kilometres of golden **beaches ★★**, among the most spectacular in the country. Coconut palms provide welcome shade while exploring on foot or on horseback. Starting in Las Terrenas and heading west, the beach

continues for 10 kilometres, passing **Playa Punta Bonita** and then **Playa Cosón**, a veritable splendour. Indeed, it extends over several kilometres and one often has the beach all to oneself. Visitors can reach the beach by either continuing further west, past Punta Bonita, or by taking a left turn at the junction leading to Punta Bonita from Las Terrenas. Heading east, the long strip of sand extends to the small town of El Portillo, about eight kilometres away. This is an ideal area for swimming, and the nearby coral reefs make for interesting scuba diving.

Cayo Levantado

Cayo Levantado has at least three superb white-sand **beaches ★★★**. The prettiest is on the west side of the island; lined with palm trees, it is washed by the turquoise waters of a lovely bay. This spot is remarkably beautiful, especially early in the morning before the beach is overrun with tourists. Wandering vendors sell snacks and drinks along the beach.

El Rincón

Playa El Rincón ★★ is a magnificent white-sand beach about one kilometre long. Bordered by a palm grove, it is nestled inside a pretty bay with calm waters. Chances are fairly good

A fruit kiosk where coconuts are sold in abundance.
- *Claude Hervé-Bazin*

A beach in the town of Monte Cristi, in the extreme northwest of the country. - *Claude Hervé-Bazin*

The Laguna Gri-Gri is an exceptional site where a multitude of bird species can be observed. - *Claude Hervé-Bazin*

La Churcha, one of Samaná's most important historic buildings.
- *Claude Hervé-Bazin*

The beach at Les Galeras on the Samaná Peninsula in the extreme northeast of the country. - *Claude Hervé-Bazin*

that you will find your-self completely alone. There are no businesses close by, but the local children will probably try to sell you some coconut.

Las Galeras

Opposite Las Galeras, and in the immediate surroundings, **wild beaches ★★** stretch several kilometres just waiting to be explored. Their waters are great for swimming and scuba diving. The half-dozen hotels in Las Galeras all have restaurants in case you get hungry.

Scuba Diving

Las Terrenas

Scuba diving is the sport par excellence in Las Terrenas, which has the best dive sites in the country. The necessary equipment can be rented on site. Excursions on the open sea are offered, as well as introductory classes (*anywhere between $60 and $70*), beginners can take a course that includes initiation in a swimming pool followed by a forty minute dive in the ocean.

There are four schools in the immediate vicinity of Las Terrenas:

The Tropical Diving Center
Tropic Banana Hotel
Las Terrenas
☎ *240-6010*

The Acaya Diving Center
Acaya Hotel
Punta Bonita

Cacao Beach
Cacao Beach Hotel
Las Terrenas
☎ *240-6000*

El Portillo Scuba Diving Center
☎ *240-6100*

Las Galeras

There is a worthwhile scuba diving centre, Dive Samaná, that arranges excursions to the local diving spots around Las Galeras.

Dive Samaná
☎ *538-0210*

Snorkelling

Snorkelling does not require much equipment and can be practised near the beach. Most hotels and diving centres in Las Terrenas, Las Galeras and Cayo Levantado have equipment and can indicate the best spots to try out this sport.

Sailing

Las Terrenas

Want to sail? Then join a group outing on a sailboat, or rent a cata-maran at:

Pura Vida
Calle La Playa
☎ *240-6070*

You can also opt for one of the tours offered by:

Jessie
Calle La Playa
☎ *240-6415*
a company that rents out 12-passenger cata-marans for either half-day (*$200*) or full-day (*$300*) excursions.

Horseback Riding

Las Terrenas

Horseback riding is a popular sport in Las Terrenas, besides being a pleasant and easy way to explore the region. Visitors can take part in excursions into the mountains, along the beaches as well as to the surrounding villages. Among the companies that organize this kind of half-day outing in the region, it would be wise to take note of the ranch next door to the

Tropic Banana Hotel where you can ride horses at *$12 an hour*. Courses are also available for those who want them. Some city hotels, notably the **El Portillo** ☎ *240-6100*, also offer horse-back riding excursions.

Las Galeras

It is also possible to go riding at the Las Galeras at **The Rancho Thikis** (*Casa Blanca Hotel*) in Las Galeras. One particularly interesting option is to ride out to the magnificent El Limón Falls (horses can be rented in El Limón or Las Terrenas).

Golf

The only golf course on the peninsula lies near the:

Gran Bahía Hotel Las Flechas *about 8 km east of Samaná* ☎ *538-3111* The nine-hole course is nice, but not quite up to par with the splendid courses at Casa de Campo, near La Romana, or at Playa Dorado near Puerto Plata. An 18-hole course is planned for the vicinity of Las Terrenas.

Hiking

Cayo Levantado

About a kilometre of trails has been cleared near the very pretty Cayo Levantado. They pass through tropical gardens on their way to beaches and lookout points offering splendid views of **Bahía de Samaná.**

El Limón

Another, more difficult hike starts in the village of El Limón, in the vicinity of Las Terrenas, and leads to the **El Limón Falls**. The freshwater pool at the base of

the falls is the perfect spot to cool off. The trip there and back takes about two hours.

Birdwatching

The **Parque Nacional Los Haïtises** is a wonderful place to go birdwatching.

Boat rides through the park usually include a trip up a river lined

with mangroves, where various species of birds nest, as well as a tour of the bird sanctuary, home to frigate birds and pelicans. Some of the park's caves, moreover, are inhabited by bats.

Whalewatching

Samaná

WhalesMarine (Humpback whale-watching excursions) *about $30* On Avenida le Malecón, one trip in the morning, another in the afternoon ☎ *538-2494* From January to March, tours are organized out of Samaná. During the winter months, humpbacks from the North Atlantic come to give birth (the gestation period is about 12 months) in the warm waters of the Caribbean Sea. About 1,000 to 2,000 of the total population of 6,000 choose the Bahía de Samaná and its surroundings. Excursions provide glimpses of these spectacular mammals, which when fully-grown measure an average of 14 metres in length and weigh 35 tons.

Several companies offer trips; the one that organizes the most interesting and the safest excursions for both you and the whales is Whales Marine. It is extremely inadvisable to head out in fishing boats, which are too unstable for this kind of activity.

All-Terrain Vehicles

Las Terrenas

If the muse overtakes you, embark on an adventure aboard one of the all-terrain vehicles that offer quick access to the most remote beaches on the peninsula. Rentals are available from

Jessie
$45 per day
Calle del Carmen de la Playa
☎ *240-6415*

Accommodations

Las Terrenas

The Las Terrenas region, including Punta Bonita and El Portillo, has about twenty hotels in all price ranges. All of the hotels in the area are situated along beautiful beaches facing the ocean.

Los Pinos
$25 for a room, $40 for a bungalow; ⊗
on the beach in Las Terrenas
☎ *240-6168*
Offering some of the cheapest rooms in Las Terrenas, the Los Pinos Hotel occupies a wood building shaded by large pines and vaguely ressembling a chalet in the Alps. Its rooms are of a spartan demeanour, in which only the beds are equipped with mosquito nets (not the windows). If you prefer a little bit more in the way of creature comforts, opt for one of the bungalows, which have been designed with a bit more of a luxurious touch. The hotel is run by French proprietors.

Las Palmeras Hotel
$30; ≋, ⊗, ℝ
road to El Portillo
☎*240-6231*
For well-priced accommodation in Las Terrenas, head to the Las Palmeras. Its houses rooms of adequate comfort, and some are equipped with air-conditioners. The rooms are found one level up from a restaurant that occupies most of the main floor.

The Casa Grande Beach Hotel
$30; ℜ, ⊗;
on Punta Bonita beach
☎ *240-6349*
↩ *240-6349*
is comprised of a few rooms distributed throughout a single building. The rooms are modest but clean. A room for four can be had for $40 US.

The Araya
$60; bkfst ℜ, ⊗
on Punta Bonita beach
☎ *240-6161*
↩ *240-6166*
is a lovely little hotel with a very convivial atmosphere. The rooms are clean, sufficiently large, ventilated and all equipped with a terrace or balcony. The upstairs rooms are particularly pleasant. Moreover, the palm-roofed restaurant adjacent to the hotel has an excellent and varied cuisine.

The Tropic Banana
$70; bkfst, ⊗, ≈, ℜ;
on the beach in Las Terrenas,
☎ *240-6010*
↩ *240-6112*
The Tropic Banana is a small hotel complex with about twenty rooms in pretty little houses shaded by palm trees. Visitors soon feel at ease in this charming place. At cocktail time, guests can enjoy a drink in the small, palm-roofed bar's relaxing atmosphere, play a game of pool or bowls. The Tropic Banana was one of the very first hotels to open in Las Terrenas and has retained a loyal clientele ever since. A scuba diving centre awaits guests on the hotel's grounds.

Coco Plaza Hotel
$60; ≋, ℝ
2 Calle Chicago Boss
☎/↩ *240-6172*
This newly-built hotel comprises a number of beautiful rooms decorated with furniture

crafted from wood and cane and painted in lively tropical colours. Everything here sparkles with cleanliness, the rooms as much as the bathrooms, which are otherwise impeccably kept. All of the rooms benefit, as well, from small balconies that overlook the ocean, adding further to the attractiveness of this property. A pool is currently under construction.

The Atlantis
$65; bkfst; ℜ, ≈, ⊗
on Punta Bonita beach
☎ *240-6111*
⇆ *240-6205*

The Atlantis is a charming little hotel housed in rococo-style buildings. Reception is friendly. The 18 rooms and common rooms have been carefully decorated. The bigger rooms cost about $20 more.

Coyamar
$48 bkfst incl., ℜ, ≈
Playa Bonita
☎/⇆ *248-2353*
Those who seek a quaint and cordial inn can end their search at the Coyamar.
Rooms are tastefully furnished and, contrary to so many of the other establishments on the island, the owner has sought to create a unique décor where violet-tinted blues and golden yellows mix together in a dance of cheerful contrasts. The property consists of two small

buildings that face the ocean at the entrance to Punta Bonita. Of course, great care is taken by the friendly proprietors to ensure that their unique establishment is well-kept and clean. A restaurant offering delicious meals is also available to ensure that everyone's culinary needs are met. (see p232).

The Aligio Beach Hotel
$130 all inclusive; ≈, ℜ, ⊗
☎*240-6255*
⇆*240-6169*
This hotel has the double advantage of offering an all-inclusive format and a more intimate atmosphere, since it only has 80 rooms. Great care has been taken in the design to ensure that guests feels at home. The rooms are all decorated with Haitian folk art, and wooden shutters adorn the windows, providing a stylish yet cozy ambience.

The pavilions housing the rooms are spread out in the heart of an attractive garden. Other considerations also cater to please: such as the two pools, one of which is especially equipped for waterpolo and the scuba-diving school that is located right on-site.

The El Portillo Beach Resort
$150 for a room, $180 for a cabana; all inclusive; ℜ, ≈, ≡
☎ *240-6100*
⇆ *240-6104*
El Portillo is a few kilometres east of Las Terrenas, close to the little village of El Portillo, along a magnificent beach. Rooms are distributed in *cabañas* that are scattered throughout a vast garden,

and they open directly out onto the beach. All are endowed with kitchenettes, a whirlpool in the bathroom, and balconies embellished with rockers. Families will feel at ease here as well, as some *cabañas* are equipped with two bedrooms and two bathrooms. For those who do not consider *cabañas* their cup of tea, regular guest rooms are available in a large building situated at a further distance from the beach.

Punta Bonita Resort
$102 US, ½b including 2 meals; ℜ, ≈
Punta Bonita
☎ *240-6082*
⇆ *240-6012*
Guests can choose between comfortable hotel rooms or cottages with kitchenettes at the large beachside Punta Bonita Resort located a few kilometres west of Las Terrenas.

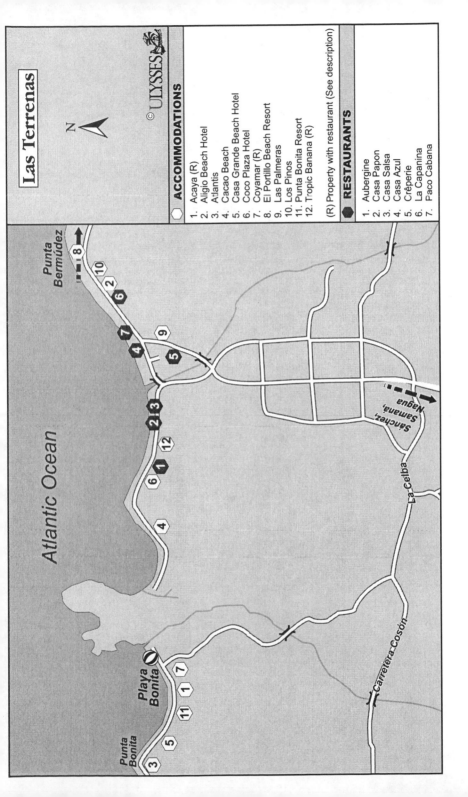

Las Terrenas

N

© ULYSSES

Atlantic Ocean

Punta Bermúdez

Punta Bonita

Playa Bonita

Sánchez, Samaná, Nagua

La Ceiba

Carretera Cosón

ACCOMMODATIONS

1. Acaya (R)
2. Aligio Beach Hotel
3. Atlantis
5. Cacao Beach
5. Casa Grande Beach Hotel
6. Coco Plaza Hotel
7. Coyamar (R)
8. El Portillo Beach Resort
9. Las Palmeras
10. Los Pinos
11. Punta Bonita Resort
12. Tropic Banana (R)

(R) Property with restaurant (See description)

RESTAURANTS

1. Aubergine
2. Casa Papon
3. Casa Salsa
4. Casa Azul
5. Crêperie
6. La Capanina
7. Paco Cabana

This hotel complex is the biggest in Punta Bonita and one of the largest in the region. The buildings are dispersed throughout a large garden.

The Cacao Beach
$150 US all-inclusive
≡, ≈, ℜ
on the beach in Las Terrenas
☎ 530-5817
The largest hotel complex in Las Terrenas, with several restaurants, nearly 150 rooms in cottages and a large swimming pool. All sorts of activities are organized for guests.

Samaná

The King Hotel
$10; ⊗, ℜ
downtown, on the road to Sanchez
☎ 538-2353
The most inexpensive rooms in town are generally those in the smaller hotels on Samaná's main street. is one of these. It offers very simple rooms, in a relatively noisy part of town. The building is tall and narrow, offering a lovely view of the city and the bay.

Plaza Taïna
$16
☎ 538-2554
A few steps from the King hotel, the Plaza Taïna offers rooms of basic comfort.

The Cotubanana
$22; ⊗, ℜ
downtown
☎ 538-2557
The Cotubanana is clean and offers moderately comfortable rooms with no frills. Check out a few rooms before settling on one, because while some are adequate, others are unbelievably tiny and have no windows. All guests have access to a common balcony overlooking the bay.

Casa de Huespedes "Leydi"
$20
43 Calle Rosario Sánchez
☎/≈ 538-2379
If you are seeking to find bargain accommodation, but are not willing to sacrifice your comfort, chances are you will find it at the Casa de Huespedes "Leydi" rather than at the Cotubananá. The well-kept rooms (like the bathrooms) are located upstairs and are decorated with wooden furniture that give them a certain character.

Casa de Huespedes "El Paraiso"
$20
53 Calle Rosario Sánchez
☎ 538-2218
On days when there is no vacancy at the Casa Huespedes 'Leydi', head to the El Paraiso where the rooms, also located upstairs, are just as clean if only slightly smaller.

Tropical Lodge
$40; ⊗, ℜ
Avenida Marina, at the eastern edge of town
☎ 538-2480
≈ 538-2068
More like a small inn than a hotel, the Tropical Lodge offers decent, well-kept rooms in a peaceful atmosphere. There is an excellent view of the bay from the front rooms, the lounge and the breakfast room. Built on a hillside just east of downtown Samaná, the Tropical Lodge is ensconced in a beautiful tropical garden.

The Cayacoa
$170; all-inclusive
≡, ≈, ℜ
take the little street on the right before the promenade
☎ 538-3131
≈ 538-2985
The Cayacoa boasts an excellent location on a hill overlooking the bay just outside the downtown area. Quality rooms and cabañas are both available. The Cayacoa has a pool, as well as its own private beach. In addition, a small footbridge leads out to the little island of Cayo Vigia. The hotel organizes various sports activities and tours of the area, including excursions to Cayo Levantado.

The Gran Bahía
$160; all-inclusive
≡, ≈, ℜ
8 km west of the city, on the
road to Las Galeras
☎ *538-3111*
⇆ *538-2764*
The Cayacoa is consid-
ered one of the best
hotels in the Domi-
nican Republic. Located
on the side of a cliff, it
offers a clear view of
the Bahía de Samaná
and Cayo Levantado.
Indeed, the layout of
the hotel makes the
most of this enchanting
spot, for a large and
beautiful terrace allows
visitors to relax com-
fortably while admiring
the water. Moreover,
the rooms also offer a
view of this wondrous
sight of the ocean as
far as the eye can see.
The hotel is beautiful,
and takes full advan-
tage of its enchanting
location. The rooms are
well furnished, and the
service impeccable; a
serene, relaxed atmo-
sphere prevails at the
Gran Bahía. Guests are
offered a wide selec-
tion of activities, in-
cluding excursions to
Cayo Levantado and all
sorts of sports, such as
tennis, golf (nine-hole
course), scuba diving,
horseback riding, etc.

Cayo Levantado

Cayo Levantado Hotel
$110 all-inclusive
ℜ, ⊗
Cayo Levantado
☎ *538-2677 or 538-3111*
The long-awaited Cayo
Levantado Hotel re-
cently opened its

doors. Set in an en-
chanting location, it
offers the level of com-
fort one would expect
from the Occidental
Hotel chain. There are
close to 30 rooms and
10 cabañas. Guests at
this hotel will enjoy the
early mornings and late
afternoons on the virtu-
ally deserted beaches
of Cayo Levantado.

Las Galeras

Moorea Beach
$30; ⊗, ℜ
200 m left of the main street,
☎ *538 2545 or 689-4105*
Until recently, the
Moorea Beach was the
only hotel in Las
Galeras. This small,
moderately comfortable
two-story building has
12 rooms, as well as a
bar and a restaurant
looking onto a beauti-
ful tropical garden. The
French owner knows
the region very well.

Paradiso Bungalow
$20; ⊗
at the edge of Las Galeras
☎/⇆ *538-0210*
On the way into Las
Galeras, you'll spot the
cottages of Paradiso
Bungalow on the left.
They are quite rudi-
mentary, but can ac-
commodate up to four
people. The beach is
close by.

The Club Bonito
$140 ½b; ≈, ≡, ℜ
☎ *538-0203*
⇆ *538-0204*
www.club-bonito.com
Once separate hotels,
the **Todo Blanco** and the
Club Bonito have since
merged into a single

hotel-club complex.
The lobby is now situ-
ated in Club Bonito's
entrance hall. Both
establishments, how-
ever, have managed to
keep their own distinct
character. The beautiful
Victorian building
housing the **Todo Blanco
Hotel** is right on the
beach in Las Galeras.
The rooms are spacious
and comfortable, and
several have balconies
and small sitting rooms.
The Club Bonito, for its
part, is the latest hotel
to open in Las Galeras
and boasts a rather
bold and unique decor.
The rooms are pleasant
and well-tended. The
establishment looks
directly onto the beach,
in the middle of the
village. At the time of
our visit, a large pool
was being built. It is
also possible to rent
large apartments
equipped with kitchen-
ettes, among other
things. These can be
found a little less than
a kilometre from the
complex.

The Villa Serena
$96; bkfst;
ℜ, ≈, ⊗
after the Moorea Beach,
☎ *223-8703*
⇆ *538-7545*
The Villa Serena is a
most charming hotel,
located close to the
beach and adorned
with magnificent tropi-
cal gardens. The quality
accommodation con-
sists of vast, elegant,
airy, well-furnished
rooms with balconies,
all in an enchanting
setting. One of the
hotel's major assets is

its huge terrace, furnished with rattan chairs, where guests can spend hours contemplating the blue ocean stretching out into the distance. The Villa Serena is one of the most pleasant hotels on the peninsula.

Casa Marina Bay
$160; all-inclusive
ℜ, ≈, ≡
on the outskirts of Las Galeras
☎ *682-8913 or 535-3450*
The largest hotel complex around Las Galeras, the Casa Marina Bay occupies a large property on the outskirts of town. Guests have direct access to the beach, and can enjoy all sorts of activities and sports, including tennis, horseback riding and scuba diving.

Restaurants

The Samaná peninsula boasts a great number of places offering excellent food. Whether in Las Terrenas, Santa Barbara de Samaná or Las Galeras, local recipes are quite often prepared with something of a European flavour.

Las Terrenas

La Crêperie
$
in the Plaza Paseo
If a craving for ice cream or crêpes suddenly overtakes you,

relief is to be found at the Crêperie. Not only do they make delicious crêpes; they serve breakfast as well.

La Capanina's
$-$$
La Capanina's consists of nothing but a dozen tables scattered under a canopy of palm trees, along with a few tables dotting the grass under the sun. It is in this relaxed and refreshing atmosphere that you can sit down to a pizza (great selection of toppings), or to a dish of beef sirloin, fish, or rock lobster. There is something here to suite everyone's palate.

Paco Cabana
$-$$
on the beach in front of Plaza Paseo
The mouth-watering fragrance of an open-air grill can be detected for blocks away. The barbecue occupies the place of honour here, and there is an extensive array of dishes to choose from. The meals are served at tables that are placed directly on the beach according to your specifications. For decor, you have the sea stretching endlessly ahead from every vantage point. A bar and pool table render the site complete.

Casa Papon
$-$$
Another address to be noted on the beach is that of Casa Papoa which offers a daily menu of appetizing

meals (spaghetti, salad, seafood, grilled fish) made from the freshest of ingredients. In this congenial space a simple hut serves as the dining room.

L'Aubergine
$-$$
Calle Chicago Boss
This restaurant has everything to delight even the most divergent of taste-buds; with a menu that includes onion soup, fish soup, and lamb stew in addition to a variety of salad, pasta, and seafood plates it is easy to see why. Walls brandishing the lively colours of yellow, orange and blue enhance the decor and warm atmosphere, which is very much like that of a bistro.

The Coyamar
$-$$
Playa Bonita
☎248-2353
The interior design of the Coyamar is a synchronised arrangement consisting of a rich red-tiled floor, a little fountain emerging from the centre of the dining room, walls dancing with spirited tones of yellow, blue, and violet, and - to top it all off - a ceiling fashioned from local palm leaves. Enclosing the restaurant is a handsome garden thriving with palm and yucca plants. It is in this most agreeable atmosphere that you savour your meal, having an extensive range of choices from a menu which proposes

omelettes, salads, sandwiches, shrimp and calamari plates, in addition to various filets of local fish.

Casa Azul
$$
Las Terrenas
Another place whose menu is suitable for any time of day is the Casa Azul, a small outdoor spot near the beach. It opens early in the morning and serves good breakfasts.

Acaya
$$-$$$
Punta Bonita
The Acaya hotel's restaurant is certainly worth a stop for dinner. Under a roof of palms, and in a rather convivial atmosphere, this establishment offers a menu including a wide variety of very well-prepared seafood, fish and meat dishes. Service is attentive.

Tropic Banana
$$-$$$
Las Terrenas
A visit to the Tropic Banana's restaurant starts during cocktail hour, as guests slowly sip their drinks in the pleasant and refreshing atmosphere of the hotel's little bar. When the proprietor is in a good mood, lucky patrons are offered tasty hors d'oeuvres to pique their appetites.

The guests can then make their way to the dining room, which opens out on the garden and the swimming pool. It is in this relaxed ambiance that guests savour dishes, each more delicious than the other, like the oven-roasted filet of sea bream in mushroom sauce or the seafood stew, brimming with large, tasty morsels.

The Casa Salsa
$$-$$$
Las Terrenas
The Casa Salsa is a romantic little palmroofed restaurant located right on the beach, an ideal place for sipping a cocktail while admiring the sunset. It is in this enchanting setting that visitors can sample one of the most refined cuisines in Las Terrenas. The menu is varied, with seafood, fish and meat dishes all prepared with equal panache. Every one of the dishes will leave you wanting more, be it the succulent Noilly sea bream, or the beef fillet with green pepper. Guests should make sure to leave a little room for dessert though, as these are also quite delectable.

Samaná

Many restaurants are clustered along Avenida le Malecón, facing the bay, on the east side of the city, where most nightlife takes place. Most have electric generators to compensate for the frequent power outages in Samaná.

The Black and White
$-$$
on the Malencón, near the port
A small open-air restaurant serving simple meals at all hours of the day.

The Café de Paris
$-$$
on Avenida le Malecón, near the port
The Café de Paris offers simple, inexpensive cuisine. Sandwiches, crepes, pizza and ice cream are the big favourites here. This pleasant spot becomes a lively bar as the evening progresses.

Camilo's
$-$$
Malecón
☎ 538-2495
Facing the port, Camilo's is another eatery to become familiar with, particularly if you are looking to experience the taste of some superb Dominican specialties - one of which is coconut fish, a plate unique to Samaná. You will have the opportunity to sample the menu in an airy dining room on the oceanfront, in a gracious atmosphere enhanced by the presence of plants, flowers, and rattan tables covered with floral tablecloths.

The Don Juan
$$
in the Tropical Lodge hotel
The Don Juan restaurant serves mainly French cuisine and seafood in a warm setting. The small bar is a relaxing place for an aperitif.

Mata Rosada
$$
in front of the port
Another cute restaurant in town where good food is served is the Mata Rosada. Every day, the menu features a host of savoury meals such as beef medallions in the gravy of wild game, filet mignon with morels, and kidneys with vine roots, not to mention the cornucopia of fish platters prepared in a variey of ways. The meals here, always artfully presented, will satiate even the most demanding of appetites.

Le France Restaurant
$$
on Avenida le Malecón, near the port
Known as a great spot for many years now, the charming Le France restaurant serves French cuisine, as its name suggests, as well as a few local delights, including succulent mérou au coco. Don't hesitate to ask the jolly, friendly host to help you pick your meal.

Cayo Levantado

Fish, seafood and chicken is sold at food stalls on the north side of Cayo Levantado.

Cayo Levantado
$$
In the Cayo Levantado Hotel
If you are looking for a more elaborate menu, try the Cayo Levantado restaurant

Las Galeras

Jardin Tropical
$$
in the centre of Las Galeras
Ideally located near the beach, the bar-restaurant Jardin Tropical serves mainly fish and seafood, prepared according to local recipes.

Shopping

Las Terranas

Las Terrenas has a certain number of shops, most of which are located near the beach. Among these are **Haitian Indian Art and Ginger Bread**, which specialize in arts and crafts.

Plaza Paseo is a new shopping centre that brings together a smattering of restaurants, several small boutiques including a jewellery shop, a cigar shop, and a **pharmacy**. Among the most interesting of these is **Nativ Art**, which sells exquisite objects of art and crafts, notably sculptures, masks, and statuettes. As its name suggests, The **Maison de la Presse** offers an excellent selection of French newspapers and magazines, as well as numerous English and foreign dailies.

Samaná

The city of Samaná is a good place to buy souvenirs. Most shops are clustered along the Melancón; **Indiana** offers a wide choice of jewellery and local handicrafts.

West of Puerto Plata

T he western part of the Atlantic coast is above all remembered for having been at the heart of an event that would irrevocably change the course of history.

I t was here, in 1493, during his second voyage to the Americas, that Christopher Columbus founded La Isabela, the first settlement in the New World. Despite its precocious beginnings, however, this portion of the coast, extending over 150 kilometres from Puerto Plata to the Haitian border, remains one of the most undeveloped regions in the country. There are no big urban centres in the area; the small population is concentrated mostly in villages where fishing and farming are the main economic activities.

S o far there has not been any major tourist development along this stretch of the coast, though a few good hotels have been built here. The beautiful sandy beaches are for the most part untouched and virtually deserted. A day trip along this part of the coast is easy from Puerto Plata.

Finding Your Way Around

The highway to Monte Cristi is in good condition, which is not always the case with the secondary roads. From this highway, secondary roads run to the main coastal communities.

Luperón

The town of Luperón lies approximately 45 kilometres from Puerto Plata. Day trips are possible from Puerto Plata if you don't want to stay overnight. To get there, take the highway to the village of Imbert. From there, a narrow winding road on the right (facing the gas station) leads to Luperón. The road is not very wide and is quite curvy in places so try to Avoid driving on this road after nightfall.

La Isabela

To get to La Isabela from Puerto Plata, first drive to Luperón, continue further west on this same road. Helpful road signs are virtually nonexistent, but the site is clearly visible from the road. If in doubt, do not hesitate to ask people in the area for directions.

Punta Rucia

Punta Rucia is accessible via the dirt road that follows the ocean from La Isabela. However, it is quicker to take the highway toward Monte Cristi, and turn right at Villa Elisa. It takes at least an hour and a half to drive the 90 kilometres between Puerto Plata and Punta Rucia.

Practical Information

Monte Cristi

Tourist Information Office
Edificio de la Gobernación
Monte Cristi
☎*579-2254*

Exploring

Luperón

Nestled alongside a pretty deepwater bay. This peaceful fishing village of about 18,000, is named after General Luperón, a hero of the Restoración. While the city is pleasant enough, and the sheltered port is picturesque, most visitors are attracted by the neighbouring **beach ★**. The area is best suited to those seeking peace and quiet outside the larger tourist centres. There is only one big hotel, the Luperón Beach Resort (see p240), located right near the beach and offering the opportunity to enjoy all sorts of water sports. The town also has some good little restaurants.

La Isabela

When, on his second voyage to America, Columbus discovered that Fuerte Navidad had been destroyed, he chose this location near the Río Bajabonico to build the first city in the New World (1493). Named La Isabela after Isabela de Castillo, it was divided into two sections, one military, the other civilian. Even today some of the remains of period buildings can be seen. At the entrance to the old town, an interesting **museum ★** has recently been constructed and displays the various objects that have been found here. The exhibition highlights the first colonists' way of life as well as that of the first peoples who inhabited the region.

Punta Rucia

Punta Rucia, a tiny fishing village bordered by a pretty white-sand **beach ★**, is located near the town of Estero Hondo. In 1959, a group opposing the Trujillo regime met here to draw up plans before battling the dictator's troops. Today this serene and picturesque village's military past seems faraway. Fishing is the main activity here, as indicated by the numerous little boats moored along the shore.

From Punta Rucia, visitors can set out on excursions to **Cayo Arenas**, a tiny island of white sand lost out in the Atlantic about 10 kilometres offshore. Swimming and snorkelling are excellent here and absolute tranquillity is guaranteed! Only those with an appreciation for deserted beaches and tranquillity should stay in Punta Rucia.

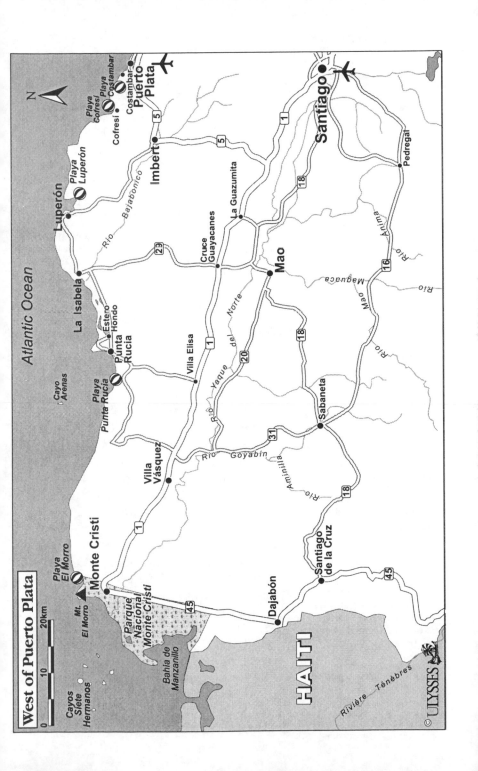

Villa Vasquez

To reach Monte Cristi from Santiago, you have to pass through the prosperous-looking little town of Villa Vasquez. Although it has little to offer in terms of sights or activities, the town does have a few decent restaurants, making it a pleasant and convenient place to stop.

Monte Cristi

Founded in the 16th century, Monte Cristi, like many towns in the region, was abandoned in 1606 when the population was forced by royal decree to move to the region around Santo Domingo. The city became active once again a century later, and enjoyed a certain prosperity at the turn of the 20th century when precious timbers and agricultural products from the centre of the country were shipped out from its port.

Today, Monte Cristi is famous primarily for its salt production, which is extracted from large evaporation sheets of salt water. Not many foreign travellers venture all the way to Monte Cristi, and a rare are those who are familiar with its long unspoiled beaches, frequented by numer-

ous species of birds, its beautiful sunsets and the extraordinary sight of **Mount El Morro** silhouetted against the sky. Monte Cristi itself is not a particularly attractive city, but it does have a certain charm. There are a number of interesting buildings here, including Victorian-style residences built during the last century, in Monte Cristi's heyday, as well as an **old clock** *(Parque Central)* purchased in France in 1895. The best time to visit Monte Cristi is in February, during **Carnival.**
Máximo Gomez's house

(free admission; open every day; Avenida Mella), where the hero of the Dominican Restoration and Cuban independence lived, has been converted into a museum, offering an interesting perspective on daily life during the last century. It was in Monte Cristi that Máximo Gomez and José Martí signed a mutual aid agreement for the liberation of the Dominican Republic and Cuba.

East of Monte Cristi, the road passes by an impressive **saltern**, runs along the ocean, then

Taino Heritage

Barely two decades after Christopher Columbus "discovered" America, Hispaniola's Taino civilization had all but vanished. A number of Taino words have survived, however, in the English language.

Notable examples are **canoe,** from the word *canoa,* designating a dugout canoe; **hammock** (the Tainos were the first to weave them); the names of various plants, including **tobacco, maize** and **guava; barbecue**, from *barbacoa*, the grill the Tainos used for cooking; and **manatee** from the word *manati.*

cuts inland to Parque Nacional Monti Cristi.

Parque Nacional Monte Cristi

This vast, uninhabited land, stretching out over more than 500 square kilometres, borders Haiti, the Siete Hermanos Islands, and several lagoons, the most prominent being the one formed by the mouth of the Dajabón River.

About three kilometres north of Monte Cristi, is the **El Morro Mountain**, some 300 meters in height and projecting its strange silhouette for miles around. A breathtaking, panaromic view of the surroundings can be had from the summit of this mountain. A small path takes one up over to the eastern slope of El Morro Mountain where a superb **beach ★** of white sand stretches out into the distance, surrounded by cliffs.

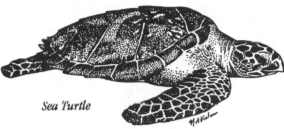
Sea Turtle

The southern slope of the mountain looks out over another long and narrow **beach** which serves as a border to the infinite, blue expanse of the sea.

Subtropical forest covers the fertile portion of the park, where a veritable tapestry composed of **frangipani, croton, mesquite**. The **red mangrove trees** of the swamp region, is rolled out in all of its splendor. In this land of sparse rainfall, (600 millimetres a year), a fauna composed mainly of reptiles has evolved. **American crocodiles** are one of the species that one should be able to see here, but due to overhunting, catching a glimpse of one would border on the miraculous. Numerous species of birds (no less than 163) also inhabit the park and its surroundings. It is possible to see, among others, the **pelican**, the **frigate bird**, the **white egret** and the **red-footed gannet**.

The seven small islands of **Los Cayos Siete Hermanos ★**, which huddle together at the edge of the Atlantic Ocean, are also included in this park. Organized excursions departing from Monte Cristi permit access to the beautiful, undeveloped beaches of these island, in addition to offering the opportunity of a more in-depth exploration of the marshes that border the mainland portion of park. Of particular renown to the islands have been the **sea turtles** which come to lay their eggs in the Bahía de Monte Cristi. Unfortunately, over the years, these reptiles have suffered the fate of overhunting and make very rare appearances.

Excellent scuba diving and snorkelling sites are found near these islands. Be aware, however, that you will need to bring your own equipment as there are no diving outfitters in Monte Cristi. On the other hand, if you want to get a closer look at the islands, the owners of the Caya Areno Hotel have a dock and can bring you to certain sites of interest. Negotiating with one of the many fishermen on the coast is another way of seeing some of the more intimate sites.

West of Puerto Plata

Dajabon

Dajabon would be a small town of no particular importance if it was not for its proximity to Haiti. As a border town, it is buzzing with commercial activity carried out between its residents and those of the nearby Haitian villages. In Dajabon, you can get a pass for several hours to go to Haiti. Every Saturday morning there is a market where beautiful Haitian art, handicrafts and clothing are sold.

Outdoor Activities

Swimming

Luperón

Playa Luperón ★, located near the Caribbean Village Luperón, is a good place for swimming and other water sports. This long ribbon of white sand is lined with coconut palms.

Punta Rucia

Playa Punta Rucia ★ is a pretty stretch of sand lined from one end to the other with coconut palms. Little fishing

vessels are pulled up on the sand. The spot is nothing if not picturesque. Swimming is possible near the Discovery Hotel, and at various other spots along the coast.

Close to Punta Rucia, you will also find a magnificent wild beach called **La Insenada ★**.

Monte Cristi

The Monte Cristi area has a few good beaches for swimming. In the national park on the western side of El Morro Mountain, there is a very beautiful and generally deserted **beach ★** surrounded by high cliffs.

Swimming is also possible at the deserted beaches of the **Los Cayos Siete Hermanos** archipelago, offshore from Monte Cristi.

Accommodations

Luperón

Caribbean Village Luperón
$130; all-inclusive; ≡, ≈, ℜ, *tv;*
☎ *571-8303*
≈ *571-8180*
The Caribbean Village Luperón is located in a charming, tranquil setting, right on Luperón's beautiful beach. The level of

comfort is what one would expect from a luxury hotel. Guests can enjoy allsorts of activities and take part in excursions to the region's major tourist centres. Ideal for people looking for an isolated spot.

Monte Cristi

The Chic Hotel
$15; ⊗
44 Calle Benito Monsion
☎ *579-2316*
The Chic hotel has rooms which may be furnished with mismatched pieces, but nevertheless offer minimal comfort. The hotel is located in downtown Monte Cristi. For a hundred pesos more, one can stay in a room enhanced with air-conditioning - something quite appreciated in Monte Cristi.

Cayo Arena
$80; ≈, ≡, *K*
near the ocean
☎*579-3145*
The most pleasant place to stay in the Monte Cristi region is unquestionably the Cayo Arena. Built next to the beach, it has about 20 comfortably furnished rooms that can sleep up to four people. Each room has a balcony. The hotel also has a boat for anyone who wants to go to the Cayos Siete Hermanos Archipelago.

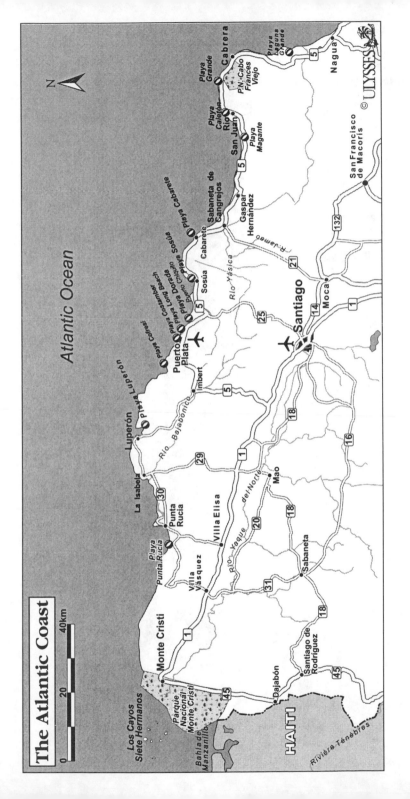

The Atlantic Coast

Atlantic Ocean

N

40km
20
0

© ULYSSES

Los Cayos
Siete Hermanos

Parque
Nacional
Monte Cristi

Bahía de
Manzanillo

Monte Cristi

Playa
Punta Rucia

Punta
Rucia

La Isabela

Luperón

Playa Luperón

Playa Cofresí

Puerto
Plata

Playa Costambar
Playa Long Beach
Playa Dorada
Playa Chiquito
Playa Sosúa

Sosúa

Playa Cabarete

Cabarete

Sabaneta de
Cangrejos

Gaspar
Hernández

Playa
Magante

San Juan

Playa
Cafetón
Río

P.N. Cabo
Frances
Viejo

Playa
Grande

Cabrera

Playa
Laguna
Grande

Nagua

5

San Francisco
de Macoris

132

Moca

Santiago

14

25

5

Río Yásica

21

Imbert

5

Río Bajabónico

Villa Elisa

29

30

Villa
Vásquez

Río Yaque del Norte

Mao

1

20

18

18

18

16

Sabaneta

31

Dajabón

Santiago de
Rodríguez

45

45

1

HAITI

Rivière Ténèbres

Hotel Los Jardines
☎579-2091
The Hotel Los Jardines is nearby; however, this little place was closed during our last visit in 1999.

Restaurants

Villa Vasquez

Mi Casa
$
on the main street as you come into town
Mi Casa serves traditional Dominican dishes, including the popular chicken, beans and rice combo.

It is an attractive, airy restaurant with a large palm-thatched roof, whose beautiful decor is somewhat surprising in a small village like Villa Vasquez.

Monte Cristi

Downtown Monte Cristi has several restaurants. However, it is much more pleasant to go out of town near the El Morro Mountain and dine at one of the restaurants by the ocean.
One of them, the **Cocomar**, always has a good selection of Dominican food.

Glossary

CONSONANTS

b   Is pronounced **b** or sometimes a soft **v**, depending on the region or the person: *bizcocho* (biz-koh-choh or viz-koh-choh).

c   As in English, *c* is pronounced as **s** before *i* and *e*: *cerro* (seh-rroh). When it is placed in front of other vowels, it is hard and pronounced as **k**: *carro* (kah-rroh). The *c* is also hard when it comes before a consonant, except before an *h* (see further below).

d   Is pronounced like a soft **d**: *dar* (dahr). *D* is usually not pronounced when at the end of a word.

g   As with the *c*, *g* is soft before an *i* or an *e*, and is pronounced like a soft **h**: *gente* (hente). In front of other vowels and consonants, the *g* is hard: *golf* (pronounced the same way as in English).

ch   Pronounced **ch**, as in English: *leche* (le-che). Like the *ll*, this combination is considered a single letter in the Spanish alphabet, listed separately in dictionaries and telephone directories.

h   Is not pronounced: *hora* (oh-ra).

j   Is pronounced like a guttural **h**, as in "him".

ll   Is pronounced like a hard **y**, as in "yes": *llamar* (yah-mar). In some regions, such as central Colombia, *ll* is pronounced as a soft **g**, as in "mirage" (*Medellín* is pronounced Medegin). Like the *ch*, this combination is considered a single letter in the Spanish alphabet, and is listed separately in dictionaries and telephone directories.

ñ   Is pronounced like the **ni** in "onion", or the **ny** in "canyon": *señora* (seh-nyo-rah).

qu   Is pronounced **k**: *aquí* (ah-kee).

r   Is rolled, as the Irish or Italian pronunciation of **r**.

s   Is always pronounced **s** like "sign": *casa* (cah-ssah).

v   Is pronounced like a **b**: *vino* (bee-noh).

z   Is pronounced like **s**: *paz* (pahss).

VOWELS

a   Is always pronounced **ah** as in "part", and never *ay* as in "day": *faro* (fah-roh).

e   Is pronounced **eh** as in "elf," and never *ey* as in "grey or "ee" as in "key": *helado* (eh-lah-doh].

i   Is always pronounced ee: *cine* (see-neh).

o   Is always pronounced oh as in "cone": *copa* (koh-pah).

u   Is always pronounced oo: *universidad* (oo-nee-ver-see-dah).

All other letters are pronounced the same as in English.

STRESSING SYLLABLES

In Spanish, syllables are differently stressed. This stress is very important, and emphasizing the right syllable might even be necessary to make yourself understood. If a vowel has an accent, this syllable is the one that should be stressed. If there is no accent, follow this rule:

Stress the second-last syllable of any word that ends with a vowel: *amigo*.

Stress the last syllable of any word that ends in a consonant, except for s (plural of nouns and adjectives) or n (plural of nouns): *usted* (but *amigos*, *hablan*).

GREETINGS

Goodbye	*adiós, hasta luego*
Good afternoon and good evening	*buenas tardes*
Hi (casual)	*hola*
Good morning	*buenos días*
Good night	*buenas noches*
Thank-you	*gracias*
Please	*por favor*
You are welcome	*de nada*
Excuse me	*perdone/a*
My name is...	*mi nombre es...*
What is your name?	*¿cómo se llama usted?*
no/yes	*no/sí*
Do you speak English?	*¿habla usted inglés?*
Slower, please	*más despacio, por favor*
I am sorry, I don't speak Spanish	*Lo siento, no hablo español*
How are you?	*¿qué tal?*
I am fine	*estoy bien*
I am American (male/female)	*Soy estadounidense*
I am Australian	*Soy autraliano/a*
I am Belgian	*Soy belga*
I am British (male/female)	*Soy británico/a*
I am Canadian	*Soy canadiense*
I am German (male/female)	*Soy alemán/a*
I am Italian (male/female)	*Soy italiano/a*
I am Swiss	*Soy suizo*
I am a tourist	*Soy turista*
single (m/f)	*soltero/a*
divorced (m/f)	*divorciado/a*
married (m/f)	*casado/a*
friend (m/f)	*amigo/a*
child (m/f)	*niño/a*
husband, wife	*esposo/a*
mother, father	*madre, padre*
brother, sister	*hermano/a*
widower widow	*viudo/a*

I am hungry	*tengo hambre*
I am ill	*estoy enfermo/a*
I am thirsty	*tengo sed*

DIRECTIONS

beside	*al lado de*
to the right	*a la derecha*
to the left	*a la izquierda*
here, there	*aquí, allí*
into, inside	*dentro*
outside	*fuera*
behind	*detrás*
in front of	*delante*
between	*entre*
far from	*lejos de*
Where is ... ?	*¿dónde está ... ?*
To get to ...?	*¿para ir a...?*
near	*cerca de*
straight ahead	*todo recto*

MONEY

money	*dinero / plata*
credit card	*tarjeta de crédito*
exchange	*cambio*
traveller's cheque	*cheque de viaje*
I don't have any money	*no tengo dinero*
The bill, please	*la cuenta, por favor*
receipt	*recibo*

SHOPPING

store	*tienda*
market	*mercado*
open, closed	*abierto/a, cerrado/a*
How much is this?	*¿cuánto es?*
to buy, to sell	*comprar,* vender
the customer	*el / la cliente*
salesman	*vendedor*
saleswoman	*vendedora*
I need...	*necesito...*
I would like...	*yo quisiera...*
batteries	*pilas*
blouse	*blusa*
cameras	*cámaras*
cosmetics and perfumes	*cosméticos y perfumes*
cotton	*algodón*
dress jacket	*saco*
eyeglasses	*lentes, gafas*
fabric	*tela*
film	*película*
gifts	*regalos*
gold	*oro*
handbag	*bolsa*
hat	*sombrero*
jewellery	*joyería*
leather	*cuero, piel*
local crafts	*artesanía*
magazines	*revistas*

newpapers	*periódicos*
pants	*pantalones*
records, cassettes	*discos, casetas*
sandals	*sandalias*
shirt	*camisa*
shoes	*zapatos*
silver	*plata*
skirt	*falda*
sun screen products	*productos solares*
T-shirt	*camiseta*
watch	*reloj*
wool	*lana*

MISCELLANEOUS

a little	*poco*
a lot	*mucho*
good (m/f)	*bueno/a*
bad (m/f)	*malo/a*
beautiful (m/f)	*hermoso/a*
pretty (m/f)	*bonito/a*
ugly	*feo*
big	*grande*
tall (m/f)	*alto/a*
small (m/f)	*pequeño/a*
short (length) (m/f)	*corto/a*
short (person) (m/f)	*bajo/a*
cold (m/f)	*frío/a*
hot	*caliente*
dark (m/f)	*oscuro/a*
light (colour)	*claro*
do not touch	*no tocar*
expensive (m/f)	*caro/a*
cheap (m/f)	*barato/a*
fat (m/f)	*gordo/a*
slim, skinny (m/f)	*delgado/a*
heavy (m/f)	*pesado/a*
light (weight) (m/f)	*ligero/a*
less	*menos*
more	*más*
narrow (m/f)	*estrecho/a*
wide (m/f)	*ancho/a*
new (m/f)	*nuevo/a*
old (m/f)	*viejo/a*
nothing	*nada*
something (m/f)	*algo/a*
quickly	*rápidamente*
slowly (m/f)	*despacio/a*
What is this?	*¿qué es esto?*
when?	*¿cuando?*
where?	*¿dónde?*

TIME

in the afternoon, early evening	*por la tarde*
at night	*por la noche*
in the daytime	*por el día*
in the morning	*por la mañana*
minute	*minuto*

month	*mes*
ever	*jamás*
never	*nunca*
now	*ahora*
today	*hoy*
yesterday	*ayer*
tomorrow	*mañana*
What time is it?	*¿qué hora es?*
hour	*hora*
week	*semana*
year	*año*
Sunday	*domingo*
Monday	*lunes*
Tuesday	*martes*
Wednesday	*miércoles*
Thursday	*jueves*
Friday	*viernes*
Saturday	*sábado*
January	*enero*
February	*febrero*
March	*marzo*
April	*abril*
May	*mayo*
June	*junio*
July	*julio*
August	*agosto*
September	*septiembre*
October	*octubre*
November	*noviembre*
December	*diciembre*

WEATHER

It is cold	*hace frío*
It is warm	*hace calor*
It is very hot	*hace mucho calor*
sun	*sol*
It is sunny	*hace sol*
It is cloudy	*está nublado*
rain	*lluvia*
It is raining	*está lloviendo*
wind	*viento*
It is windy	*hay viento*
snow	*nieve*
damp	*húmedo*
dry	*seco*
storm	*tormenta*
hurricane	*huracán*

COMMUNICATION

air mail	*correos aéreo*
collect call	*llamada por cobrar*
dial the number	*marcar el número*
area code, country code	*código*
envelope	*sobre*
long distance	*larga distancia*
post office	*correo*
rate	*tarifa*

stamps	estampillas
telegram	telegrama
telephone book	un guia telefónica
wait for the tone	esperar la señal

ACTIVITIES

beach	playa
museum or gallery	museo
scuba diving	buceo
to swim	bañarse
to walk around	pasear
hiking	caminata
trail	pista, sendero
cycling	ciclismo
fishing	pesca

TRANSPORTATION

arrival, departure	llegada, salida
on time	a tiempo
cancelled (m/f)	anulado/a
one way ticket	ida
return	regreso
round trip	ida y vuelta
schedule	horario
baggage	equipajes
north, south	norte, sur
east, west	este, oeste
avenue	avenida
street	calle
highway	carretera
expressway	autopista
airplane	avión
airport	aeropuerto
bicycle	bicicleta
boat	barco
bus	bus
bus stop	parada
bus terminal	terminal
train	tren
train crossing	crucero ferrocarril
station	estación
neighbourhood	barrio
collective taxi	colectivo
corner	esquina
express	rápido
safe	seguro/a
be careful	cuidado
car	coche, carro
To rent a car	alquilar un auto
gas	gasolina
gas station	gasolinera
no parking	no estacionar
no passing	no adelantar
parking	parqueo
pedestrian	peaton
road closed, no through traffic	no hay paso
slow down	reduzca velocidad

stop	*alto*
stop! (an order)	*pare*
traffic light	*semáforo*

ACCOMMODATION

cabin, bungalow	*cabaña*
accommodation	*alojamiento*
double, for two people	*doble*
single, for one person	*sencillo*
high season	*temporada alta*
low season	*temporada baja*
bed	*cama*
floor (first, second...)	*piso*
main floor	*planta baja*
manager	*gerente, jefe*
double bed	*cama matrimonial*
cot	*camita*
bathroom	*baños*
with private bathroom	*con baño privado*
hot water	*agua caliente*
breakfast	*desayuno*
elevator	*ascensor*
air conditioning	*aire acondicionado*
fan	*ventilador, abanico*
pool	*piscina, alberca*
room	*habitación*

NUMBERS

1	*uno*	30	*treinta*
2	*dos*	31	*treinta y uno*
3	*tres*	32	*treinta y dos*
4	*cuatro*	40	*cuarenta*
5	*cinco*	50	*cincuenta*
6	*seis*	60	*sesenta*
7	*siete*	70	*setenta*
8	*ocho*	80	*ochenta*
9	*nueve*	90	*noventa*
10	*diez*	100	*cien*
11	*once*	101	*ciento uno*
12	*doce*	102	*ciento dos*
13	*trece*	200	*doscientos*
14	*catorce*	300	*trescientos*
15	*quince*	400	*quatrocientoa*
16	*dieciséis*	500	*quinientos*
17	*diecisiete*	600	*seiscientos*
18	*dieciocho*	700	*sietecientos*
19	*diecinueve*	800	*ochocientos*
20	*veinte*	900	*novecientos*
21	*veintiuno*	1,000	*mil*
22	*veintidós*	1,100	*mil cien*
23	*veintitrés*	1,200	*mil doscientos*
24	*veinticuatro*	2000	*dos mil*
25	*veinticinco*	3000	*tres mil*
26	*veintiséis*	10,000	*diez mil*
27	*veintisiete*	100,000	*cien mil*
28	*veintiocho*	1,000,000	*un millón*
29	*veintinueve*		

Glossary

Index

Index

Index

Index

The Caribbean

The Islands Of The Bahamas

Vacationers will find extensive coverage of the big favourites of New Providence (Nassau) and Grand Bahama (Freeport) with their spectacular beaches, glittering casinos and great scuba diving, but they will also find the most extensive coverage of the Out Islands. Here island-hoppers enjoy world-class fishing, scuba diving and boating, friendly people and pristine deserted beaches.
Jennifer McMorran
288 pages, 25 maps, 8 pages of colour photos
ISBN 2-89464-123-0
$24.95 CAN $17.95 US   £12.99

Cuba, 2nd edition

Already a second edition for this unique guide to Cuba. The island's spirit is revealed, from colonial Havana, to the world-heritage site of Trinidad and to Santiago with it Afro-Cuban culture. The guide also covers the famous beaches and provides travellers with countless shortcuts and tips for independent travel in Cuba.
Carlos Soldevila
336 pages, 40 maps, 8 pages of colour photos
ISBN 2-89464-143-5
$24.95 CAN $17.95 US   £12.99

Guadeloupe, 3rd edition

This is the only guide to provide such extensive cultural and practical coverage of this destination. The charm of this dramatically beautiful Caribbean island is revealed along winding picturesque roads through typical villages and towns. Magnificent colour plates help to identify Guadeloupe's birds and plants.
Pascale Couture
208 pages, 15 maps, 8 pages of colour photos
ISBN 2-89464-135-4
$24.95 CAN $17.95 US   £12.99

Martinique, 3rd edition

A perfect marriage of cultural and practical information provides the best coverage of Martinique. Numerous tours lead across the island of flowers, from Fort-de-France to Saint-Pierre, with stops in Grande Anse and Montagne Pelée. Everything you need to know about hiking and water sports. Magnificent colour plates help to identify birds and plants.
Claude Morneau
256 pages, 18 maps, 8 pages of colour photos
ISBN 2-89464-136-2
$24.95 CAN $17.95 US   £12.99

Saint Martin - Saint Barts, 2nd edition
Jewels of the French and Dutch Caribbean, Saint Martin and Saint Barts offer a kaleidoscope of attractions – beautiful beaches, charming villages, first-class tourist facilities – and they have been combined for this guide. Whether it's international Saint Martin or tiny Saint Barts, or both, this handy pocket guide has all the great restaurants, luxurious hotels, outdoor activities, plus a glossary, maps and a historical overview.
Pascale Couture
192 pages, 10 maps,
ISBN 2-89464-071-4
$16.95 CAN $12.95 US   £8.99

MEXICO

Acapulco, 2nd edition
A fresh look at Acapulco, the most famous Mexican resort: Acapulco Bay, its beaches, restaurants and nightlife, as well as the neighbouring mountains and an enlightened overview of the people and history of this spot.
Marc Rigole, Claude-Victor Langlois
176 pages, 6 maps
ISBN 2-89464-213-X
$14.95 CAN $9.95 US   £7.99
current edition 2-89464-062-5

Cancún & Riviera Maya, 2nd edition
The resort of Cancún on the Yucatán Peninsula attracts visitors from the world-over, who come to enjoy a unique experience that includes fabulous archaeological sites and excursions to nearby Cozumel, a scuba-diver's paradise.
Caroline Vien, Alain Théroux
304 pages, 18 maps
8 pages of colour photos
ISBN 2-89464-214-8
$19.95 CAN $14.95 US   £9.99
current edition 2-89464040-4

Puerto Vallarta,
What began as a tiny fishing village has blossomed into one of the Mexican Riviera's most magnificent resorts. This guide reveals the splendour of Puerto Vallarta, from its luxuriant flora to its countless excellent restaurants.
Richard Bizier, Roch Nadeau
192 pages, 8 maps
ISBN 2-89464-150-8
$14.95 CAN $10.95 US   £7.99

CENTRAL AMERICA

Costa Rica
Yves Séguin, Francis Giguère
This fresh look at Costa Rica places special emphasis on eco-tourism, independent travel and the culture, history and natural wonders of this Central American gem.
368 pages, 35 maps, 8 pages of colour photos, Spanish-English glossary
ISBN 2-89464-144-3
$27.95 CAN $19.95 US   £13.99

Panamá, 3rd Edition
Marc Rigole, Claude-Victor Langlois
Famous for its impressive canal and a diverse ethnic and cultural environment, Panamá offers magnificent beaches on two different oceans. Travellers will discover an infinite variety of landscapes with unequalled flora and fauna.
288 pages, 24 maps, 8 pages of colour photos, Spanish-English glossary
ISBN 2-89464-129-X   September 1999
$24.95 CAN $17.95 US   £12.99

Nicaragua, 2nd edition
Carol Wood
Once a headline-maker the world-over, Nicaragua is more often featured in the "Travel" section these days. Besides the capital city of Managua and the popular resort of Montelimar, this guide crosses the whole country, discovering the impressive cities of León and Granada, among other places along the way.
208 pages, 18 maps, Spanish-English glossary
ISBN 2-89464-148-6   August 1999
$24.95 CAN $17.95 US   £12.99

Honduras, 2nd edition
Eric Hamovitch
Honduras is a land of gorgeous complexity and myriad sights. Ulysses helps travelers discover all the possibilities that lie just off the beaten track: the Mayan ruins of Copán, the colonial bustle of Tegucigalpa, or the luscious islands off the Caribbean coast.
224 pages, 20 maps, Spanish-English glossary
ISBN 2-89464-132-X   August 1999
$24.95 CAN $17.95 US   £12.99

El Salvador
Eric Hamovitch
This guide provides everything a traveller needs to discover this fascinating Central American country: explanation of cultural and political contexts, advice on how to travel in the area, descriptions of the various attractions, detailed lists of accommodations, restaurants, entertainment and more.
152 pages, 7 maps
ISBN 2-92144489-5
$22.95 CAN $14.95 US   £11.50

Belize
Carlos Soldevila
This tiny Central American country encompasses part of the ancient Ruta Maya and is rimmed by spectacular coral reefs. Its archaeological and natural treasures make it an explorer's paradise. Practical and cultural information will help you make the most of your vacation.
272 pages, 29 maps
ISBN 2-89464-179-6
$16.95 CAN $12.95 US   £8.99

Guatemala
Carlos Soldevila, Denis Faubert
Historic peace talks have once again allowed tourism to develop in Guatemala, providing travellers with a glimpse of this spectacular country whose vibrant traditions are so much a part of everyday life.
288 pages, 30 maps, Spanish-English glossary
ISBN 2-89464-175-3   October 1999
$24.95 CAN $17.95 US   £12.99

SOUTH AMERICA

Ecuador and the Galápagos Islands
Alain Legault
Extensive coverage of the colonial capital city, Quito, the extraordinary diversity of the Galapagos Islands and the beautiful Andean highlands.
320 pages, 39 maps, 8 pages of color photos, Spanish-English glossary
ISBN 2-89464-059-5
$24.95 CAN $17.95 US   £12.99

Peru
Alain Legault
Ulysses reveals the stunning scenery of this varied land: the Inca Trail and the ancient Inca city of Macchu Pichu, the depths of the Amazon rainforest, the high reaches of the Cordillera Blanca, modern and bustling Lima and beautiful Arequipa.
336 pages, 59 maps, 8 pages of color photos, Spanish-English glossary
ISBN 2-89464-122-2
$27.95 CAN $19.95 US   £13.99

Colombia
Marc Lessard
Beyond the headlines is a fascinating country full of possibilities for adventure seekers. Ulysses explains all the ins and outs, how to get beyond the wild streets of Bogota, discover the magic of the Ciudad Perdida (lost city) and the majesty of the World Heritage Site of Cartagena and explore national parks that protect jungles, deserts, beaches and mountains.
320 pages, 46 maps, 8 pages of colour photos, Spanish-English glossary
ISBN 2-89464-089-7
$29.95 CAN $21.95 US   £14.99

Travel Notes

Travel Notes

Travel Notes

_____
_____
_____
_____
_____
_____
_____
_____
_____
_____
_____
_____
_____
_____
_____
_____
_____
_____
_____
_____
_____
_____
_____
_____
_____
_____

Travel Notes

Travel Notes

Travel Notes

Travel Notes

Travel Notes

ORDER FORM

ULYSSES TRAVEL GUIDES

☐ Atlantic Canada .... $24.95 CAN $17.95 US	☐ Lisbon .... $18.95 CAN $13.95 US
☐ Bahamas .... $24.95 CAN $17.95 US	☐ Louisiana .... $29.95 CAN $21.95 US
☐ Beaches of Maine .... $12.95 CAN $9.95 US	☐ Martinique .... $24.95 CAN $17.95 US
☐ Bed & Breakfasts .... $13.95 CAN in Québec $10.95 US	☐ Montréal .... $19.95 CAN $14.95 US
☐ Belize .... $16.95 CAN $12.95 US	☐ New Orleans .... $17.95 CAN $12.95 US
☐ Calgary .... $17.95 CAN $12.95 US	☐ New York City .... $19.95 CAN $14.95 US
☐ Canada .... $29.95 CAN $21.95 US	☐ Nicaragua .... $24.95 CAN $16.95 US
☐ Chicago .... $19.95 CAN $14.95 US	☐ Ontario .... $27.95 CAN $19.95US
☐ Chile .... $27.95 CAN $17.95 US	☐ Ottawa .... $17.95 CAN $12.95 US
☐ Colombia .... $29.95 CAN $21.95 US	☐ Panamá .... $24.95 CAN $17.95 US
☐ Costa Rica .... $27.95 CAN $19.95 US	☐ Peru .... $27.95 CAN $19.95 US
☐ Cuba .... $24.95 CAN $17.95 US	☐ Portugal .... $24.95 CAN $16.95 US
☐ Dominican .... $24.95 CAN Republic $17.95 US	☐ Provence - .... $29.95 CAN Côte d'Azur $21.95US
☐ Ecuador and .... $24.95 CAN Galapagos Islands $17.95 US	☐ Québec .... $29.95 CAN $21.95 US
☐ El Salvador .... $22.95 CAN $14.95 US	☐ Québec and Ontario .... $9.95 CAN with Via $7.95 US
☐ Guadeloupe .... $24.95 CAN $17.95 US	☐ Toronto .... $18.95 CAN $13.95 US
☐ Guatemala .... $24.95 CAN $17.95 US	☐ Vancouver .... $17.95 CAN $12.95 US
☐ Honduras .... $24.95 CAN $17.95 US	☐ Washington D.C. .... $18.95 CAN $13.95 US
☐ Jamaica .... $24.95 CAN $17.95 US	☐ Western Canada .... $29.95 CAN $21.95 US

ULYSSES DUE SOUTH

☐ Acapulco .... $14.95 CAN $9.95 US	☐ Cartagena .... $12.95 CAN (Colombia) $9.95 US
☐ Belize .... $16.95 CAN $12.95 US	☐ Cancun Cozumel .... $17.95 CAN $12.95 US

ULYSSES DUE SOUTH

☐ Puerto Vallarta .... $14.95 CAN $9.95 US	☐ St. Martin and .... $16.95 CAN St. Barts $12.95 US

ULYSSES TRAVEL JOURNAL

☐ Ulysses Travel Journal .... $9.95 CAN
(Blue, Red, Green, Yellow, Sextant) $7.95 US

☐ Ulysses Travel Journal 80 Days ..... $14.95 CAN
                                          $9.95 US

ULYSSES GREEN ESCAPES

☐ Cycling in France .... $22.95 CAN
                                       $16.95 US
☐ Cycling in Ontario .... $22.95 CAN
                                       $16.95 US

☐ Hiking in the .... $19.95 CAN
  Northeastern U.S. $13.95 US
☐ Hiking in Québec .... $19.95 CAN
                                       $13.95 US

TITLE	QUANTITY	PRICE	

Name _____

Address _____

_____

_____

Payment : ☐ Money Order ☐ Visa ☐ MasterCard

Card Number _____

Expiration date _____

Signature _____

Sub-total	
Postage & Handling	$8.00*
Sub-total	
G.S.T. in Canada 7%	
TOTAL	

ULYSSES TRAVEL PUBLICATIONS
4176 St-Denis,
Montréal, Québec, H2W 2M5
(514) 843-9447 fax (514) 843-9448
www.ulysses.ca
*$15 for overseas orders

U.S. ORDERS: **GLOBE PEQUOT PRESS**
P.O. Box 833, 6 Business Park Road,
Old Saybrook, CT 06475-0833
1-800-243-0495 fax 1-800-820-2329
www.globe-pequot.com